CW00926182

ANIMAL SUBJECTS

Animal Subjects identifies a new understanding of animals in modernist literature and science. Drawing on Darwin's evolutionary theory, British writers and scientists of the late nineteenth and early twentieth centuries began to think of animals as subjects dwelling in their own animal worlds. Both science and literature aimed to capture the complexity of animal life, and their shared attention to animals pulled the two disciplines closer together. It led scientists to borrow the literary techniques of fiction and poetry, and writers to borrow the observational methods of zoology. *Animal Subjects* tracks the coevolution of literature and zoology in works by H. G. Wells, Aldous Huxley, D. H. Lawrence, Virginia Woolf, and modern scientists including Julian Huxley, Charles Elton, and J. B. S. Haldane. Examining the rise of ecology, ethology, and animal psychology, this book shows how new, subject-centered approaches to the study of animals transformed literature and science in the modernist period.

CAROLINE HOVANEC earned her Ph.D. in English from Vanderbilt University, where she won the Edgar Hill Duncan Award for academic achievement. She is Assistant Professor of English and Writing at the University of Tampa. Her research interests include modernism, literature and science, environmental humanities, and contemporary literature. She has published essays on aestheticism and science fiction, the melting of glaciers, and the 1918 flu pandemic. She is a member of the Society for Literature, Science, and the Arts, and the Modernist Studies Association.

ANIMAL SUBJECTS

Literature, Zoology, and British Modernism

CAROLINE HOVANEC

University of Tampa

CAMBRIDGE
UNIVERSITY PRESS

CAMBRIDGE
UNIVERSITY PRESS

University Printing House, Cambridge CB2 8BS, United Kingdom

One Liberty Plaza, 20th Floor, New York, NY 10006, USA

477 Williamstown Road, Port Melbourne, VIC 3207, Australia

314–321, 3rd Floor, Plot 3, Splendor Forum, Jasola District Centre, New Delhi – 110025, India

79 Anson Road, #06-04/06, Singapore 079906

Cambridge University Press is part of the University of Cambridge.

It furthers the University's mission by disseminating knowledge in the pursuit of education, learning, and research at the highest international levels of excellence.

www.cambridge.org
Information on this title: www.cambridge.org/9781108428392

DOI: 10.1017/9781108552752

First published 2018

Printed and bound in Great Britain by Clays Ltd, Elcograf S.p.A.

A catalogue record for this publication is available from the British Library.

Library of Congress Cataloging-in-Publication Data

NAMES: Hovanec, Caroline, author.
TITLE: Animal subjects : literature, zoology, and British modernism / Caroline Hovanec, University of Tampa.
DESCRIPTION: Cambridge, United Kingdom ; New York, NY : Cambridge University Press, 2018.
IDENTIFIERS: LCCN 2018009351 | ISBN 9781108428392 (hardback)
SUBJECTS: LCSH: Zoology—Great Britain—19th century—History. | Zoology—Great Britain—20th century—History. | Animals in literature—Great Britain—19th century. | Animals in literature—Great Britain—20th century.
CLASSIFICATION: LCC QL255 .H68 2018 | DDC 591.941—dc23 LC record available at https://lccn.loc.gov/2018009351

ISBN 978-1-108-42839-2 Hardback

Contents

Contents

Acknowledgments

I would like to thank the many colleagues and friends at Vanderbilt University and the University of Tampa who have supported me and this project over the past six years: Jay Clayton, Mark Wollaeger, Rachel Teukolsky, Mona Frederick, and everyone at the Robert Penn Warren Center for the Humanities, Donika Kelly, Heather Freeman, Elizabeth Barnett, David Reamer, Joe Letter, Andy Plattner, Kyle McIntosh, Yuly Restrepo, Sarah Fryett, and many others. Thanks to the staff of the Fondren Library at Rice University for allowing me to access the Julian Huxley Papers. I am grateful to Ray Ryan at Cambridge University Press and the anonymous readers for their guidance and feedback, which made this book better. An earlier version of Chapter 4 first appeared as "Philosophical Barnacles and Empiricist Dogs: Knowing Animals in Modernist Literature and Science" in *Configurations* 21.3 (2013): 245–69. Thanks to Melissa M. Littlefield, Rajani Sudan, and the Johns Hopkins University Press for permission to reprint it here.

For their unwavering support and love, and for instilling in me a love of reading, I thank my parents, Tom and Donna Hovanec. And for his patience, extremely unhelpful writing suggestions, and endless kindness, I thank my partner, Andrew Leathers.

Introduction

In the spring of 1924, the London Zoo unveiled a new and improved aquarium to great fanfare – its opening was presided over by no less than the king and queen themselves. It had been seventy-one years since the zoo had built the "Fish House," the very first public aquarium, which had sparked an "aquarium craze" among the Victorians. In the intervening years, the marine life on display had continued to draw large crowds, necessitating larger facilities in Regent's Park.[1] *The Nation and Athenaeum* ran a short review of the new aquarium a couple of weeks after its opening, an odd bit of prose which declined to offer any concrete information about the zoo's history, the renovation project, the public reception, or the species stocked. This review, penned by an up-and-coming writer named Virginia Woolf, reads as follows:

> Aesthetically speaking, the new aquarium is undoubtedly the most impressive of all the houses at the zoo. Red fish, blue fish, nightmare fish, dapper fish, fish lean as gimlets, fish round and white as soup plates, ceaselessly gyrate in oblong frames of greenish light in the hushed and darkened apartment hollowed out beneath the Mappin terraces. Scientifically, no doubt, the place is a paradise for the ichthyologist; but the poet might equally celebrate the strange beauty of the broad-leaved water plants trembling in the current, or the sinister procession of self-centred sea-beasts forever circling and seeking perhaps some minute prey, perhaps some explanation of a universe which evidently appears to them of inscrutable mystery. Now they knock the glass with their noses; now they shoot dart-like to the surface; now eddy slowly contemplatively down to the sandy bottom. Some are delicately fringed with a fin that vibrates like an electric fan and propels them on; others wear a mail boldly splashed with a design by a Japanese artist. That crude human egotism which supposes that Nature has wrought her best for those who walk the earth is rebuked at the aquarium. Nature seems to have cared more to tint and adorn the

[1] "The History of the Aquarium," *ZSL London Zoo*: www.zsl.org/zsl-london-zoo/exhibits/the-history-of-the-aquarium.

fishes who live unseen at the depths of the sea than to ornament our old, familiar friends, the goat, the hog, the sparrow, and the horse.[2]

Woolf perceives the aquarium as simultaneously a space of scientific observation, where ichthyologists might study a multitude of living fish, and a source of aesthetic inspiration for the writer. The aquarium harbors a "strange beauty" of abstract colors and moving shapes, "sinister" and "inscrutable" rather than classical, reminiscent of the Japanese art forms that many poets and artists in Woolf's milieu appreciated and appropriated – in short, a modernist beauty.[3]

At the same time that Woolf links the zoological display of the aquarium to modernist aesthetics, she also pursues a Darwinian project of decentering humans. The review is resolutely secular in its assumption that nature is not for humans, that it was never created for us, and that to believe otherwise is arrogant and "crude." When Woolf points out that the fishes, rarely seen by human eyes, are more beautiful than the animals we live with, she echoes one of Darwin's most controversial claims: that the beauty of birds, orchids, butterflies, and other living beings was not designed by God for our enjoyment, but instead evolved for the species' own benefit.[4] As Darwin pointed out in *The Origin of Species*, some naturalists "believe that very many structures have been created for beauty in the eyes of man, or for mere variety. This doctrine, if true, would be absolutely fatal to my theory."[5] He doubled down on this notion in *The Descent of Man*, writing, "I know of no fact in natural history more wonderful than that the female Argus pheasant should be able to appreciate the exquisite shading of the ball-and-socket ornaments and the elegant patterns on the wing-feathers of the male."[6] Yet it is that bird's taste that selected for such beautiful plumage. Woolf, likewise, marvels at the

---

[2] Virginia Woolf, *The Essays of Virginia Woolf*, vol. 3, ed. Andrew McNeillie (Harcourt Brace Jovanovich, 1985), 404–5.

[3] On Anglo-American modernism's engagement with Japan and Japanese art, see Yoko Chiba, "Japonisme: East-West Renaissance in the Late 19th Century," *Mosaic* 31.2 (1998): 1–20; Andrew Thacker, "'Mad After Foreign Notions': Ezra Pound, Imagism and the Geography of the Orient," in *Geographies of Modernism: Literatures, Cultures, Spaces*, ed. Peter Brooker and Andrew Thacker (Routledge, 2005), 31–42; and Rupert Richard Arrowsmith, *Modernism and the Museum: Asian, African, and Pacific Art and the London Avant-Garde* (Oxford University Press, 2011), 103–27.

[4] For an account of how Darwin's evolutionary aesthetics disturbed Victorian thinkers, most notably John Ruskin, see Jonathan Smith, *Charles Darwin and Victorian Visual Culture* (Cambridge University Press, 2006), 3.

[5] Charles Darwin, *On the Origin of Species by Means of Natural Selection* [1859], ed. J. W. Burrow (Penguin Books, 1985), 227.

[6] Charles Darwin, *The Descent of Man and Selection in Relation to Sex*, vol. 1 (John Murray, 1871; repr. in *The Complete Work of Charles Darwin Online*, ed. John van Wyhe: www.darwin-online.org .uk), 400–1.

fishes' splendor, the ornamentation that, evolutionary theory instructs, is not for us but for them.

Those "self-centred sea-beasts," displaced into tanks in metropolitan London for people to look at, subjected to the scientific gaze and to aesthetic contemplation, are also mysterious subjects in their own right. Woolf supposes that they are up to something when they gambol about the aquarium, looking for food or for answers, "perhaps some explanation of a universe which evidently appears to them of inscrutable mystery." They look back at the viewer, "knock[ing] the glass with their noses." The nature of their experience is impossible to surmise, but Woolf attributes some intention, however, nebulous and inaccessible, to their motions. They inhabit a "universe," a world overlapping with but utterly distinct from our own.

This book proposes that Woolf's review, which makes the aquarium a site of scientific interest, aesthetic novelty, and animal worlds, is not just a one-off, but represents a broader pattern in modern British culture. Woolf belonged to a network of writers and biologists who were deeply invested in the question of how to represent animal subjectivity, and whose forays into animal worlds shaped their understanding of science and literature. Coming of age after Darwin, these figures knew that there was good scientific reason for supposing that we evolved from animals and share with many animals some version of our "higher" traits, including the capacities for pain and pleasure, emotion, communication, some forms of intelligence, and, as Darwin made clear in the writings quoted above, an appreciation of beauty. They assumed, in other words, that many animals were sentient subjects rather than Cartesian automatons. Yet Woolf and her contemporaries also recognized the enduring difficulty of knowing or saying anything definitive about animal subjectivity, other than that it exists. Any claims they could make about it were speculative, provisional, open to accusations of anthropomorphism or excessive imagination. As the philosopher Thomas Nagel expressed the problem, "there is something that it is like to be a bat," but "there is no reason to suppose that it is subjectively like anything we can experience or imagine."[7] This quandary – one must understand animals as subjects, one cannot know animals' subjective experience – drove Woolf and her contemporaries to the very limits of literary and scientific representation.

---

[7] Thomas Nagel, "What Is It Like to Be a Bat?" *The Philosophical Review* 83.4 (1974): 435–50, quote on 438.

The obscurity of animal minds, however, did not preclude a blossoming of new zoological knowledge in the late nineteenth- and early twentieth centuries. An explosion of scientific and popular zoology was made possible by new technologies, new scientific approaches, and the new evolutionary theory, which created order out of the undifferentiated mass of facts collected by naturalists. Around the turn of the century, Christina Alt explains, "the long domination of taxonomic natural history was brought to an end by the combined impact of evolutionary theory and the new biology of the laboratory. As the twentieth century began, ethology [the study of animal behavior] and ecology also emerged as recognized disciplines and added a further dimension to the study of nature."[8] The change, she argues, was fundamental: the cataloging and categorizing of preserved specimens in museums gave way to a study of "the living organism, its behavior, and its interactions with its environment."[9] It was an age that saw the invention of the "ecosystem" and "niche" concepts; an era in which many naturalists traded in their guns for cameras; a time when behaviorists, ethologists, and psychologists, not to mention poets, competed over which theory afforded the best explanations of animal behaviors. It was also a period of mutual legibility between literature and science. Writers and scientists during this period went to the same movies, belonged to the same clubs, and wrote for the same presses. Drawing on each other's insights, they recognized the unsolved (and sometimes unsolvable) mysteries of animal life, but that recognition did not stymie their attempts to pursue greater knowledge.

This book examines animals in the literature of H.G. Wells, Aldous Huxley, D.H. Lawrence, and Virginia Woolf, as well as scientific and philosophical writings by Charles Darwin, Thomas H. Huxley, Charles Elton, Henry Eliot Howard, Julian Huxley, J.B.S. Haldane, Bertrand Russell, and C. Lloyd Morgan. These figures represent a wide range of intellectual approaches to animals and a variety of rhetorical tactics for writing about them, from the free verse animal poems of Lawrence to the spare, objective descriptions of Aldous Huxley; the revelatory calculations of Elton to the rich, ritualistic courtship scenes of Julian Huxley; the sensuous animal perspectives of Woolf to the ironic fables of Wells. Yet all of these writers and scientists can be understood as responding to the same two questions: how should we understand animal life after Darwin? and, how can we capture animals in words that are true

---

[8] Christina Alt, *Virginia Woolf and the Study of Nature* (Cambridge University Press, 2010), 38.
[9] Ibid., 39.

to life? The pursuit of answers to these questions led even further down the rabbit hole, to the question of what constitutes "true" for each discipline. The scientists found themselves turning to the methods of fiction and poetry to better express animal subjectivity, while the literary writers found themselves adopting the observational techniques of science. The study of animals thus blurred the boundaries between literary and scientific forms of description, and indeed between literary and scientific ways of knowing.

Science and literature, in late nineteenth- and early twentieth-century Britain, shared a common environment in which they coevolved, sometimes in symbiotic and other times in antagonistic ways. They exchanged zoological ideas and representational strategies, producing science writing that feels strangely modernist and literature that is surprisingly committed to realism. Together, they created new species of thought about animals, ones that ventured outside the well-trodden paths of scientific reductionism, primitivism, and anthropocentric humanism.

Animal Subjectivity: Darwin, Freud, James

To call animals "subjects" requires some explanation, since many philosophical understandings of subjectivity would seem to exclude animals. If one becomes a subject by tacitly signing the Enlightenment social contract (cf. Hobbes, Locke), or by learning language and entering the Lacanian Symbolic, or by the interpellation of the state and ideological state apparatuses, as Althusser proposed, then it makes little sense to speak of animal subjects.[10] Animals, after all, lack human language and exist primarily as objects under the state.[11] If, on the other hand, we take a posthumanist point of view, the very notion of a "subject" may seem antiquated and objectionable. Bruno Latour's actor-network theory, the rhizomes of Deleuze and Guattari, Donna Haraway's companion species, Stacy Alaimo's transcorporeality, the distributed agency of Jane Bennett's

---

[10] Western philosophy's exclusion of animals has been deftly explored by a number of philosophers and critics, including Giorgio Agamben in *The Open: Man and Animal*, transl. Kevin Attell (Stanford University Press, 2004), Kelly Oliver in *Animal Lessons: How They Teach Us to Be Human* (Columbia University Press, 2009), and Carrie Rohman in *Stalking the Subject: Modernism and the Animal* (Columbia University Press, 2009).

[11] Recent developments such as legal protections for great apes in some countries challenge the notion that animals exist as objects under the state but, with a few exceptions, the general claim is still true. A few researchers believe that certain animals – most famously Koko the gorilla, Kanzi the bonobo, and Alex the grey parrot – have demonstrated human-like language use, but these claims are controversial and not widely accepted among linguists or primatologists.

"vibrant matter": what these influential posthumanist concepts have in common is that they emphasize the interconnected, multiplicitous, entangled nature of things.[12] For posthumanism, it makes little sense to speak of a subject, human or animal, when it is intersubjectivity – and intercorporeality – all the way down.

These posthumanist concepts are generative and insightful, but rather than apply them to modernism, I would like to bracket them and ask instead, in a historicist mode, how British writers and scientists of the late nineteenth- and early twentieth centuries would have understood subjectivity. We will find in this period a conception of the subject that embraces both human and nonhuman animals. The evolutionary biology and psychology of that age produced a more elemental definition of a subject as any being capable of subjective experience. This school of thought emphasized continuity, not rupture, between humans and animals. It was not posthumanist in the sense of being after, or over, humanism and all its structuring binaries – subject/object, mind/matter, culture/nature, etc. But it did resist anthropocentrism and envision a permeable border between self and world, traits that resonate with post-humanist projects today.

Darwin's work provides a foundation for this notion of subjectivity by outlining a naturalistic worldview and an evolutionary understanding of mind. His groundbreaking *Origin of Species* (1859) proposed that the species in the world today evolved from one or a few ancestors, without divine intervention. Famously, the *Origin* barely mentions the evolution of humans, devoting only a single sentence to it in the conclusion: "Light will be thrown on the origin of man and his history."[13] Darwin understood that while his book might convincingly show that plants and animals had evolved via natural selection, to persuade readers that people, too, had evolved, he would have to amass another kind of evidence. He would have to offer some plausible naturalistic explanation for the most apparently magical trait of *Homo sapiens* – its mind. It was one thing to say that human lungs or kidneys or even eyes evolved via natural selection from some ancient animal ancestor, but what about human

---

[12] Bruno Latour, *Reassembling the Social: An Introduction to Actor-Network Theory* (Oxford University Press, 2005); Gilles Deleuze and Félix Guattari, *A Thousand Plateaus: Capitalism and Schizophrenia*, transl. Brian Massumi (University of Minnesota Press, 1987); Donna Haraway, *When Species Meet* (University of Minnesota Press, 2008); Stacy Alaimo, *Bodily Natures: Science, Environment, and the Material Self* (Indiana University Press, 2010); Jane Bennett, *Vibrant Matter: A Political Ecology of Things* (Duke University Press, 2010).
[13] Darwin, *Origin of Species*, 458.

language or art or morality? Those seemed much harder to explain within the evolutionary framework.

Darwin aimed to answer these unresolved questions in his 1871 follow-up to the *Origin, The Descent of Man*. In order to show that the human mind evolved under the same forces of natural and sexual selection that shaped the body, Darwin needed to demonstrate that every mental trait in humans exists, in some related form, in other animals. "If no organic being excepting man possessed any mental power, or if his powers had been of a wholly different nature from those of the lower animals," then Darwin's theory of humans' evolution would have been proven wrong, for evolution does not make leaps. "But," he argues, "it can be clearly shewn that there is no fundamental difference of this kind. We must also admit that there is a much wider interval in mental power between one of the lowest fishes, as a lamprey or lancelet, and one of the higher apes, than between an ape and man; yet this immense interval is filled up by numberless gradations."[14] Accordingly, Darwin devoted two chapters to "Comparison of the Mental Powers of Man and the Lower Animals." He claimed that animals were capable of emotions, a capacity for attention, memory, reason, self-consciousness, a sense of beauty, even a primitive kind of religious belief. While the immediate aim of these chapters was to show that each human mental trait reflected a natural development of animals' mental traits, the result was a rich and detailed portrait of animal subjective life that remains deeply important for both zoology and literary animal studies.

After the *Descent of Man*, psychology diverged into two streams that would prove influential for twentieth-century biology and literary modernism. The better known of these is Freudian psychoanalysis. Freud saw himself as a successor to Darwin in more than one sense. Both men's theories, like that of their Renaissance precursor Copernicus, dealt "severe blows" to "the universal narcissism of men," as Freud argued. Copernicus showed that Earth (and therefore humankind) was not the center of the universe; Darwin showed that "[m]an is not a being different from animals or superior to them; he himself is of animal descent"; and Freud showed that the unconscious determined human actions and thus that "*the ego is not master in its own house*."[15] As Gillian Beer points

---

[14] Darwin, *Descent of Man*, 34–5.

[15] Sigmund Freud, "A Difficulty in the Path of Psychoanalysis," in *The Standard Edition of the Complete Psychological Works of Sigmund Freud*, vol. 17, ed. James Strachey (Hogarth Press, 1971), 141, 143; quoted in Gillian Beer, *Darwin's Plots: Evolutionary Narrative in Darwin, George Eliot, and Nineteenth-Century Fiction* [1983] (Ark Paperbacks, 1985), 12–13.

out, the triad seems to imply that the process of debunking anthropocentric humanism is complete: "[t]he magical number three belies the possibility of a fourth great wound."[16] Freud's self-aggrandizing mythopoesis notwithstanding, he makes an important point. Evolutionary theory and psychoanalysis, like heliocentrism, are humbling doctrines. They figure the human as an ape, a well-adapted one in Darwin's view or a neurotic one in Freud's, but in either case an ape.

Freud's psychoanalytic theory borrows from Darwin in more direct ways too. Chief among them is his allegorical retelling of the story of human evolution in his account of individual psychological development. As Carrie Rohman shows, Freud drew on recapitulation theory, the belief (prominent in late nineteenth- and early twentieth-century biology but now mostly discredited) that the biological development of an individual from embryo to adult repeats the evolutionary changes undergone by its ancestors.[17] The same, Freud held, was true for the human psyche – as infants develop, they recapitulate the stages their ancestors went through on their journey from animal to civilized human being. In *Totem and Taboo* (1913), Freud cites Darwin's hypothesis that the earliest form of human society resembled the social organization of the gorilla, a primal horde in which one powerful male ruled over many wives and other subservient males.[18] At some point in human prehistory, Freud conjectured, a group of less powerful sons had banded together to kill the father who had dominated or expelled them, and their subsequent guilt over this crime led them to create the first law of human civilization: the prohibitions against murder and incest.[19] The child's passage through the Oedipal stage, for Freud, recapitulates and helps to decode this ancient transition from human as primal animal to human as subject of law and religion.[20] The originary desires to kill the father and sexually possess the mother must be repressed, the taboos against patricide and incest established, in order for the individual and the species to become truly human.

For Freud, the crucial stages in that journey are those that repress the animal self, which encompasses the drives of sex and aggression, in favor of the mores of civilization. Yet the primitive animal self remains potent in the unconscious, resurfacing in dreams, art, and neuroses.

---

[16] Beer, *Darwin's Plots*, 13.
[17] Rohman, *Stalking the Subject*, 6–7.
[18] Sigmund Freud, *Totem and Taboo* [1913], transl. James Strachey (W.W. Norton, 1950), 155–6.
[19] Ibid., 176–81.
[20] Ibid., 178.

In *Civilization and Its Discontents* (1930), Freud uses animal imagery to argue that the repressed instinct of aggression continues to pose a threat to human civilization. "[M]en are not gentle creatures who want to be loved, and who at the most can defend themselves if they are attacked," he claims; "they are, on the contrary, creatures among whose instinctual endowments is to be reckoned a powerful share of aggressiveness ... *Homo homini lupus*" – man is wolf to man.[21]

Freud understood the human as essentially conflicted, torn between the primitive animal unconscious and the demands of civilization, internalized as the superego. This understanding offers extensive insight into the writings of Lawrence, Wells, and many of their contemporaries, and it has been deftly explored within the field of modernist animal studies, particularly in Rohman's *Stalking the Subject* and Philip J. Armstrong's *What Animals Mean in the Fiction of Modernity*. However, while Freud's theory offers an extraordinarily influential account of human subjectivity, it has much less to say about the subjectivity of actual nonhuman animals. One can surmise from Freud only that animal subjectivity is dominated by the sexual and aggressive instincts, and that it is fundamentally different from human subjectivity in lacking the conflict introduced by civilization. Freud did express curiosity about nonhuman subjectivity, but only as an aside. "Why do our relatives, the animals, not exhibit any such cultural struggle?" he asks, speculating that perhaps "a temporary balance has been reached between the influences of their environment and the mutually contending instincts within them ... There are a great many questions here to which as yet there is no answer."[22] Darwin's account of animal life in the *Descent* was much fuller. It examined animal subjectivity in the service of describing humans' lineage, but it did not reduce animals to a mere metaphor for the primitive parts of human nature.

To understand how the writers and scientists under study in this book conceived of animal subjectivity, the more important school of psychology is not Freud's but William James's. James, too, was a Darwinian, but his evolutionism took a different, more concrete, form than Freud's. James saw psychological traits as at root physical traits, theoretically reducible to actions of the brain and nervous system. The goal of psychology, he claimed in *The Principles of Psychology*, is to "[ascertain] the empirical correlation of the various sorts of thought or feeling with

[21] Sigmund Freud, *Civilization and Its Discontents* [1930], transl. James Strachey (W.W. Norton, 1961), 68–9.
[22] Ibid., 83.

definite conditions of the brain," taking a "strictly positivistic point of view."[23] The first chapter of *The Principles* focus on physiology and neuroscience, reflecting James's wish to disentangle psychology from metaphysics and make it scientific.

James believed that psychological traits evolved just as physical traits did, and that they existed in different forms and degrees throughout the animal kingdom. "It is very generally admitted," he wrote, "though the point would be hard to prove, that consciousness grows the more complex and intense the higher we rise in the animal kingdom. That of a man must exceed that of an oyster."[24] Though he uses the anthropocentric metric of "higher" and "lower" to rank animals, in fact James's theory suggests that the oyster's form of consciousness is just as well adapted to its form of life as the human's is to hers. As Mark Nielsen and R.H. Day point out, one of James's early lectures argued that the simple *Aplysia*, a sea slug without a cerebellum, is a fine example of evolutionary adaptation; James said that its nervous system is responsive "to few stimuli but to them strongly and well."[25] Other animals in other walks of life benefit from more complex forms of consciousness, which, according to James, allow them to select which sensations from the external environment to pay attention to: "consciousness is at all times primarily *a selecting agency* ... choosing one out of several of the materials so presented to its notice, emphasizing and accentuating that and suppressing as far as possible all the rest."[26] Consciousness thus benefits the organism by allowing it to respond flexibly to small changes in its environment. In the claim that consciousness is evolutionarily *useful* and thus operates under the action of natural selection, James was making an innovative argument. Thomas H. Huxley, another follower of Darwin, had declared the opposite: that consciousness was an extra, a by-product of evolution but with no efficacy of its own. "We are conscious automata," he wrote, referring to both humans and nonhuman animals.[27] James, on the other hand, assumed that consciousness evolved because it served an adaptive purpose.

For T.H. Huxley, then, consciousness constitutes subjective experience but does not affect the workings of the body; for James,

[23] William James, *The Principles of Psychology*, vol. 1 (Henry Holt, 1890), vi.
[24] Ibid., 138.
[25] William James, *Manuscript Lectures* (Harvard University Press, 1988), 25; quoted in Mark Nielsen and R. H. Day, "William James and the Evolution of Consciousness," *Journal of Theoretical and Philosophical Psychology* 19.1 (1999): 90–113, quote on 100.
[26] James, *Principles of Psychology*, 1:139.
[27] Thomas H. Huxley, "On the Hypothesis that Animals are Automata, and Its History" [1874], in *The Huxley File*, ed. Charles Blinderman and David Joyce: alepho.clarku.edu/huxley/.

consciousness directs many of our observable actions. This tenet allows a fuller understanding of the distinction James makes, in the introductory chapter of *The Principles*, between nonliving and living things. He argues that living beings have "ends," or intents, and nonliving things do not. He illustrates his meaning with three examples. A piece of metal, attracted to a magnet but separated from it by a card, will never move around the card to get closer to the magnet. The "attraction" of conscious things is different; it finds a way to reach its goal. Romeo, if separated from Juliet by a wall, will go around, over, or under the wall to reach her; he has *ends* and will try a variety of means to meet them. Likewise, a frog suspended in water, seeking air at the surface, will not stop if it finds itself trapped under a roof. It will keep searching until it finds another path to the surface. James takes these actions as evidence that the frog, like Romeo, is conscious, and that its consciousness modifies its activity.[28] Later in *The Principles*, James cites a host of other experiments on frogs and other animals to elucidate where, in the brain and nervous system, different psychological activities are "located." These descriptions of vivisected animals and their addled behaviors are disturbing to read, but many of them offer further evidence of James's point that consciousness and volition exist in the "normal" animal specimens.

James's influence on literature, while not as well known as Freud's, is nevertheless firmly established in modernist studies. Most notably, his notion of the "stream of consciousness," which he considered the elementary data of introspective psychology, has been tied to the experimental prose of writers like Marcel Proust, James Joyce, Virginia Woolf, and Dorothy Richardson. And Judith Ryan's *The Vanishing Subject* shows how James and other "empiricist" psychologists of the late nineteenth century influenced literary understandings of subjectivity, spurring writers to experiment with different methods for representing the self as a collection or flow of sensations (an idea we'll revisit in Chapter 4).[29] Within literary animal studies, Jamesian psychology has received less attention. Yet his notion of animal consciousness – that it is a power of focusing attention on particular things in the environment, that it guides the animal's actions – is arguably just as important as Freud's idea of animal instincts for influencing early twentieth-century literature and science.

---

[28] James, *Principles of Psychology*, vol. 1, 6–8.
[29] Judith Ryan, *The Vanishing Subject: Early Psychology and Literary Modernism* (University of Chicago Press, 1991).

In James's theory, animals aren't just embodiments of sex and violence. They are conscious subjects, perceiving and responding with intention to the things in their worlds.

Triangulating Literature, Science, and Animals

To discuss Darwin, Freud, or James in a work of literary criticism hardly requires defense. Though all three were trained in science and considered themselves scientific thinkers, the relevance of their ideas for any study of late nineteenth- and twentieth-century Anglo-American literature is so well established as to be obvious. The names of the other scientists studied in this book – Charles Elton, Julian Huxley, Henry Eliot Howard, J.B.S. Haldane, C. Lloyd Morgan – are probably less familiar within literary studies, and their inclusion might thus seem to demand some further explanation. To begin, they are all major figures in the history of biology, part of the field's expansion in the post-Darwinian era. Elton was the founder of animal ecology in Britain, and Morgan of comparative psychology, a subfield which compared human and animal minds. Howard, an ornithologist, wrote influential behavior studies of birds that are retrospectively considered key works of early ethology. He is best known for his work theorizing territoriality in birds. And Julian Huxley and J.B.S. Haldane were the two most prominent popularizers of science in early twentieth-century Britain, in addition to being productive research scientists. Huxley's studies of bird courtship were landmarks in ethology, while Haldane participated in the "evolutionary synthesis," weaving together evolutionary theory with Gregor Mendel's heredity studies to create the modern understanding of genetics. Further, these biologists knew, read, and cited each other. Julian Huxley was at the center of this network. He and Haldane studied together at Oxford and were close friends; Elton was his student; and he corresponded with Morgan and Howard. The world of biological science in the early twentieth century was still small, and even as its practitioners were beginning to specialize, they were not so deep in the process as to lose contact with the wider field or the general public.

This network of biologists overlapped significantly with the literary network that included Wells, Aldous Huxley, Lawrence, and Woolf. Wells and Aldous Huxley are known as writers deeply conversant with scientific culture. The former studied biology under Thomas H. Huxley, made his name writing evolutionary fables in the 1890s, and in the 1920s collaborated with Julian Huxley and G.P. Wells on the textbook project

The Science of Life. The latter was Thomas H. Huxley's grandson and Julian's brother. He frequently made science and scientists the subjects of his fiction, most famously in the 1934 dystopian novel *Brave New World*. Lawrence and Woolf, in contrast, are not usually associated with the world of science, except as part of a general humanist backlash against instrumental reason (the Enlightenment drive to make all things calculable and thereby exploitable). But they, too, engaged with science and scientists in more specific ways. Lawrence was a close friend of Aldous Huxley and spent the winter of 1928 arguing with the Huxley brothers about science and evolution, an experience his late poetry seems to reflect. Woolf, too, knew the Huxley brothers and probably Haldane socially, and she even cited an essay by Julian in *Three Guineas*. Her writing is strewn with allusions, some obvious and some opaque, to modern science, as critics including Christina Alt and Holly Henry have shown.[30]

The newness of ecology, ethology, and comparative psychology meant that the late nineteenth- and early twentieth-century culture of zoology was in an incomplete state of professionalization and specialization, and therefore more permeable to literary and popular culture than science is today. This permeability between science and literature has been obscured, however, by the "two cultures" narrative. C. P. Snow's 1959 Rede Lecture, which argued that the sciences and arts had split into two mutually incomprehensible, indeed mutually hostile, discourses, continues to cast a shadow over the first half of the twentieth century.[31] From the paradisiacal "one culture" of the nineteenth century, the narrative goes, the sciences and arts had specialized, retreating into the two cultures, which Snow decried. Scientists, newly employed in universities, began publishing in disciplinary journals unsuited to untrained readers; writers, meanwhile, withdrew into aestheticism and modernism, refusing usefulness or mass appeal. Such a master narrative, of course, is by now a straw man that few, if any, scholars would endorse without at least half a dozen caveats, exceptions, and qualifications. But even without a legion of true believers, it remains a forceful story that exerts a pull on literary criticism. It is probably the reason why there is still so much more literature and science scholarship in Victorian studies than in modernist studies. And it is the reason why I was surprised to discover that Charles Elton, as late as 1958 in his book *The Ecology of Invasions by Animals and*

---

[30] Alt, *Virginia Woolf and the Study of Nature*; and Holly Henry, *Virginia Woolf and the Discourse of Science: The Aesthetics of Astronomy* (Cambridge University Press, 2003).
[31] C. P. Snow, "The Two Cultures" [1959], *Leonardo* 23.2–3 (1990): 169–73.

Plants, was quoting poetry and fiction; that Julian Huxley wrote poems, many inspired by scientific developments; that both men called for collaboration between professional scientists and amateur naturalists, whose knowledge they respected; and that so much of what Elton, Huxley, Howard, Morgan, and Haldane wrote is perfectly accessible to nonspecialists, indeed is designed for them.

Just as there is reason to think the scientists in this book were culturally literate and engaged with a wider public, there is also reason to think the writers were acquainted with scientific ideas. Perhaps the most successful competitor to the two cultures master narrative is the notion of a public culture of science. As historians have shown, scientific ideas circulated in a public discourse in the early twentieth century, one that may be called popular science or vernacular science, and one to which Woolf, Lawrence, Aldous Huxley, and Wells were certainly exposed. Museums, zoos and aquariums, science films, science journalism, public lectures, radio broadcasts, and educational materials all represent what Katherine Pandora and Karen A. Rader call "science in the everyday world," and all flourished in this period.[32] Scholars including David Elliston Allen, Peter J. Bowler, and Oliver Gaycken have explored this vibrant culture of popular science in the amateur natural history, science journalism, and scientific film of the early twentieth century.[33] Meanwhile literary critics such as Christina Walter, Holly Henry, Christina Alt, and Katherine Ebury have described modernist writers' uptake of popular science, ranging from the optical toys and illusions of the nineteenth century to the astronomy of Edwin Hubble, the natural history of writers like W.H. Hudson, and the "new physics" popularized by Arthur Eddington and James Jeans.[34] Literary modernism, they show, was energized by the public culture of science that developed in the nineteenth- and early twentieth centuries. The zoology of Julian Huxley, Haldane, Howard, Morgan, Elton, and others should be considered a key part of that culture.

[32] Katherine Pandora and Karen A. Rader, "Science in the Everyday World: Why Perspectives from the History of Science Matter," *Isis* 99.2 (2008): 350–64.

[33] David Elliston Allen, *The Naturalist in Britain: A Social History* (Allen Lane, 1976); Peter J. Bowler, *Science for All: The Popularization of Science in Early Twentieth-Century Britain* (University of Chicago Press, 2009); and Oliver Gaycken, *Devices of Curiosity: Early Cinema and Popular Science* (Oxford University Press, 2015).

[34] Christina Walter, *Optical Impersonality; Science, Images, and Literary Modernism* (Johns Hopkins University Press, 2014); Henry, *Virginia Woolf and the Discourse of Science*; Alt, *Virginia Woolf and the Study of Nature*; Katherine Ebury, *Modernism and Cosmology: Absurd Lights* (Palgrave Macmillan, 2014).

The writers and scientists under study here had a common cultural context in a more general sense as well. All were British; all were familiar with Darwin's evolutionary theory and, with the partial exception of Lawrence, accepted its tenets and implications; all were born in the Victorian era and sought to modernize or overturn Victorian conventions in their respective fields. That they should be British is more important than it might initially seem. While science and literature were fairly transnational enterprises in the early twentieth century, important local and national differences in flora, fauna, and the myths surrounding them persisted. A brief sketch of differences between US and British perceptions of nature and animal life is instructive here. As Joshua Schuster's book *The Ecology of Modernism* shows, key influences on American modernism's environmental thought included Thoreau's transcendentalism, a nineteenth-century belief in nature as plenteous and inexhaustible, the near-extinction of the bison, and the racial terror of the US South.[35] These were formative for twentieth-century American literature but their impact on British modernism was less direct. An outdoorsy American like Teddy Roosevelt or Ernest Hemingway could write about hunting the bear or fishing for trout in the American West, but in Britain the locales, the animals, and the history were different. A wildlife observer in early twentieth-century England might have seen rabbits, hedgehogs, bats, and many varieties of birds, perhaps a fox if he were lucky, but no wolves, bears, or panthers. Jeffrey McCarthy's *Green Modernism* argues that, in 1920s England, "nature" and "nation" were closely tied together, but British nature was more about hay-making, apple orchards, and an ancestral affinity to the land than about rugged wilderness.[36] It was domesticated and cozy, befitting a small island; perhaps it was best encapsulated in Elton's love for hedgerows, which he considered miniature nature reserves and emblems of Britishness.[37] British nature discourse typically dealt with "primitive" and predatory nature by relocating it to the colonies. This comparison suggests that, while it is important to study literary animals on a global scale, there is also good reason to study them within particular national traditions.

---

[35] Joshua Schuster, *The Ecology of Modernism: American Environments and Avant-Garde Poetics* (University of Alabama Press, 2015): 11–15, 82–102, and *passim*.

[36] Jeffrey Mathes McCarthy, *Green Modernism: Nature and the English Novel, 1900 to 1930* (Palgrave, 2016), 7–8, 116–22, and *passim*.

[37] Charles Elton, *The Ecology of Invasions by Animals and Plants* [1958] (University of Chicago Press, 2000), 155–8.

The shared intellectual network, cultural setting, and national environment justify examining British zoologists and writers side by side. But the question of how to conceptualize any connections found between the two disciplines remains open. The notion of a common *zeitgeist*, the historical period animated by a unitary spirit of the age, has largely fallen out of favor among literature and science scholars for being too vague. Yet the opposite extreme, a strict empiricism that allows the critic to posit only those connections between literature and science which are clearly and unambiguously demarcated in the historical record, is also objectionable. As John Holmes argues, "if we are discouraged from putting forward interpretations because they are not sufficiently empirically robust, we may end up consigning to oblivion that very substantial tranche of the past's engagement with science which has not left a firm enough imprint to be traced in more definite lines."[38] A middle ground can be found in the work of Gillian Beer, who defends the importance of "loose accords" across intellectual fields.[39] As Beer argues, an exacting systematicity in the study of literature and science is not always possible or even desirable. "[I]f we are to appraise the presences of scientific ideas and activities in literature," she writes, we must "take account also of the local: the fugitive allusion, the half-understood concept, the evasive reference whose significance takes us only some way."[40]

Beer's middle way, the unsystematic study of "loose accords," is largely the approach I have taken throughout this book. I have chosen literary and scientific figures who were linked by one or two degrees in a common intellectual network, but I have not limited my analysis of the traffic of ideas among them only to claims that can be proven via concrete historical evidence. I know that D.H. Lawrence and Julian Huxley argued about evolution in Switzerland, but I do not know if Lawrence had those arguments in mind when he wrote the poem "Self-Protection." Likewise, I know that Virginia Woolf met Julian Huxley and that she read some of his work, but I do not know if she read his essay "Philosophic Ants," or J.B.S. Haldane's essay "Possible Worlds," even though I see resonances between those essays and her novel *Flush*. Nevertheless, I have cited these and other instances as loose accords, possibly but not necessarily cases of

[38] John Holmes, "Literature and Science vs. History of Science," *Journal of Literature and Science* 5.2 (2012): 67–71, quote on 67.
[39] Gillian Beer, "Translation or Transformation? The Relations of Literature and Science," in *Open Fields: Science in Cultural Encounter*, by Gillian Beer (Clarendon Press, 1996): 173–95, quote on 195.
[40] Ibid., 185.

direct influence, which shed significant light on each figure's understanding of animal subjectivity. In the cases of H.G. Wells and Aldous Huxley, the literature mostly predates the ecological and ethological writing with which it shares ideas and rhetoric. In these cases, direct influence from fiction to science is unlikely; the more plausible explanation is that both the writers and the scientists were entering an existing post-Darwinian discourse about animal life, to which they all had access.

This book also follows Gillian Beer in its strategy of reading scientific texts *as* literature. Beer's field-defining *Darwin's Plots* (1983) performed close readings of *Origin of Species*, tracing Darwin's use of metaphor, narrative, and imagery with as much care as she lavished on the novels of George Eliot and Thomas Hardy. Paul Peppis's *Sciences of Modernism* takes a similar approach. Instead of treating the sciences as background context for modernist literature, Peppis affords equal attention to scientific and literary works, scrutinizing both through the eyes of the literary critic.[41] Like Peppis, I see scientific texts "as innovative texts in their own right, worthy of sustained, close, 'literary' analysis."[42] It is worth adding that Charles Elton thought the inverse was true too. In his 1927 book *Animal Ecology*, he wrote, "[T]here is more ecology in the Old Testament or the plays of Shakespeare than in most of the zoological textbooks ever published!"[43] This belief persisted in his 1958 *Ecology of Invasions by Animals and Plants*, in which he asserted that "[t]he first person to draw a picture of a food-chain was Peter Brueghel the Elder," in his engraving of a large fish.[44] If literary critics like Beer, Peppis, and me find literary tropes and storytelling structures within science, scientists like Elton perceive factual knowledge within literary and artistic works as well. The boundary between the two fields thus blurs from both sides.

Animal subjectivity, the third term in this book's equation, is perhaps the final rationale for reading zoology and literature together, for both science and literature aim to represent animals, and each has valuable methods for understanding animal life. Where science contributes techniques of observation, experimentation, and measurement, literature contributes techniques of empathy, intuition, and speculation. Animal subjectivity may thus be regarded as a shared domain, an area of inquiry inherently unbounded by discipline, and a space where

[41] Paul Peppis, *Sciences of Modernism: Ethnography, Sexology, and Psychology* (Cambridge University Press, 2014), 8–9.
[42] Ibid., 9.
[43] Charles Elton, *Animal Ecology* (Macmillan, 1927), 7.
[44] Elton, *Ecology of Invasions by Animals and Plants*, 126.

literature and science are changed by their encounters with each other. Leah Knight suggests that one possible avenue for future literature and science studies lies in "triangulation," the addition of a third term to the "literature and science" pairing.[45] This move is, she suggests, paradoxically, a way to narrow and expand the scope of research at the same time. While Knight remains somewhat wary of the trend, triangulation makes visible certain patterns that might otherwise go unnoticed. It gives us a new vantage point from which to look at old materials. In triangulating literature, science, and animals, it is this book's wager that all three will look different. It is not only that the scientists and literary writers under study here can show us some new things about animals; it is also that attention to animals reshaped their very understanding of what "science" and "literature" are.

Physics, Biology, and the Defamiliarization of the World

During the 1920s, the "new physics" was an object of interest for many writers. Its principles – relativity, uncertainty, a world of particles radically different from the ordinary world of visible matter – seemed to fit naturally with the values of literary modernism. Einstein's relativity meant that observers with different positions and velocities would measure the same event differently, the only constant being the speed of light; Heisenberg's uncertainty principle meant that a particle's position and momentum could not be precisely known at the same time. Both ideas undermined the notion of a stable, objective observer position, which helps to explain their popularity among a generation of writers who felt the grounds of knowledge shifting under their feet. D.H. Lawrence's 1929 poem "Relativity" is a classic example of the modernist attraction to modern physics:

> I like relativity and quantum theories
> because I don't understand them
> and they make me feel as if space shifted about
> like a swan that can't settle
> refusing to sit still and be measured;
> and as if the atom were an impulsive thing
> always changing its mind.[46]

---

[45] Leah Knight, "Historicising Early Modern Literature and Science: Recent Topics, Trends, and Problems," *Journal of Literature and Science* 5.2 (2012): 56–60, quote on 58.
[46] D. H. Lawrence, *The Complete Poems of D.H. Lawrence*, ed. Vivian de Sola Pinto and F. Warren Roberts (Penguin, 1993), 524, lines 1–7.

Lawrence, like most of his fellow writers, made no pretense to fully grasping the science of Einstein and Heisenberg, but he saw something alluring in its defamiliarization of the universe we thought we knew. In contrast, Lawrence did *not* like modern biology, which he considered mechanistic and disenchanting. Lawrence's view still reverberates in literary studies today, as critics explore the role of relativity theory and the uncertainty principle in twentieth-century intellectual culture but say little about the life sciences. Modern physics was revolutionary, unmooring knowledge itself, revealing all grounds for observation as unstable. Modern biology, meanwhile, was evolutionary, a mechanical process of slow, gradual change. At the risk of oversimplifying the critical perception, biology seemed Victorian, physics modernist.[47]

However, Lawrence's very frame of reference for understanding physics is zoological. He visualizes matter under the uncertainty principle as resembling a fidgety swan, resisting precise measurement just as animals in the field often do. The atom itself seems like a tiny, unpredictable animal with a "mind" of its own, one that scientists can't quite read. And at the same time that Lawrence was using his observations of animals to imagine quantum particles, J.B.S. Haldane and Julian Huxley were using the new physics to reimagine their own discipline. Twentieth-century biology was by no means exempt from the relativity craze. The thought experiments of Haldane and Huxley's essays show that modern biology did not always cling to the outdated positivistic notion of an objective observer. They made way for the epistemological shifts triggered by the physicists, and they aimed to show that zoology, too, could contribute to the ongoing defamiliarization of the visible world.

In "Kant and Scientific Thought," one of the essays in his 1927 book *Possible Worlds*, Haldane suggested that the current transformations in science and philosophy could be understood as a shift from a Cartesian worldview to a Kantian one. The Cartesian view assumed a material world of homogeneous space and time, one that scientists could study without worrying too much about the role of mind in shaping their observations. Around the beginning of the twentieth century, however, the Cartesian understanding of space began to break down. The failures of ordinary physics to explain or predict certain observed events led, Haldane explains, to the breakthroughs of Einstein. For Haldane, the

---

[47] For explorations of modernism, physics, and astronomy, see Michael H. Whitworth, *Einstein's Wake: Relativity, Metaphor, and Modernist Literature* (Oxford University Press, 2001); Ebury, *Modernism and Cosmology*; and Henry, *Virginia Woolf and the Discourse of Science*.

general theory of relativity meant "that the action of mind in perceiving homogeneous space and time is truly constitutive, and it is dubious
how far the space-like character of the event-manifold is not a mere con-
cession to our ideas of what a 'real' world ought to be like."[48] In other
words, properties previously thought to belong to the material world, like
the regularity of space and time, now appeared to be properties of mind
instead – we project regularity onto the world. Presumably drawing on
Kant's distinction between *noumena* and *phenomena*, things as they are
versus things as they are perceived, Haldane writes that physics had thus
arrived at "approximately the position reached by Kant in the *Critique of
Pure Reason*."[49] The world-in-itself and the world-known-to-humans cannot
be completely reconciled.

Like modern physics, modern biology is, per Haldane, "in a curiously
Kantian position."[50] It is caught between purposive and mechanistic
explanations of nature. Kant saw living organisms as purposive, having
some kind of teleological "natural end," although he was careful to say
that such purposes appear to us but cannot be proven objectively: "if
we want to investigate the organized products of nature by continued
observation, we find it completely unavoidable to apply [*unterlegen*] to
nature the concept of an intention, so that even for our empirical use of
reason this concept is an absolutely necessary maxim."[51] The twentieth-
century mechanists, by contrast, rejected purpose and the divine design
it implied, believing that all life processes follow the same laws of physics and chemistry that govern inorganic matter. As Haldane points out,
"[t]he mechanistic interpretation has nowhere broken down in detail."[52]
Yet biologists constantly found themselves thinking in Kantian terms,
speaking *as if there were* purpose in nature, discussing an organ's "function"
or its value as an "adaptation." The mechanistic approach does not afford
an explanation for the existence of self-organizing living creatures for
whom an organ might be understood as functional or adaptive, Haldane
argues. "At present," he writes, "with Kant, we are compelled to leave open
the question 'whether in the unknown inner ground of nature the physical
and teleological connection of the same things may not cohere in principle; we only say that our reason cannot so unite them.'"[53] Haldane did

[48] J. B. S. Haldane, *Possible Worlds* [1927] (Transaction, 2009), 126.
[49] Ibid., 127.
[50] Ibid.
[51] Immanuel Kant, *The Critique of Judgment* [1790], transl. Werner S. Pluhar (Hackett, 1987), 280.
[52] Haldane, *Possible Worlds*, 127.
[53] Ibid., 128.

not suppose that the Kantian standpoint of modern biology was the final word, but he made no predictions as to how the two modes of understanding life – mechanism versus purposiveness – would be reconciled. The current state of scientific knowledge, in his view, was too limited to see that far ahead.

Haldane wasn't the only one to link modern biology to Kantian philosophy. In Aldous Huxley's 1936 novel *Eyeless in Gaza*, one character suggests to another that she should read "one or two of the modern Kantians," perhaps "von Uexküll's *Theoretical Biology*. You see, Kant's behind all our twentieth-century science. Just as Newton was behind all the science of the eighteenth and nineteenth ..."[54] The remark is presented as an aside, and the author does not explain what it means, but the reference is to twentieth-century German biologist Jakob von Uexküll. Uexküll is best known for introducing the idea of *Umwelten*, the phenomenological worlds of animals, to biology. As Malte Herwig explains, Uexküll studied Kant with the poet Rainer Maria Rilke. Kant's transcendental idealism, which held that we construct our notion of the world from sense impressions (phenomena) but cannot know the world in itself (noumena), was a major influence on Uexküll's conceptualization of *Umwelten*.[55] Uexküll, Herwig writes, wanted to add to the objective approaches of physics, chemistry, and traditional biology "a new 'subjective biology,' which focuses on the qualities and characteristics of objects and how they are perceived by an organism."[56] The subjective biologist must know about the ecology, behavior, and physiology of the creature he is studying, but he also must be able to perform thought experiments into the animal's *Umwelt*. As Herwig sums up, "the ethologist has to put himself in the place of the animals he observes ... sometimes by trying to think in terms of 'their world' in order to understand their behavior and not apply human standards."[57]

Haldane and Julian Huxley, too, described forays into the *Umwelten* of animals in their writing, and these thought experiments led them to posit another connection between physics and biology: the two sciences had analogous notions of relativity. In his 1923 essay "A Journey in Relativity" (an alternative version of "Philosophic Ants," discussed in Chapter 4), Huxley writes, "Relativity is in the air. It is so much in the

[54] Aldous Huxley, *Eyeless in Gaza* [1936] (Harper Perennial, 1964), 141.
[55] Malte Herwig, "The Unwitting Muse: Jakob von Uexküll's Theory of Umwelt and Twentieth-Century Literature," *Semiotica* 134:1 (2001): 553–93.
[56] Ibid., 571.
[57] Ibid., 568.

air that it becomes almost stifling at times; but even so, its sphere so far has been the inorganic sciences, and we have heard little of the equally important biological relativity."[58] The rest of the essay aims to show that the human understanding of the world is shaped by our biology: our size, the range of vibrations audible to our ears, the range of wavelengths visible to our eyes, our biological rhythms. Evidently inspired by H.G. Wells's *The Time Machine*, Huxley imagines an inventor creating a machine that could speed up his biological processes, revealing a new world of colors he has never seen and sounds he has never dreamt of. Huxley concludes with a "moral": alongside Occam's razor, the principle of parsimony, "[w]e want another razor – a Relativist Razor; and with that ... we will shave the Absolute."[59] Huxley's reflections here and in the related essay "Philosophic Ants" inspired Haldane's piece "Possible Worlds," which envisions how an intelligent barnacle, bee, dog, and alien might construct their science and philosophy. These essays show that scientific knowledge is shaped and limited by humans' biological capacities. Scientists are animals too and, Huxley and Haldane demonstrate, the world of science is just one *Umwelt* among many.

A final point about modern biology: not only did it accept epistemological relativity and a Kantian divide between what may be perceived and what is, it also harbored the negative capability described by Keats – "that is, when a man is capable of being in uncertainties, mysteries, doubts, without any irritable reaching after fact and reason."[60] One sees negative capability in certain passages by Haldane and Lloyd Morgan, but it is Howard who expresses it most fully. In his preface to *The Nature of a Bird's World*, Howard makes no effort to advertise the findings or scientific value of his book. Instead he writes the following:

> In this book I seek the nature of a bird's world, not with any hope of finding it but to know what to find. There is more joy in finding a problem than in trying to solve one, for to solve a problem is vain delusion.

> There is a mystery of flight, a mystery of song, a mystery of a nest; and yet, not three mysteries but one: a bird is the mystery, for it steals our values of beauty and mingles them strangely in form no less than in feathers; in colour no less than in song; and in what we value most, devotion to its home.

---

[58] Julian Huxley, "A Journey in Relativity," *North American Review* 218.1 (1923): 67–75, quote on 67.

[59] Ibid., 75.

[60] John Keats, *The Complete Poetical Works and Letters of John Keats* (Houghton, Mifflin and Company, 1899), 277.

> And no less strangely it seems to mingle the blindness of an insect with the intelligence of an ape; and because nothing is really blind and no one is likely to know what intelligence really is, mysteries will be mysteries still. I would not change it.[61]

A reader expecting to find dull, disenchanting mechanism or pretensions of objectivity in modern biology will be perplexed by this preface. And the author cannot be dismissed as an overly mystical outlier – he knew as much as anyone about avian ethology, and his fellow zoologists frequently cited his work. Howard went out looking for new scientific knowledge about birds, but the birds showed him something beyond science. As with many of his peers, encounters with animals and thought experiments about animal worlds reshaped his understanding of the scientific endeavor. Mystery alongside mechanism, relativity alongside reductionism, and subjective experience alongside objective fact: modern zoology made space for these possibilities.

Real Toads, Imaginary Gardens

If one had to identify a starting point for modernist animal studies, one could do worse than W.H. Auden's essay "Two Bestiaries" (published in the 1962 collection *The Dyer's Hand and Other Essays*). Auden is best known as a late-modernist poet, but in this essay he takes on the role of a critic, meditating on the work of D.H. Lawrence and Marianne Moore. Though Lawrence and Moore might appear to have little in common – Lawrence's expressive, passionate free verse seems the opposite of Moore's careful, restrained syllabic verse – Auden pairs them because "many of [their] best poems are, overtly, at least, about animals."[62] And not merely "about animals," but "about animals" in the same way. Auden offers a taxonomy of animals in literature that places Lawrence and Moore in the same genus. Literary animals, he writes, may be (1) the subjects of fables, (2) the vehicles of similes, (3) "allegorical emblems" (i.e. symbols), (4) props for the "romantic encounter of man and beast"; or, as in the "bestiaries" of Lawrence and Moore, (5) "objects of human interest and affection."[63] In Lawrence's case, Auden argues that animals offer a respite from his usual misanthropy: "Whenever, in his writings, he forgets about men and women with proper names and describes the anonymous life of

---

[61] H. Eliot Howard, *The Nature of a Bird's World* (Cambridge University Press, 1925), vii.

[62] W. H. Auden, *The Dyer's Hand and Other Essays* (Random House, 1962), 300.

[63] Ibid., 300–2, quote on 302.

stones, waters, forests, animals, flowers, chance traveling companions or passers-by, his bad temper and his dogmatism immediately vanish and he becomes the most enchanting companion imaginable."[64] In Moore's case, her "animal poems are those of a naturalist; the animals she selects are animals she likes" – pangolins, elephants, jerboas, even humans.[65] As Kelly Sultzbach shows, this assessment of Lawrence and Moore reflects Auden's own interest in and affection for animals, who are frequent subjects of his late poetry.[66] He links scientific curiosity about animals with a poetic warmth, so that liking animals, studying them, and writing good poetry about them are all of a piece, and Lawrence, Moore, and Auden himself are birds of a feather.

Auden's five categories of literary animals offer a useful way of mapping modernist animal studies since then. The fable, which Auden explains may be "educative" or "satirical" but rarely "realistic" about animal life, is an important modernist genre for writers including Franz Kafka, Marianne Moore, and H.G. Wells. As Joshua Schuster points out, fables have gotten rather a bad rap – critics accuse them of saying little about human psychology and even less about animals.[67] Yet Moore herself liked fables and translated those of La Fontaine, and Schuster suggests that her animal poems can be read as "modernist fables" which "offer an alternative world of form, style, wit, fantasy, embodiment, and utopian longing for animal communion compared to a modernity primarily driven by capitalist expediency and human-centered agendas."[68] Read as fables, modernist animal poems offer an important critique of instrumental reason, which makes little space for either Moorean virtues like restraint, grace, and wit or Lawrentian virtues like vivacity and free expression. As I argue in Chapter 1, in Wells's hands the fable even becomes a mode of critiquing anthropocentrism itself – the "moral" is typically a warning against human hubris, a reminder that we do not stand outside of "nature."

The animal simile, a favorite technique of Aldous Huxley, identifies commonalities between animals and humans. For example, a man is like a wolf (to paraphrase Freud) because both are violent and predatory. Animal similes and metaphors have been fruitful objects of analysis for

---

[64] Ibid., 289.
[65] Ibid., 303.
[66] Kelly Sultzbach, *Ecocriticism in the Modernist Imagination* (Cambridge University Press, 2016), 176–7.
[67] Schuster, *The Ecology of Modernism*, 27.
[68] Ibid., 46.

modernist animal studies, yet they also produce a lot of critical anxiety. Partly this is because, as Carrie Rohman shows, modernist writers often used them to dehumanize marginalized people. T. S. Eliot, for example, combined anti-Semitic stereotypes with animal imagery in his Sweeney poems, and in "Burbank with a Baedeker" directly compared Jews to rats; Joseph Conrad, meanwhile, portrayed Africans as animalistic beings whose loincloths "[waggle] to and fro like tails" in *Heart of Darkness*; and Lawrence used animal similes to demean Mexicans in *The Plumed Serpent*.[69] In some cases, more generous readings of these similes are possible – "Does Marlow consciously equate the men with animals," asks Rohman, "[o]r does he perceive that they are *being treated like animals* by the machinery of imperialist conquest?"[70] In other cases, though, the complicity with racist stereotypes is obvious. Modernist writers were neither the first nor the last to use animal similes to prop up racist ideologies, but this recurrent pattern has made critics justly suspicious of animal comparisons in modernist literature.

Another reason animal similes and metaphors raise critics' hackles is because they seem bound up with an anthropocentrism that assumes literary representations of animals are only worthy of attention insofar as they are "really" about humans. As Susan McHugh argues in *Animal Stories*, critics have traditionally been ready to grant poetic animals like Shelley's nightingale literary value only insofar as they metaphorically represent some facet of human experience. "[T]he aesthetic structures of metaphor," she argues, "seem unable to bear animal agency."[71] As the metaphorical meaning becomes visible, the literal animal recedes. Like McHugh, Philip J. Armstrong argues that most cultural criticism "read[s] animals as screens for the projection of human interests and meanings"; the task of animal studies, in response, is to recognize animals as agents, material actors, or subjects.[72] Even Auden, in "Two Bestiaries," seems cognizant of this problem, writing that while the animal simile "is more realistic than the beast fable ... what is described is the behavior considered typical for that animal; everything else about it is considered irrelevant."[73] It is hard for comparative figures like the simile and metaphor to do justice to the full complexity of animal life.

[69] Rohman, *Stalking the Subject*, 34–6, 43–4, 55–6.
[70] Ibid., 44.
[71] Susan McHugh, *Animal Stories: Narrating Across Species Lines* (University of Minnesota Press, 2011), 7.
[72] Philip J. Armstrong, *What Animals Mean in the Fiction of Modernity* (Routledge, 2008), 2.
[73] Auden, *The Dyer's Hand*, 300.

The "allegorical emblem" is likewise a figure that makes animals represent some human implication, but here the ambiguity of meaning seems to hold more promise for animal studies scholarship. Allegory has been an important interpretive method for modernist animal studies, in part because it can accommodate the broad significance of animal representations without evacuating their literal referents. For example, Akira Mizuta Lippit, in *Electric Animal*, reads modern representations of animals in literature, film, and psychoanalysis as symbols of a bygone era in which real animals flourished. Drawing on John Berger's influential claim that "Everywhere animals disappear," Lippit argues that the modern animal is a spectral animal, one in "a state of perpetual vanishing."[74] As real animals diminished in number during the nineteenth- and twentieth centuries, becoming endangered in the face of environmental destruction or hidden away in factory farms and slaughterhouses, they began to appear everywhere in "humanity's reflections on itself: in philosophy, psychoanalysis, and technological media such as the telephone, film, and radio."[75] Under Western modernity, the human and natural worlds came to be understood as essentially severed, Lippit writes, and the animal became an object of repeated sacrifice and mourning. Cinema is, for Lippit, the paradigmatic case: the film stock becomes the last refuge of animals and a space where they remain alive in death.

Like Lippit, Kari Weil reads the animals of modernist literature as symbolizing things excluded from modernity. The process of Enlightenment pushes the animal back into a lost past that can be mourned but not accommodated. Weil discusses Kafka's "A Report to an Academy" as a key example of modernism's theme of half-remembered animality. The story is an allegory of civilization and the animalistic ways of being it disavows.[76] Red Peter, the narrator, is an ape who has learned to talk and become human, a process of "progress" he could achieve only by harsh self-discipline: "My ape nature fled out of me, head over heels and away."[77] The animal represents, Weil suggests, the repressed, the traumatic, the unrepresentable – all that is excommunicated from Enlightenment reason. This understanding of the animal's role in modernism, I would add, bears strong affinities to Freud's account of

---

[74] Akira Mizuta Lippit, *Electric Animal: Toward a Rhetoric of Wildlife* (University of Minnesota Press, 2000), 1.
[75] Ibid., 3.
[76] Kari Weil, *Thinking Animals: Why Animal Studies Now?* (Columbia University Press, 2012), 12–14.
[77] Franz Kafka, "A Report to an Academy" [1917], transl. Willa and Edwin Muir, in *The Complete Stories*, by Franz Kafka (Schocken Books, 1971), 281–91, quote on 289.

animality as a part of human history that still resides in the unconscious, buried but not gone.

In *Stalking the Subject*, the most important treatment to date of animals in British modernism, Carrie Rohman envisions animals less as vanished than as forcibly expelled from modernity, and yet still lurking at its borders, reminding the humans inside of what they have had to exclude to justify their ways of thinking and living. Although this problem is as old as Western humanism itself, it became a particular preoccupation in the early twentieth century, when it was "refracted ... through the lenses of evolutionary theory, British imperialism, antirationalism, and even the discourse of psychoanalysis."[78] Rohman argues that while some modernist texts, like the aforementioned works of Eliot, Conrad, and Lawrence, reinscribe the boundary around the (typically male, European) human by displacing animality onto racial and sexual others, other modernist texts erase the divide, embracing the possibility of becoming-animal. In works like Djuna Barnes's *Nightwood*, this process culminates in an animalization of language itself: in "the modernist rejection of traditional forms ... animality is instantiated in the language as well as the thematics of canonical literature."[79] For Rohman, modernism's "discourse of species" makes and unmakes the human subject, which is constituted by its difference from animal others and radically transformed when that difference is erased.

Key to all of these allegorical readings is that, while the textual animals within them come to signify a premodern past, a part of human nature disavowed by modern civilization, or an experience that is unrepresentable within human language, they do not stop signifying themselves. They are not arbitrary symbols; they are also historically connected to these meanings. It is because human activity has driven many species to the brink of extinction that Lippit sees animals as ghostly symbols of the past. It is because evolutionary theory taught the modernist generation that we are phylogenetically related to other animals that Rohman sees animals as encroaching on the belief in human exceptionalism. And it is because intellectuals have increasingly come to realize that animals have some phenomenological experience, even though they cannot communicate it to us directly, that Weil sees animals as pointing, obliquely, to what lies outside language.

---

[78] Rohman, *Stalking the Subject*, 21.
[79] Ibid., 27.

However, the danger with modernism's allegorical animals is that they may slide into a more abstract primitivism, bolstering the culture/nature divide while ignoring the specificity and diversity of actual animals. Auden, for example, criticizes literature featuring a "romantic encounter of man and beast" because "in these encounters, the nature of the animal itself has little, if anything, to do with the thoughts and emotions he provokes in the human individual"; only the human's thoughts and emotions matter. Such representations tend to be "[in]-accurate in their natural history," since the actual animal at hand is mostly irrelevant to the artist's point.[80] In *What Animals Mean in the Fiction of Modernity*, Philip J. Armstrong levels a similar critique at a particular type of human-animal encounter prominent in modernism: the hunt. Armstrong points out that primitivist modernists, including Lawrence and Ernest Hemingway, turned against modernity as they dreamed of restoring a way of life in which animals including humans could be wild again. They felt that "it was time for art to break loose, go feral and return to a revitalizing savagery."[81] For Hemingway especially, it was the hunt which offered the best escape from the deadening abstractions of modern civilization – in the hunt one could *be* an animal, an apex predator. However, Armstrong sees this movement as a failed project in its efforts to return animals to their lost glory. "For all its insistence on the urgency of a renewed intimacy between humanity and animality – either hostile or symbiotic – modernist therio-primitivism thus repeats the modern transformation of the animal into an abstraction," he writes. "Where industrial modernity reduces animals to a collection of raw materials or a sequence of processes, modernist aesthetic sublimates them into essence. As a consequence, actual animals always prove inadequate."[82] In other words, the modernist encounter of man and beast falls prey to the same trap of anthropocentrism and abstraction as the romantic encounter that Auden described.

While many of the animal representations under study in this book can be classified as fable, simile or metaphor, allegorical symbol, or romantic encounter, they are best described by Auden's fifth category of literary animals: those that draw out the poet's interest and affection. This category overlaps the others, but its particular characteristics include a

---

[80] Auden, *The Dyer's Hand*, 302.
[81] Armstrong, *What Animals Mean in the Fiction of Modernity*, 134.
[82] Ibid., 149.

keen interest in observing animals, akin to a naturalist's; an admiration
and fondness for animals; a willingness to use "anthropomorphic terms"
of description; and, paradoxically, a recognition of animals' separateness
from us. On the surface Auden's language to name this category may
seem old-fashionedly humanist – "animals as *objects* of *human* interest
and affection" (my emphasis). Yet, as Sultzbach argues, this category actually "avoids a human-centered approach" and "anticipates the 'respecere'
advanced by current animal advocate Donna Haraway," *respecere* meaning
both to re-see and to respect.[83] When Auden praises the type of poet who
would "describe [an animal] in the same way that he would describe a
friend, that is to say, every detail of the animal's appearance and behavior
will interest him," he captures something of that *respecere*.[84]

Auden's calm acceptance of anthropomorphism may surprise some
readers, since anthropomorphism has, like the fable, gotten a bad rap.
Lorraine Daston and Gregg Mitman, for example, call it "the irresistible
taboo."[85] But in some circumstances anthropomorphism offers a way of
re-seeing and respecting animals within our necessarily human framework. The traditional critique of anthropomorphism is that it is unscientific and sentimental, projecting human traits onto creatures who are
very different from us. Yet, as Auden points out, anthropomorphism is
often necessary to make "a description communicable to others."[86] And,
as Eileen Crist argues, in the hands of careful and observant writers like
Darwin, anthropomorphism cannot be dismissed as "erroneous," untutored, or naïve; on the contrary, it reflects a "perception of subjectivity
in the animal world" and a belief "that living is experientially meaningful for animals and that their actions are authored."[87] The primatologist
Frans de Waal has warned against "anthropodenial" – "the a priori
rejection of shared characteristics between humans and animals when
in fact they may exist" – as a standpoint that may lead to error just as
anthropomorphism sometimes does.[88] Kneejerk, careless forms of anthropomorphism warrant criticism, as Chapter 2 discusses, but writers like

---

[83] Sultzbach, *Ecocriticism in the Modernist Imagination*, 176–7.
[84] Auden, *The Dyer's Hand*, 302.
[85] Lorraine Daston and Gregg Mitman, "Introduction: The How and Why of Thinking with
Animals," in *Thinking with Animals: New Perspectives on Anthropomorphism*, ed. Lorraine Daston
and Gregg Mitman (Columbia University Press, 2005): 1–14, quote on 1.
[86] Auden, *The Dyer's Hand*, 302.
[87] Eileen Crist, *Images of Animals: Anthropomorphism and Animal Mind* (Temple University Press,
1999), 12.
[88] Frans de Waal, "Anthropomorphism and Anthropodenial: Consistency in Our Thinking About
Humans and Animals," *Philosophical Topics* 27.1 (1999): 255–80, quote on 258.

Woolf and scientists like Julian Huxley also used anthropomorphism
in more thoughtful ways as they attempted to represent animal life
accurately and fully.

   Curiosity, observant seeing, and respect for animals are the values that
Auden and Haraway share, and this book argues that, at their best, the
modernist literature and science writing under study here foster these
virtues. For Haraway, we have an obligation to our "companion species,"
the species with which we share our lives and our planet, to take interest in them. The trouble with much animal philosophy, from Derrida to
Deleuze and Guattari, is that it does not sustain this curiosity.[89] Derrida
may begin his philosophical meditation *The Animal That Therefore I
Am* by looking at his cat, "a real cat, truly, believe me, *a little cat.*"[90] But
once the philosophizing begins, "the cat [is] never heard from again."[91]
Similarly, Haraway argues, Deleuze and Guattari's notion of the wolf-
pack has nothing to do with "[m]undane, prosaic, living wolves."[92]
Haraway suggests that zoological science might fill a gap here. True,
much science objectifies animals; many scientists throughout the history
of biology "observe real animals and write about them but never meet
their gaze." But not all. "What if not all such Western human workers
with animals have refused the risk of an intersecting gaze, even if it usually has to be teased out from the repressive literary conventions of scientific publishing and descriptions of method?" Haraway asks. "Why did
Derrida not ask, even in principle, if a Gregory Bateson or Jane Goodall
or Marc Bekoff or Barbara Smuts or many others have met the gaze of
living, diverse animals and in response undone and redone themselves
and their sciences?"[93] This is not a reactionary defense of old-school,
objective, scientific positivism; it is rather a defense of biologists as people who are curious about animals for their own sake, who work and live
with them, and who develop forms of knowledge *with* them. The same
might be said of the early twentieth-century literary writers under study
here. Their animal representations may be seen as exhibits of folk zoology
as well as of literary modernism.

   To read modernism's animals as folk zoology, or as the expressions
of writers inhabiting the guise of naturalists, is not to deny any useful

[89] Haraway, *When Species Meet*, 20.
[90] Jacques Derrida, "The Animal That Therefore I Am (More to Follow)," transl. David Wills, *Critical
    Inquiry* 28.2 (2002): 369–418, quote on 374.
[91] Haraway, *When Species Meet*, 20.
[92] Ibid., 27.
[93] Ibid., 21.

distinction between science and literature. It's still the case that scientists are predominantly after the production of knowledge about the material world, and literary writers are predominantly after the creation of aesthetic experiences within humans. But if we temporarily bracket that distinction, we will better perceive the ways that scientific writing about animals creates aesthetic experiences, and the ways that literary writing about animals produces knowledge. We will see that scientific and literary modes of description shade into each other, and that curiosity motivates both. Curiosity is an epistemic and aesthetic virtue, and it can be an ethical virtue too in its assumption that animals are subjects worth getting to know. Auden writes of Marianne Moore that "[t]he approach of her poetry is that of a naturalist but, really, their theme is almost always the Good Life."[94] But these two things are not opposed. For Moore, Auden, Wells, Huxley, Lawrence, and Woolf, as well as for the modern zoologists discussed in these pages, animals are part of the Good Life – living with them, observing them, admiring them, learning about and from them.

In "Poetry" (1920), Moore offers one of the most famous, and most enigmatic, manifestos of modernist literature, and it is one centered on an animal. Poets, she writes, must be "'literalists of/the imagination'" who "can present/for inspection, imaginary gardens with real toads/in them."[95] The call here has long struck critics as puzzling and paradoxical – how can something be both real and imaginary? There is a tension between the material immediacy of "real toads" and the "imaginary gardens" that house them, a tension which charges "Poetry" and literature about animals more generally. If we think of the garden as a human production, carefully cultivated to sustain toads, flowers, and other species, perhaps we can better understand Moore's point. A garden is a living frame, demarcating a space where our *Umwelt* and an animal's overlap. A poem might be a similar frame; so is anthropomorphism; so is an aquarium tank. They are the forms that give form to our encounters with animals. As Joshua Schuster argues, "Moore's poetics make clear [that] mediation is the means by which we share our human-animal worlds in the first place."[96] Likewise, I would argue, for the other modernist writers and scientists in this book. Their works reflect the draw of animals in their alluring otherness, and at the same time

---

[94] Auden, *The Dyer's Hand*, 304.
[95] Marianne Moore, "Poetry," in *Others for 1919: An Anthology of the New Verse*, ed. Alfred Kreymborg (Nicholas L. Brown, 1920): 131–2, lines 34–5, 36–8.
[96] Schuster, *The Ecology of Modernism*, 46.

they recognize that human frameworks always shape our understanding of other species. The goal of this book is not to extricate the "real toads" from the "imaginary gardens," but to study them together, in natural history and modernist poetry and everything in between.

Animal Subjects takes on the study of these "imaginary gardens" in the works of four modernist writers and a handful of modern zoologists. It begins with texts that look at animals from an external perspective, regarding their minds as existent but mysterious and less knowable than their ecology or behavior. And it ends with texts that aim for thick descriptions of animals' inner lives, including their emotions, sensations, and thoughts. The book's arc thus moves from objective to empathic ways of knowing. Chapter 1, "H.G. Wells, Charles Elton, and the Struggle for Existence," focuses on Wells as a transitional figure between Victorian and modernist cultures. Wells grew up in the world reinterpreted by Darwin, and his early writings reveal an unflinching view of the most disturbing aspects of Darwinism – nature's indifference to humans, the probability of extinction, the waste endemic to the struggle for existence. His fin-de-siècle stories represent a transitional form between Darwinian evolution and the twentieth-century ecology of figures like Charles Elton, who made the struggle for existence measurable. Wells and Elton both fixated on animal invasions as events in which that struggle for existence might be witnessed. For Wells, invasions signified resistance to human efforts at controlling nature, especially the efforts of the British Empire. For Elton, invasive species produced doubts about the efficacy of ecology itself as a means of control. Both saw in the "entangled banks" of nature a challenge to human sovereignty, a grotesque profusion of life and death that was disquieting but that could also be pleasurable in its carnivalesque upsetting of the hierarchies inherited from natural theology.

Like Wells, Aldous Huxley occupies a transitional space between the Victorian and twentieth-century cultures of science. In Huxley's novels of the 1920s and 30s – the subject of Chapter 2, "Aldous Huxley, Henry Eliot Howard, and the Observational Ethic" – animals frequently appear as test subjects for laboratory biologists. Huxley's depiction of laboratory biology adapts the discourse of the Victorian antivivisection movement, aiming to shine an unflattering light on animal experimentation without falling into the traps of sentimentality. His fiction also offers an alternative to the violent intrusions of vivisection, as characters adopt noninterventional forms of observation and empirical description. For Huxley, who was on the brink of his 1930s turn to vegetarianism and pacifism, this noninvasive, epistemologically modest kind of observation represented a more ethical way of being. It was also methodologically close to a new branch of zoology: ethology, or the study of animals' behaviors in their normal habitats. Huxley's brother Julian and the ornithologist Henry Eliot Howard were among the pioneers of scientific ethology, a field which reached its classical period in the 1950s under the guidance of Konrad Lorenz and Niko Tinbergen. Howard's work occupies a liminal position between the anthropomorphic, subjectively rich descriptions of natural history and the strictly objective descriptions of Tinbergen and Lorenz, and its outlook is quite close to Aldous Huxley's. For both, empirical observation and thin description reflected not a belief that animals are mindless machines, but a respect for animals as conscious subjects whose experience is only partly knowable.

Julian Huxley and D.H. Lawrence shared Aldous Huxley and Henry Eliot Howard's commitment to observing animals, but they were much less reluctant to pen subjective, speculative, thick descriptions of animal life, as Chapter 3, "Romantic Ethologies: D.H. Lawrence and Julian Huxley," illustrates. Lawrence and Julian Huxley, who met through Aldous, saw themselves as oppositional figures – Lawrence hated the scientific rationalism that Huxley stood for, while Huxley found Lawrence's embrace of vitalism and "the dark loins of man" ridiculous. Despite their apparent opposition, the two had a good deal in common when it came to their understanding of animals. Both were essentially Romantics, rather than mechanists, who saw animals as creatures of instinct and emotion. And both employed empathy – imagining themselves in an animal's place – as a method of knowing. Their thick descriptions of animal behaviors are more ambitious than Howard's or Aldous Huxley's, but their evocative representations of animal life also involved a certain amount of risk. Their interpretations might always be wrong, their claims about animal subjectivity ungrounded. Lawrence and Julian Huxley can both be justly accused of projecting their own values onto the animal world, seeing what they are predisposed to see. They can also be justly praised, however, for their empathetic outlook, which insists that animals are not reducible to scenery or machinery but are the subjects of their own lives.

The writers under study in Chapter 4, "Bloomsbury's Comparative Psychology: Bertrand Russell, Julian Huxley, J.B.S. Haldane, Virginia Woolf," likewise sought to represent animal subjectivity from the inside. Russell, Julian Huxley, Haldane, and Woolf drew on the discipline of comparative psychology as they attempted to construct animals'

Umwelten and see the world from animals' perspectives. Unlike the works analyzed in Chapter 3, however, which focused on animal instincts and emotions, the writers discussed in Chapter 4 considered sensations – visual, aural, tactile, olfactory, gustatory – the key to animal life. Building on the same empiricist framework that structured comparative psychology, these writers approached animal subjectivity by imagining animals' sensory experiences. In the process, they came to recognize the human world as a construct of the human sensorium, and science as a relativistic picture of the world that is limited by our biological capabilities. What Woolf and her peers realized was that "the world" is better conceptualized as a set of overlapping phenomenological worlds, animal and human. Even further, they saw that our only hope of understanding animal worlds is to combine the careful observational techniques of science with the empathic power and negative capability of literature.

In its conclusion, *Animal Subjects* asks how modernism's animal worlds relate to popular science narratives today. Looking at four contemporary case studies – the tardigrade, the octopus, the whale, and the mantis shrimp – it finds that modernist ideas about animal subjectivity resonate in many ways with twenty-first-century animal discourse. The major historical shift has been that, while the modernists had some inkling that human activities were putting many animals and plants in environmental distress, they did not know, as we do, that they were living in a new age of global warming and mass extinction. Modernism's animals speak to us differently now. They still invite us into strange, enchanting animal worlds, but now, when we enter those worlds, (to borrow a phrase from Eliot) at our backs in a cold blast we hear the ticking clock of climate change, ever louder. The ethical call is louder too; it calls us to find ways to bring forth a livable, vibrant multispecies world.

CHAPTER I

H. G. Wells, Charles Elton, and the Struggle for Existence

Killer ants, three-eyed amphibians, man-eating cephalopods, vicious flying lemurs, and one vengeful extinct bird populate the landscapes of H. G. Wells's early short fiction – not to mention the Morlocks, Beast People, and insectoid Martians of his novels. His animals are rarely cute and never cuddly. They represent a "nature red in tooth and claw," a nature that preys on humans and threatens our precarious dominion over the globe. Aggressive, inscrutable, and occasionally cartoonish, the animals of Wells's fin-de-siècle writing dare to compete with humans in the scramble for territory and preeminence. Today, hyper-intelligent, predatory creatures are a staple of campy sci-fi movies, but in the 1890s Wells was inventing a new genre. Why did he write so many of these animal horror stories?

The answer, this chapter argues, is that Wells was remixing Darwin's concept of the struggle for existence for the fin de siècle, a period obsessed with cultural, biological, and imperial decadence. Wells popularized a new kind of fable which dramatized the struggle for existence among animals, including humans, in order to teach his readers lessons about their place in the world. These stories have mostly received critical attention as precursors or supplements to his scientific romances – *The Time Machine*, *The War of the Worlds*, *The Island of Doctor Moreau*, and so on – but they also warrant study as an innovative form in their own right. To some extent, Wells's short stories conform to the conventions of late Victorian print culture. They were first published in newspapers and magazines like the *Pall Mall Gazette*, *Pearson's Magazine*, and *The Strand*, which, as Winnie Chan shows in her study of the fin de siècle boom in short stories, demanded of would-be writers both commercial appeal and highbrow aesthetic effect.[1] Like many writers of the period, Wells was trying to get paid and managed to find a profitable formula.

[1] Winnie Chan, *The Economy of the Short Story in British Periodicals of the 1890s* (Routledge, 2007).

But he was also up to something more peculiar in his stories, something that exceeds their marketplace context.[2] The stories blended imperial anxieties with zoological knowledge and grotesque aesthetics, resulting in a generic novelty: a decadent Darwinian fable.

In many ways, Wells's short stories are barometers of 1890s literary trends. Like so many classics of the period – Joseph Conrad's *Heart of Darkness* and *Lord Jim*, Henry James's *Turn of the Screw*, Bram Stoker's *Dracula*, Arthur Conan Doyle's *Hound of the Baskervilles* – these tales use framing devices and stories-within-a-story to incorporate multiple narrative points of view, troubling the epistemological certainty of the omniscient narrator. Like Conrad's novels and the work of Robert Louis Stevenson and H. Rider Haggard, they take on – and ironize – the conventions of the imperial romance. And like Oscar Wilde's *Picture of Dorian Gray*, Thomas Hardy's *Tess of the d'Urbervilles*, and Stevenson's *Strange Case of Dr. Jekyll and Mr. Hyde*, they fixate on the specter of degeneration, often using gothic imagery to illustrate the threat to civilization (Wells's gothicism tends to be tinged with ironic humor). Wells did not have much regard for either Wilde or Stevenson, rejecting both art for art's sake and literature as imperial propaganda. Nevertheless, critics have recognized for some time that despite his oppositional stance, Wells was very much enmeshed in, and influenced by, 1890s literary culture.[3]

In British literary history, "decadence" is usually associated with Oscar Wilde, Algernon Charles Swinburne, Aubrey Beardsley, and the *Yellow Book* contributors – writers and artists who, like their counterparts in France, embraced art for art's sake and "perversity" of both style and

---

[2] Though Wells was quite successful in the 1890s, especially after *The Time Machine* became a hit, he was never solely about commercial success. In fact, when Joseph Conrad and Ford Madox Ford got the idea to write a *Treasure Island*-style romance together in the hopes of making a lot of money, Wells objected vociferously on political and aesthetic grounds, as Linda Dryden shows in *Joseph Conrad and H. G. Wells: The Fin-de-Siècle Literary Scene* (Palgrave Macmillan, 2015), 40–58.

[3] A number of recent critical works have sought to frame Wells's writing in the 1890s context, of which I can mention only a few that have shaped my own understanding of the early Wells. Simon J. James's *Maps of Utopia: H. G. Wells, Modernity and the End of Culture* (Oxford University Press, 2012), which looks at Wells's literary didacticism, begins with the context of late Victorian print culture and reading practices, identifying the period as a time when fiction was cheaper and more plentiful than ever, and simultaneously a source of considerable anxiety for the sages of culture who feared that the love of novels was lowbrow or even pathological. Paul A. Cantor and Peter Hufnagel's "The Empire of the Future: Imperialism and Modernism in H. G. Wells," in *Studies in the Novel* 38.1 (2006): 36–56 argues that the British Empire was a key influence on, and target of, Wells's fiction, and an impetus for his modernist style in the scientific romances. Finally, Dryden's *Joseph Conrad and H. G. Wells* offers an in-depth account of Conrad and Wells's friendship and mutual literary influence, their points of aesthetic divergence, and their responses to other contemporary writers, including Stevenson and Ford Madox Ford.

subject matter. "Decadent" is notoriously hard to define, since Victorian critics made liberal use of the term as a pejorative and not all decadent writers adopted it as a badge. Nevertheless, Dennis Denisoff offers a useful characterization of decadence as a literature against "progress": "Western culture, the decadent argument goes, has habitualised a view of birth and growth as positive, and decay and death as negative, when in fact they are all part of one indivisible, non-progressive package."[4] To its critics, decadence was morbid and amoral, even symptomatic of biological degeneration. To its practitioners, Denisoff suggests, it held the promise "that one's private utopia is at hand," a temporary aesthetic fulfillment amid a decaying civilization.[5]

Wells is almost never labeled a decadent writer because his writing is so different from Wilde's or Baudelaire's. Yet it has long been clear to Victorian scholars that literary decadence is linked to a contemporaneous biological discourse of degeneration or evolutionary retrogression. Bernard Bergonzi, for example, draws together Max Nordau's *Degeneration*, Wilde's aestheticism, Darwinian theory, Nietzschean nihilism, and many other intellectual currents to illustrate the *fin du globe* mood permeating the decade in which Wells came to prominence as a writer.[6] John Batchelor, too, places Wells in the context of "the decadence" by showing how he shared its concerns with "biological decline," the denouement of the century, and "the primitive forces at work within the self."[7] However, I want to make a more specific claim that Wells's fin-de-siècle short stories should be understood as decadent works themselves. Not only do they share with decadent literature a skepticism about progress, they also foster a perverse pleasure in decay, retrogression, and extinction, which Wells understands to be part of the same "indivisible" package as life and growth. The difference is that, while other decadent writers were primarily focused on "civilization" or "culture" as the arena of decline, Wells transposed their vision onto what we would call "nature."

---

[4] Dennis Denisoff, "Decadence and Aestheticism," in *The Cambridge Companion to the Fin de Siècle*, ed. Gail Marshall (Cambridge University Press, 2007): 31–52, quote on 32.

[5] Ibid., 33.

[6] Bernard Bergonzi, *The Early H. G. Wells: A Study of the Scientific Romances* (Manchester University Press, 1961). This book, particular its first chapter, remains an extremely useful account of Wells's historical context more than fifty years after its first publication.

[7] John Batchelor, "Conrad and Wells at the End of the Century," *The Critical Review* 38 (1998): 69–82, quote on 70.

To dramatize decadence in nature, Wells turned to an old form: the animal fable. He updated the fable form to comment on fin-de-siècle anxieties about evolutionary retrogression, imperialism, and humans' place in nature.[8] Drawing on his zoological education, Wells wrote stories that explored the uneasy relationships of humans to the rest of the animals with whom we share the planet. The unstated moral of these fables is typically a warning against Anglocentrism, anthropocentrism, and the Victorian faith in upward progress. All species, Wells implies, are locked in the struggle for existence, and all victories are temporary. The predator can become prey; small creatures can defeat large; nature cares not.[9] This lesson could be disturbing, but what pleasure Wells's stories do offer readers is the perverse pleasure of toppling giants. His early writings take humans, mostly English gentlemen, off their presumed thrones and place them down in the muck with the other creatures of the world.

Wells's fables also represent a missing link between the Victorian culture of evolution and the twentieth-century culture of ecology. If Wells remixed the "struggle for existence" for the 1890s, animal ecologist Charles Elton remixed it again for the twentieth century. Animal ecology might be said to have begun in the 1920s, though its founding figure, Elton, disputed its newness, writing that "Ecology is a new name for a very old subject. It simply means scientific natural history."[10] Elton's research aimed to measure and quantify the struggle for existence.[11] Like Wells's fables, animal ecology's narratives were frequently disconcerting. While plant ecologists found a comforting form of progress in ecological succession (the stages through which biotic communities evolve in their path toward a complex, stable "climax community") and

---

[8] Some other writers, most notably Arthur Conan Doyle and William Hope Hodgson, picked up the animal horror story in the first decade of the twentieth century with stories such as "The Terror of Blue John Gap" (Doyle, 1910) and "A Tropical Horror" (Hodgson, 1905). I think it likely that they were inspired by Wells's earlier experiments with this genre.

[9] Wells's challenge to anthropocentrism is perhaps the most enduring theme in the criticism, probably because it is the most constant theme in his early writing. To give just three classic examples, Robert Philmus and David Y. Hughes, editors of *H. G. Wells: Early Writings in Science and Science Fiction* (University of California Press, 1975), say that the idea "which most fascinated Wells and evoked some of his most imaginative work from the late 1880s until at least the turn of the century concerns the precarious position of man in the universe" (148). J. R. Hammond, in *H. G. Wells and the Short Story* (St. Martin's Press, 1992), agrees that the "precariousness of man" is one of the overarching themes of Wells's oeuvre (22). Patrick Parrinder refers to it as "a sense of dethronement," noting that "[t]he loss of human mastery over nature is a source of fear, horror, and irony throughout the scientific romances"; see *Shadows of the Future: H. G. Wells, Science Fiction, and Prophecy* (Syracuse University Press, 1995), 49.

[10] Elton, *Animal Ecology*, 1.

[11] Ibid., vii.

admired plant associations as holistic "superorganisms," animal ecologists like Elton were looking at population flux and trying to calculate the cycles of growth and die-off in animal communities.[12] The hope was that, if ecologists could better understand these cycles of boom and bust in animal populations, they could control them, creating order out of the grotesque profusion of nature and thereby serving the needs of the British Empire. The fear, which Elton came to voice later in his career as he turned to the study of invasive species, was that human intervention in the animal world was a quixotic endeavor, one that would only lead to more chaos and more victims of the struggle for life.

Today, the word "ecology" connotes a balanced, peaceful view of nature and an ethic of care for the environment. But Elton did not believe in any balance of nature. For him, as for Wells, nature did not conform to cultural ideals of proportion and harmony; it was instead a realm of disproportionate waste and grotesque materiality. Wells railed against the "bio-optimism" of some of his peers because he thought they did not truly understand the upshot of Darwin's theory of natural selection. His outlook at the end of the century and Elton's outlook at the end of his career were sometimes tragic, sometimes comic, but always assured that animal existence is a dark, dirty, and decadent business.

1.1   The Roots of Wells's Bio-pessimism

In 1859, the year that Darwin first published his theory of evolution by natural selection, "ecology" did not yet exist as a word, much less as a science. But in retrospect, it is tempting to locate the origin of ecological science in *Origin of Species*. It has become a cliché in ecological writing to quote Darwin's famous final paragraph, which begins, "It is interesting to contemplate an entangled bank, clothed with many plants of many kinds, with birds singing on the bushes, with various insects flitting about, and with worms crawling through the damp earth, and to reflect that these elaborately constructed forms, so different from each other, and dependent on each other in so complex a manner, have all been produced by laws acting around us."[13] This image of a vibrant, symbiotic,

---

[12] For the history of scientific ecology, including the concepts of succession and the superorganism, the best sources are Donald Worster's *Nature's Economy: A History of Ecological Ideas*, 2nd edn. (Cambridge University Press, 1994) and Peder Anker's *Imperial Ecology: Environmental Order in the British Empire, 1895–1945* (Harvard University Press, 2001), both of which have guided my own thinking about ecology.

[13] Darwin, *Origin of Species*, 460.

multispecies habitat has prompted many readers to see Darwin as a proto-ecological thinker.[14] The famous conclusion is not the only reason for believing that Darwin anticipated many of the themes of scientific ecology. Chapter 3, "The Struggle for Existence," also lays down threads that ecologists would pick up many decades later. The chapter illustrates the interdependence of species that share a habitat: insectivorous birds rely on insects for food, while plants rely on insects for pollination, while cattle rely on plants for food, "and so onwards in ever-increasing circles of complexity."[15] From food cycles to parasitism to epidemics to checks on population growth, most topics of study that Charles Elton would identify as falling under the purview of animal ecology appear somewhere in "The Struggle for Existence."

The author of the *Origin* was obviously a nature lover who greatly admired the many "beautiful adaptations" that had been produced through natural selection, from the "structure of the beetle which dives through the water" to the "plumed seed which is wafted by the gentlest breeze."[16] Yet he was also painfully aware of the immense waste, suffering, and death that inhered in the struggle for existence, and it was this side of Darwin's vision that would prove formative for Wells at the fin de siècle. Darwin exhorts his readers to hold in their minds at once the beauty of nature and its ugliness. "We behold the face of nature bright with gladness, we often see superabundance of food," he writes. But there is a darker underside to nature as well:

> [W]e do not see, or we forget, that the birds which are idly singing round us mostly live on insects or seeds, and are thus constantly destroying life; or we forget how largely these songsters, or their eggs, or their nestlings, are destroyed by birds and beasts of prey; we do not always bear in mind, that though food may be now superabundant, it is not so at all seasons of each recurring year.[17]

Famine, predation, disease, and competition are all part of the organic world, and one cannot understand natural selection without them.

But we "forget," in Darwin's parlance; to borrow a term from Freud, we repress. Knowledge of the waste endemic in nature threatens any

---

[14] Historians of ecology frequently accord Darwin a place of central importance; see, for example, Worster's *Nature's Economy*, Joel B. Hagen's *An Entangled Bank: The Origins of Ecosystem Ecology* (Rutgers University Press, 1992), and Frank N. Egerton's *Roots of Ecology: Antiquity to Haeckel* (University of California Press, 2012).

[15] Darwin, *Origin of Species*, 124.

[16] Ibid., 114.

[17] Ibid., 116.

preexisting belief we may have that the world is kind, just, or designed by God to be harmonious. No wonder Darwin's theory hit a nerve for so many Victorians. At the end of "The Struggle for Existence," Darwin tries to minimize the queasiness that his vision may have induced by saying, "When we reflect on this struggle, we may console ourselves with the full belief, that the war of nature is not incessant, that no fear is felt, that death is generally prompt, and that the vigorous, the healthy, and the happy survive and multiply."[18] Not all readers were consoled, however. Indeed, one powerful (albeit oversimplified) way of understanding the literary naturalism of writers like Thomas Hardy is as an expression of those who remained haunted by the unyielding struggle in the processes of nature.

Among those readers more affected by Darwin's imagery of struggle than his imagery of flourishing was Thomas H. Huxley. It is well known that Wells studied under Huxley at the Royal College of Science, and that Huxley's evolutionary thought exerted a major influence on the young Wells. Huxley's *Evolution and Ethics* (1893–4), which argues that ethical behavior means combating the "cosmic process" of nature, offers particular insight into Wells's preoccupations in the 1890s. Huxley's essay was written as a counterargument to the Social Darwinists and eugenicists of his era who believed that society should imitate natural selection by culling its weakest members. In the "Prolegomena," Huxley counters this viewpoint, explaining that a eugenics program, modeled after the artificial selection of breeders and gardeners, could never play a significant role in human social progress because it could not "be practiced without a serious weakening, it may be the destruction, of the bonds which hold society together."[19] In "Evolution and Ethics" itself, he makes an even stronger statement, declaring that "the ethical progress of society depends, not on imitating the cosmic process, still less in running away from it, but in combating it."[20] Nature may be full of beautiful adaptations, but it has nothing to teach us about justice or mercy; it is a wild, amoral jungle. For Huxley, nearly seventy when he delivered "Evolution and Ethics" as a lecture, promoting evolution by natural selection had been his life's work. But one detects in this essay's view of nature something like nausea.

---

[18] Ibid., 129.
[19] Thomas H. Huxley, *Evolution and Ethics; and Science and Morals* [1886–94] (Prometheus, 2004), 36.
[20] Ibid., 83.

The state of nature, Huxley believed, only appears an innocent, Edenic paradise to untutored eyes. Drawing on *Origin of Species*, he describes it in terms of an eternal struggle that might not always be visible to us but that is always going on beneath the surface: "what we call rest is only unperceived activity; that seeming peace is silent but strenuous battle."[21] This is the dark side of the "entangled bank" that Darwin marveled at, where "endless forms most beautiful and most wonderful have been, and are being, evolved."[22] The struggle for existence relies on an overpopulation of plants and animals, "too menny" to borrow a phrase from Hardy's *Jude the Obscure*, so that the fit may survive and the unfit may perish. It means a world where dying young is common, a world where animals, including humans, experience undeserved pain. "[S]uffering is the badge of all the tribe of sentient things," Huxley explained; "it is no accidental accompaniment, but an essential constituent of the cosmic process."[23] Animals, in this view, are amoral but sentient creatures, swept up in a drama they cannot control, predestined to suffer and to inflict suffering.

The only way out of this perpetual strife, Huxley believed, was through human social progress. People can act ethically by "combating" the processes of nature and creating for themselves a peaceful "garden" that offers a respite from the struggle for existence. Just as the gardener can create a space outside of the forces of natural selection by protecting his or her plants and giving them ample space, sunlight, water, nutrients, etc., so human society can build a world where people can survive and thrive. But that world is inevitably opposed to the forces of nature.

Huxley further identifies two checks on social progress that make the elimination of suffering forever out of reach. First is the Malthusian problem, the issue of "too menny": humans living in a nurturing, balanced society will tend to multiply until they outstrip their resources, thus reintroducing the struggle for existence into their world.[24] (Little wonder that, thirty years later, Huxley's grandson Julian would become an ardent advocate of birth control.) Second is what Huxley considered the cyclical nature of evolution: "If, for millions of years, our globe has taken the upward road, yet, some time, the summit will be reached and the downward route will be commenced."[25] Humans can probably progress for a while, but they cannot progress forever. All creatures die, all empires fall,

[21] Ibid., 49.
[22] Darwin, *Origin of Species*, 460.
[23] Huxley, *Evolution and Ethics*, 54.
[24] Ibid., 21.
[25] Ibid., 85.

and "retrogressive evolution" is always a possibility.[26] Between these two cosmic pressures, ethics amounts to a battle against nature that we are destined to lose in the long run but obligated to keep fighting anyway.

It is easy to see how *Evolution and Ethics* ties in with Wells's *The Time Machine* (1895) in its shared concern with cyclical, retrogressive evolution, which the novel dramatizes so famously. But the connection runs much deeper than that – Huxley's dark, nauseated vision of nature suffuses Wells's fin-de-siècle writing. It reaches a peak in "Bio-Optimism," a scathing review of the new little magazine *The Evergreen* which Wells penned for *Nature* in 1895. *The Evergreen*, the work of J. Arthur Thomson and Patrick Geddes, offered a pleasant and pastoral vision of nature, full of allusions to symbiosis and odes to spring and illustrations of butterflies. Reading Wells's evisceration of its first volume is a bit like watching a hawk swoop down on an innocent and fuzzy mouse. Wells ridicules the art, which is zoologically inaccurate: "the beautiful markings on the carapace of a crab and the exquisite convolutions of a ram's horn are alike replaced by unmeaning and clumsy spirals, the delicate outlines of a butterfly body by a gross shape like a soda-water bottle."[27] He criticizes the literary content, which comprises "amateurish short stories about spring, 'descriptive articles' of the High School Essay type," and bad poetry.[28] Above all, he condemns *The Evergreen*'s misrepresentation of natural selection.

What really made Wells angry was that Thomson had written that "the conception of the Struggle for Existence as Nature's sole method of progress … was to be sure a libel projected upon nature, but it had enough truth in it to be mischievous for a while."[29] Thomson went on to call the theory "false to natural fact," and to announce that science has now discovered "how love, not egoism, is the motive which the final history of every species justifies."[30] To Wells, this was not only disrespectful to Darwin – "So zoologists honour their greatest!" he exclaims sarcastically – but also bad science.[31] His response is worth quoting at length because it illustrates the bio-pessimism that Wells saw as biology's true inheritance from Darwin and Huxley:

> There is nothing in Symbiosis or in any other group of phenomena to warrant the statement that the representation of all life as a Struggle for

[26] Ibid., 88.
[27] H. G. Wells, *H. G. Wells: Early Writings in Science and Science Fiction*, ed. Robert Philmus and David Y. Hughes (University of California Press, 1975), 206.
[28] Ibid., 209.
[29] Quoted in ibid., 207.
[30] Quoted in ibid., 208.
[31] Ibid., 207.

Existence is a libel on Nature. Because some species have abandoned fighting in open order, each family for itself, as some of the larger carnivora do, for a fight in masses after the fashion of the ants, because the fungus fighting its brother fungus has armed itself with an auxiliary algae, because man instead of killing his cattle at sight preserves them against his convenience, and fights with advertisements and legal process instead of with flint instruments, is life therefore any the less a battle-field? ... In brief, a static species is mechanical, an evolving species suffering – no line of escape from that *impasse* has as yet presented itself. The names of the sculptor who carves out the new forms of life are, and so far as human science goes at present they must ever be, Pain and Death.[32]

If anything, Wells's vision here is bleaker than Huxley's, for while Huxley believed that, at least temporarily, human society could replace the battlefield with a carefully tended garden, Wells implies that the state of nature operates in human society no less than in the forest or the savanna. Pain, death, and struggle are, for Wells, the watchwords of evolution for all species.

If there is any payoff to the pain and death that evolution necessitates, it is that while the individual may perish, the species endures, becoming better adapted to its environment with each trial it survives. But Wells knew that not even that small consolation was guaranteed, for the story of evolution is also always a story of extinction. Extinction was a relatively new and controversial idea in the nineteenth century. Throughout the 1700s, most naturalists did not believe in extinction because they considered it incompatible with natural theological ideas about the divine design of nature. Only through the work of Georges Cuvier at the end of the eighteenth century did extinction come to be considered scientific fact, and even by 1859 Darwin expected his readers to find it surprising and difficult to account for – "so profound is our ignorance, and so high our presumption, that we marvel when we hear of the extinction of an organic being; and as we do not see the cause, we invent cataclysms to desolate the world, or invent laws on the duration of the forms of life!"[33] Before the theory of natural selection, it was difficult for scientists to understand what could make an entire species die out, short of the earth-shaking upheavals and deluges of catastrophism.[34]

---

[32] Ibid., 208–9.

[33] Darwin, *Origin of Species*, 124.

[34] The debate between catastrophists like Cuvier, who believed that major, violent natural disasters had occurred in the earth's past and caused extinctions, and uniformitarians like Charles Lyell, who believed that geological changes had occurred gradually through forces that are still observable in

The Victorian period, however, also marks the dawning of scientific awareness that humans are sometimes responsible for the extinction of other species. What the Cambridge zoology professor Alfred Newton called the "extermination" of the great auk became a well-known example of human-driven extinction and a touchstone for the bird protection movement. By the end of the century, a number of laws had been passed in Britain and throughout the empire intended to preserve animal species endangered by overhunting.[35] Alongside these efforts at preservation, however, was a sense of inevitability: the progress of "civilization," i.e. imperialism, required a diminution of wild animals. As Harriet Ritvo explains, "if new territories were to be appropriated by white settlers, who intended to exploit them more productively, their previous inhabitants, non-human as well as human, would inevitably have to give way."[36] Ritvo argues that as the century drew to an end, this sense of inevitability "was replaced by one that viewed [wild animals] as a valuable resource requiring protection."[37] But not fully replaced; as Wells's essay "On Extinction" (1893) demonstrates, the belief in an inexorable and environmentally destructive form of progress still had some currency at the fin de siècle.

"On Extinction" is nonfiction, but it reads like a miniature naturalist novel, its characters doomed from the start. Its dominant mode of storytelling is tragic. Its opening paragraph draws a direct line from Greek tragedy to naturalist drama to biological extinction:

> The passing away of ineffective things, the entire rejection by Nature of the plans of life, is the essence of tragedy. In the world of animals, that runs so curiously parallel with the world of men, we can see and trace only too often the analogies of our grimmer human experiences; we can find the equivalents to the sharp tragic force of Shakespeare, the majestic

---

the present, is well known to historians of science. Lyell's uniformitarianism is widely regarded as a key influence on Darwin's evolutionary theory, showing Darwin that the earth was old enough for species to have had time to evolve into their present forms. For more on the history of extinction and its role in Darwin's thought, see Henry M. Cowles's "A Victorian Extinction: Alfred Newton and the Evolution of Animal Protection," *British Journal for the History of Science* 46.4 (2013): 695–714, and Gillian Beer's "Darwin and the Uses of Extinction," *Victorian Studies* 51.2 (2009): 321–31. Elizabeth Kolbert's *The Sixth Extinction: An Unnatural History* (Henry Holt, 2014) also offers an excellent non-academic account of Cuvier and the discovery of extinction (23–46).

[35] See Cowles's "A Victorian Extinction" for an analysis of Newton's study of human-caused extinctions and his influence on the animal protection movement. See also Harriet Ritvo, "Destroyers and Preservers: Big Game in the Victorian Empire," *History Today* 52.1 (2002): 33–9 for the history of animal protection laws in the British colonies.

[36] Ritvo, "Destroyers and Preservers," 37.

[37] Ibid.

inevitableness of Sophocles, and the sordid dreary tale, the middle-class misery, of Ibsen ... This is the saddest chapter of biological science – the tragedy of Extinction.[38]

Wells elevates the endangered animals by comparing them to human characters in highly esteemed plays and thus implying that their loss is tragic. Like the downfall of Oedipus or Macbeth, extinction is also a predetermined outcome, a necessary result of the crossed wires of inheritance and environment.

For Wells, this predeterminism applies whether the animals are driven to extinction through the ancient process of natural selection or through human action. Unlike Newton, who differentiated between "natural" extinctions and "exterminations" at the hand of man, Wells naturalized the latter by portraying them as part of the same inexorable drama. "One Fate still spins, and the gleaming scissors cut," as he puts it. "In the last hundred years," he continues, "the swift change of condition throughout the world, due to the invention of new means of transit, geographical discovery, and the consequent 'swarming' of the whole globe by civilized men, has pushed many an animal to the very verge of destruction."[39] The rhetorical move here, which makes Fate and change (rather than people) the grammatical subjects, implies that both environmental destruction and colonialism are natural and inevitable forces, not qualitatively different from the forces of natural selection that existed for eons before humans came on the scene.

"On Extinction" naturalizes colonialism even more explicitly in its reflection on the decline of the American bison, "many Australian and New Zealand animals and birds ousted by more vigorous imported competitors," and other endangered and recently extinct creatures. Wells directly compares the bison to the Native Americans: "Can any of these fated creatures count? Does any suspicion of their dwindling numbers dawn upon them? Do they, like the Red Indian, perceive the end to which they are coming?"[40] There is no acknowledgement here that the colonization of North America, Australia, and New Zealand, which proved so disastrous for human and nonhuman inhabitants alike, was a conscious political choice. The simultaneous decimation of Native Americans and the bison was not a coincidence or a convenient analogy – it was the result of US government policy, which encouraged

[38] Wells, *Early Writings in Science and Science Fiction*, 169.
[39] Ibid., 170.
[40] Ibid., 171.

the destruction of herds of buffalo in order to clear the plains of Native Americans.[41] Wells's references to the "Red Indian" echo a well-worn nineteenth-century discourse that mourned the vanishing of noble Indians while effacing the state-sanctioned violence that continued to oppress them. It is a discourse that allowed Wells and others to lament the destruction wrought by white Europeans and Americans without having to do anything about it. There is an undertone of social Darwinism in Wells's essay, implying that the dwindling of Native American populations, like the dwindling of animal species, is a natural consequence of the struggle for existence in which only the strongest and fittest (i.e. the Europeans) survive.

The tragic rhetoric of "On Extinction," then, reflects Wells's bio-pessimism, which regarded death, loss, and suffering as central to the drama of nature. But it also demonstrates a deep, unreflective complicity with Victorian ideology. It naturalizes the imperialism and racial hierarchies that were so central to nineteenth-century Anglo-Americans' understandings of themselves and their place in history. In other writings of this period, however, Wells loosened up on the unyielding tragic tone that dominates "On Extinction," finding comic elements in nature as well. This loosening up allowed him to write a number of essays and stories that denaturalized the Victorian conception of man's place in nature, making challenges to political and environmental imperialism thinkable.

1.2 The Wellsian Grotesque

If Wells's fin-de-siècle vision of nature was a pessimistic one, it was not entirely devoid of pleasure. True, Wells fixated on retrogression, extinction, violence, and waste in his 1890s fiction and nonfiction alike. The "re-enchantment of the world" that George Levine finds in Darwin's writing is not quite as forthcoming in Wells's.[42] But Wells inherited from Darwin a compensatory pleasure of a different sort. He found in the animal world a carnivalesque overturning of the pecking order, and a grotesque aesthetic that celebrated materiality without masking its continual decay and transformation. Mikhail Bakhtin, in *Rabelais and His World*,

---

[41] Andrew C. Isenberg, *The Destruction of the Bison: An Environmental History, 1750–1920* (Cambridge University Press, 2000), 123–63.

[42] George Levine, in *Darwin Loves You: Natural Selection and the Re-enchantment of the World* (Princeton University Press, 2008), argues that Darwin "finds in non-human nature the energy, diversity, beauty, intelligence, and sensibility that might provide a world-friendly alternative to otherworldly values" (xv). This predominantly affirming view of a secularized nature is less conspicuous in Wells's fiction.

famously defines the carnivalesque as a festive atmosphere ruled by "the peculiar logic of the 'inside out' (*à l'envers*) of the 'turnabout,' of a continual shifting from top to bottom, from front to rear, of numerous parodies and travesties, humiliations, profanations, comic crownings and uncrownings."[43] Wells's fables revel in this process, "uncrowning" humans and making them into animals, "crowning" animals and making them into intelligent subjects. Before Darwin, it made sense to think of species as "lower" or "higher," and to classify them in tiers, with humans at the top of the pyramid. After Darwin, all such hierarchies were suspended, resulting in a carnivalesque democracy of living things. Few saw that as clearly as Wells.

For Bakhtin, the carnivalesque was intimately connected to the concept of grotesque realism, a literary and aesthetic mode that celebrated the body in all its physical excess – its fertility and decay, consumption and waste, life and death. "The essential principle of grotesque realism," he explains, "is degradation, that is, the lowering of all that is high, spiritual, ideal, abstract; it is a transfer to the material level, to the sphere of earth and body in their indissoluble unity."[44] Darwin's view of nature, as critics including Jonathan Smith have pointed out, embraces grotesque realism. Smith identifies the "Darwinian grotesque" in Darwin's writings about barnacles, birds, and above all earthworms. These writings capture Darwin's delight in elevating the lowliest of creatures and substances, right down to "worm shit," which he "lovingly rendered as an object of wonder."[45] Nicola Bown argues that the "entangled bank" itself is a grotesque image, one "in which death leads to life in endlessly new and different forms."[46] For Bown, the Darwinian grotesque encompasses the instability of species and their interdependent "tangling together," which refuses the orderliness of Linnaean taxonomic biology.[47]

---

[43] Mikhail Bakhtin, *Rabelais and His World* [1965], transl. Helene Iswolsky (Indiana University Press, 1984), 11.

[44] Ibid., 19–20.

[45] Smith, *Charles Darwin and Victorian Visual Culture*, 247.

[46] Nicola Bown, "'Entangled Banks': Robert Browning, Richard Dadd and the Darwinian Grotesque," in *Victorian Culture and the Idea of the Grotesque*, ed. Colin Trodd, Paul Barlow, and David Amigoni (Ashgate, 1999): 119–42, quote on 120.

[47] Ibid., 123. For additional explorations of the Darwinian grotesque, see Donald Ulin, "A Clerisy of Worms in Darwin's Inverted World," *Victorian Studies* 35.3 (1992): 295–308, which argues that Darwin's writings challenged Victorian hierarchies of culture; George Levine's *Darwin the Writer* (Oxford University Press, 2011), particularly the final chapter, which explores Thomas Hardy's uptake of the Darwinian grotesque in *The Woodlanders*; and Beer's *Darwin's Plots*, always the go-to book on Darwinian aesthetics, especially 123–30 on the simultaneously beautiful and alarming fecundity Victorians saw in nature.

There is a Wellsian grotesque as well, one that draws on Darwin's and is even more nakedly subversive of Victorian ideology. Sometimes Wells's vision of nature resembles the Romantic grotesque more than the Rabelaisian version, portraying "a terrifying world, alien to man," in which everything familiar "suddenly becomes meaningless, dubious, and hostile."[48] There is, as Kelly Hurley shows, a form of gothic horror in many of Wells's early stories.[49] At other times, Wells's fables reflect an ironic humor, a delight in debunking, and a relishing of the bizarre. A sense of campy fun pervades many of these stories; they are full of the humorousness that, Bakhtin emphasized, is a key part of the Rabelaisian grotesque.

"Zoological Retrogression" (1891) exemplifies this side of Wells's outlook on nature. The essay's goal is to correct the popular belief in what Wells calls "Excelsior evolution" – the notion that biological evolution represents a story of steady upward progress. This "optimistic evolution" is a little too pat for his taste, and he writes that if the truth were known, "the too sweet harmony of the spheres would be enhanced by a discord, this evolutionary antithesis – degradation."[50] The metaphor reveals that for Wells, this is an aesthetic as well as a scientific issue. A little discord enhances the song; a little grotesquerie enhances the picture of nature.

Wells goes on to enumerate instances of retrogressive evolution, including the sea squirt, an exemplar of the Wellsian grotesque. The sea squirt is a mobile, seeing, hearing, tadpole-like creature in its youth, but develops into a sessile, eyeless, earless lump in its maturity. As Wells explains, it evolved from more complex ancestors who resembled the form it takes in its early life; it has retrogressed into "a merely vegetative excrescence on a rock."[51] The description of this creature's life history is full of comic asides; for example, "We have then, as I have read somewhere – I think it was in an ecclesiastical biography – a career not perhaps teemingly eventful, but full of the richest suggestion and edification."[52] The sea squirt's life is, for Wells, comparable to that of a person who, in his youth, "shocks his aunts," but eventually settles down into a dull, respectable life, his "Bohemian tail" lost and his "wild ambitions" forsaken.[53] The parallels between the lowly sea squirt and the human are typical of Wells's zoological sense of humor: he looks into the

---

[48] Bakhtin, *Rabelais and His World*, 38–9.
[49] Kelly Hurley, *The Gothic Body: Sexuality, Materialism, and Degeneration at the Fin de Siècle* (Cambridge University Press, 1996).
[50] Wells, *Early Writings in Science and Science Fiction*, 158.
[51] Ibid., 162.
[52] Ibid.
[53] Ibid., 163.

face of a weird and unattractive animal, sees the human in it, and laughs at the unflattering comparison.

The culminating example of retrogression in "Zoological Retrogression" is not just presented as a parallel to humans – it is our very progenitor. Describing several anatomical features in higher vertebrates that reveal our descent from a fish-like ancestor, Wells says, "Everywhere we should find the anatomy of a fish twisted and patched to fit a life out of water; nowhere organs built specially for this very special condition."[54] *Natural Theology* author William Paley would probably faint if he could read this line, which figures the "highest" animals, including humans, not as beautiful designs of an omniscient watchmaker but as grotesquely distorted variations on a fish. Looking back at the Silurian period (over 400 million years ago), Wells identifies a mud-fish, creeping in the dirt of a dried-up river bed, as the ancestor of lung-breathing mammals today – as, in fact, *our* ancestor. "Why were they living thus in inhospitable rivers and spending half their lives half baked in river mud?" he asks. "The answer would be the old story of degeneration again; they had failed in the struggle, they were less active and powerful than their rivals of the sea, and they had taken the second great road of preservation – flight."[55] Wells evidently delights in the dirty, degenerate materiality of this slimy river fish, and in the notion that humans, who consider themselves the pinnacle of evolution, sprung from such a creature.

An early short story, "A Vision of the Past" (1887), likewise aims to debunk human hubris through an imaginary trip backwards in geological time. This story exemplifies not just Wells's ongoing challenge to anthropocentrism, but also his tendency to poke fun at English gentlemen-scientists. The narrator, hiking down an old Roman road (a metonym for transient empires) on a hot day, finds a shady spot to rest and dozes off. He dreams that he has been transported back in time, presumably to the age of the dinosaurs. There he encounters huge, lumbering reptilian creatures who are apparently masters of the earth. "[M]ore surprising than all the other grotesque features I had observed," the narrator says, is that "this strange beast had three eyes, one being in the center of its forehead."[56] This, presumably, is an allusion to the mystical notion of a third eye that sees on a higher plane; it signals that these apparently primitive monsters might have a wisdom the narrator lacks.

[54] Ibid., 165.
[55] Ibid., 166.
[56] Ibid., 154.

This hint of an advanced consciousness is confirmed when the narrator stumbles upon a group of these animals listening to a "philosophic discourse."[57] "[L]ook at the wondrous world around, and think that it is for our use that this world has been formed," intones the creatures' leader. They, it declares, are "the culminating point of all existence, the noblest of all beings who have ever existed or will ever exist."[58] The narrator, amused by "the absurd claims to such a lofty position, made by a creature so inferior to myself in all respects as this philosophic amphibian," speaks up to inform the creature of its foolishness. He is in the middle of declaring that these animals will soon be extinct and that humans will evolve to take over the earth when the creatures start converging upon him. "Nearer and nearer they came, their huge mouths opened; they seemed ready to crush me between their powerful jaws" – and right at the moment of imminent attack, he wakes up.[59]

"A Vision of the Past" feels like a lost chapter from *The Time Machine*, which Wells first began dreaming up during that period.[60] Like that novel and "Zoological Retrogression," it aims to orient readers to the ephemerality of the here and now by showing them an evolutionary time scale on which the history of the human species is a mere blip. "A Vision" also represents a comic, zoological variation on the "Ozymandias" theme. Shelley's sonnet describes a ruined monument in the desert, with the words "My name is Ozymandias, King of Kings; Look on my Works, ye Mighty, and despair!" etched on its base. Like the poem, Wells's story reminds readers that eventually, all "mighty" rulers die, their works decay, and they are forgotten. The three-eyed amphibians reign for a time and then go extinct; so, the story implies, will humans.

The narrator of "A Vision of the Past," however, is blind to these evolutionary ironies. He is a proponent of what Wells called "Excelsior evolution," eager to announce to the dinosaurian creatures that

> higher forms than you will, by insensible gradations, spring from you and succeed you; that you are here only for the purpose of preparing the earth for the reception of those higher forms, which in turn will but prepare

---

[57] Ibid., 155.
[58] Ibid., 156.
[59] Ibid., 157.
[60] "The Chronic Argonauts," first published in 1888, was Wells's first story to feature a time machine and is often regarded as a precursor to the novel. In the novel version of *The Time Machine* (Penguin, 2005), the Time Traveler disappears at the end and the frame narrator imagines him "among the grotesque saurians, the huge reptilian brutes of the Jurassic times" or "wandering on some plesiosaurus-haunted Oolitic coral reef, or beside the lonely saline lakes of the Triassic Age" (91).

it for the advent of that glorious race of reasoning and soul-possessing beings, who, through the endless aeons of the future, will never cease their onward march towards infinite perfection – a race of which I –.[61]

This grandiloquent speech is cut short by the creatures' predatory approach. It shows, however, more clearly than any other part of the story, the distance between this narrator and Wells himself. For this is exactly the view of evolution that Wells ridicules in "Zoological Retrogression." This is a narrator who has read his Darwin but has not grasped the philosophical challenge to anthropocentrism that evolutionary theory entails.

This early short story thus anticipates a theme that Wells went on to develop further in novels like *The Time Machine* and *The War of the Worlds*: a mockery of the scientifically educated English gentleman, who knows about evolution and the struggle for existence but cannot grasp his own bodily enmeshment in it. The narrator of "A Vision of the Past" seems to be a paleontologist; when he sees the long-extinct amphibian creature, his initial impulse is to study it "[w]ith the intent to benefit science ... but, being only accustomed to identify by means of bones and of teeth, I could not do so in this case, because its bones were hidden by its flesh."[62] Habituated to the safety and scientific distance of the fossil museum, the narrator is out of his element in the field. At the museum, he is used to exerting a kind of scientific mastery over the dusty, long-dead creatures he studies, but when confronted with one face-to-face, he finds himself no longer standing above nature, but part of it. The dig at paleontology in this story likely reflects the influence of T. H. Huxley. Huxley's agenda for professional science, Christina Alt points out, promoted "secular, speculative biology centred in the laboratory ... over the museum-based, theologically justified taxonomic cataloguing" that dominated Victorian natural history.[63] Wells, too, seems to imply in "A Vision" that museum-based paleontology is backward, its methods inadequate for the new biology of the lab and the field.

Being part of nature, engaged in the struggle for existence, means being physically vulnerable in a way that discomfits the narrator. He euphemistically nods to this discomfort by mentioning that, along with the difficulty in studying a living, breathing creature rather than the bones and teeth he is used to, "a certain diffidence, that I now

---

[61] Wells, *Early Writings in Science and Science Fiction*, 156.
[62] Ibid., 154.
[63] Alt, *Virginia Woolf and the Study of Nature*, 42.

feel inclined to regret, prevented any examination of its teeth."[64] Wells's zoological humor resurfaces here in the narrator's understatement. In the story's climactic scene, right before the narrator awakens from his dream, scientific mastery is again contrasted with the bodily violence of predation, and again the narrator is posed as the loser of this battle. He may be able to give a thousand reasons why humans and not amphibians will inherit the earth, but argumentation will not save him in the face of a group of intelligent predators with "powerful jaws" encircling him. His failure, like that of the Time Traveler and *The War of the Worlds* narrator, is the failure to recognize that scientific knowledge does not exempt one from bodily vulnerability or allow an exit from the inexorable struggle.

Ecocriticism today urges us to think of ourselves as embodied creatures enmeshed in a material environment. Kelly Sultzbach, for example, argues that modernist texts like E. M. Forster's *A Passage to India* reveal an "intercorporeality of human and environment" – *inter* emphasizing the connectedness of human, nonhuman animal, and natural object, and *corporeality* emphasizing their physical nature. Forster's India, which he describes as having "flesh" and as animated by a "hundred voices," refuses anthropocentrism in favor of a biocentric, materialist pluralism, according to Sultzbach's reading.[65] Likewise, Jeffrey M. McCarthy finds in some modernist novels a vision of "dwelling as a material intermingling between the actors in a place," an ecoconsciousness that grounds human bodies in particular habitats.[66] This recognition of our physical enmeshment in nature can be enchanting, as in the novels McCarthy analyzes, or disturbing, as in *A Passage to India*. In Wells's fables, it is simultaneously disturbing and comic. His version of "ecomaterialism" means embedding humans in the Darwinian struggle for existence, where death and life are part of the same organic cycle. Thus "A Vision," a story about extinction and evolution, should also be understood as a story about predation in a material environment. The grotesque reptilians, with their "ungainly" forms and "ludicrous" movements, challenge Victorian values of continual progress, English supremacy, and scientific mastery. They represent Wells's conviction that we are subject to the same laws of evolution and made of the same decaying matter as every other animal.

---

[64] Wells, *Early Writings in Science and Science Fiction*, 154.
[65] Sultzbach, *Ecocriticism in the Modernist Imagination*, 68.
[66] McCarthy, *Green Modernism*, 189.

1.3   Animal Empires

The struggle for existence as an animating concept is most visible in a series of stories Wells wrote between 1894 and 1905. These stories, which include "Aepyornis Island" (1894), "In the Avu Observatory" (1894), "The Sea Raiders" (1896), "The Valley of Spiders" (1903), and "The Empire of the Ants" (1905), narrate strange animal encounters with an ironic sensibility. They are fables of colonialism, issuing sly warnings to the Briton who considers himself heir of all the ages and master of an empire that spans the globe. Wells's animal subjects turn British colonial administrators into prey and the seat of empire into an invaded territory. The creatures that effect these reversals prefigure the "Coming Beast" that, Wells warned in "Zoological Retrogression," may one day supplant humans in the evolutionary future. They also represent, metaphorically, the colonized people of the British Empire rising up, and literally, the unpredictable animals that resist human efforts to control nature.

"Aepyornis Island," a story of rivalry between a bad-tempered extinct bird and a bad-tempered collector of natural history specimens, stages a showdown at the edges of empire. Like so much fin-de-siècle fiction, it is a story within a story, a yarn spun to an unnamed frame narrator by a collector named (with all of Wells's characteristic subtlety) Butcher. The frame structure sets up Butcher's narrative as a tall tale, hovering somewhere between truth and humbug. (Wells knew that humbug was a not-insignificant part of the natural history business, having written about fraudulent specimens in his satirical short story "The Triumphs of a Taxidermist.") Butcher's story goes like this: he is hunting for specimens in Madagascar when he and two African workers find intact eggs of the Aepyornis, an extinct giant bird whose fossilized bones and eggs had been "discovered" by Western naturalists in the 1850s.[67] When one of the workers, bitten by a centipede, drops an egg, Butcher hurls abuse at him, and later that night, both workers try to escape in a canoe. Butcher chases them in a rage, killing one with his revolver; the other dies as well, presumably of poison from the centipede bite. Butcher finds himself lost at sea in a tiny boat, alone with three Aepyornis eggs for sustenance.

---

[67] Thomas J. Anderson's "*Aepyornis* as Moa: Giant Birds and Global Connections in Nineteenth-Century Science," *British Journal for the History of Science* 46.4 (2013): 675–93 offers useful historical context for "Aepyornis Island" by analyzing the Western "discovery" of the extinct *Aepyornis*, the ongoing hope through the 1850s that a living specimen might still be found, and the (fairly hypocritical) blame that Western naturalists placed on Malagasy natives for driving the bird to extinction.

Eventually, Butcher makes it to an unpopulated island, where, to his shock, the one remaining Aepyornis egg hatches and a small bird emerges. At first, the collector is fond of the bird, sharing food with him and talking to him. He even names the Aepyornis, calling him Friday after Robinson Crusoe's companion. After a couple of years, however, the bird grows up; "he began to cock his comb at me and give himself airs, and show signs of a nasty temper ..."[68] When food becomes scarce, the two begin to compete for resources. As Butcher recalls, "I was hungry, too, and when at last I landed a fish I wanted it for myself. Tempers were short that morning on both sides. He pecked at it and grabbed it, and I gave him a whack on the head to make him leave go. And at that he went for me."[69] Soon it becomes an all-out war between bird and man. Eventually, after a period of sleeping in trees to avoid the creature's attacks, Butcher devises a way to kill him, but the act wracks him with guilt. "I don't like to think of that even now," he says; "I felt like a murderer while I did it, though my anger was hot against him. When I stood over him and saw him bleeding on the white sand, and his beautiful great legs and neck writhing in his last agony ... Pah!"[70]

The irony of Butcher's spasms of guilt is that he *is* a murderer – he has killed one of the African workers in Madagascar and contributed to the death of the other. He expresses no qualms about those deaths, but regrets the death of the beautiful Aepyornis. In both cases, it is Butcher's violence that turns his former friends into enemies. With the African worker, he admits, "I hit him about rather" when the man had dropped the egg; with the bird, "I gave him a whack on the head to make him leave go."[71] The repetition of violence which begets rebellion, then more violence, ending with Butcher killing his companion turned enemy, is a microcosm of colonialism. "It was the brutal ingratitude of the creature," Butcher says in an echo of the Briton's confusion at colonial resistance – *why aren't they grateful to us for bringing them civilization?* "I'd been more than a brother to him. A great, gawky, out-of-date bird! And me a human being – heir of the ages and all that."[72] Butcher's words here make clear the parallel Wells wishes to establish between "Excelsior evolution," which makes humans the pinnacle of evolution, and European imperialism, which makes Europeans "rightful" lords of earth. The return of the

[68] H. G. Wells, *The Complete Short Stories of H. G. Wells* (Ernest Benn, 1974), 60.
[69] Ibid.
[70] Ibid., 62.
[71] Ibid., 55, 60.
[72] Ibid., 61.

extinct bird suggests a metaphorical reincarnation of the dead African men. But, to put it in Freudian terms, Butcher cannot name his earlier crime, and repeats what he has repressed.

It should, in fairness, be noted that Wells as an author is not exactly overcome with compassion for the characters he has killed off either. The above summary may make "Aepyornis Island" sound grave and serious, but Wells opted for a humorous writing style that deflects the story's grim implications. However, Wells seems to have been subject to his own repetition compulsion, and he revisits this plot event in his 1908 novel *Tono-Bungay*. The protagonist of that novel, the huckster George Ponderevo, reaches the nadir of his moral arc when, on a West African island on a quest to collect quap (a fictitious substance that George and his uncle hope to process and sell), he shoots in the back a black man who is running away from him. Ponderevo reenacts the murder Butcher commits in "Aepyornis Island," suggesting that Wells remained haunted by this episode, the primal crime of European racism and colonialism, and needed to write it again. As Suzanne Keen argues, even in *Tono-Bungay*, a more mature work, the protagonist – and, it seems, Wells as an author – fails to fully reckon with the depravity of shooting a man in the back: "what really permeates the novel is a point of view emanating from a murderer," though neither George nor Wells can name it as such.[73] Still, the return to this scene suggests that Wells recognized on some level that cold-blooded violence against African people could not be merely an incidental plot point, a convenient way of getting from point A to point B.

Though it is hard to swallow after Butcher's careless account of the workers' deaths, a humorous tone does pervade the story's second half, once he reaches the island. There is something absurd in the images of an irascible English collector climbing trees (rather like a squirrel or monkey) to escape from an enormous and angry flightless bird, or railing against "this extinct animal mooning about my island like a sulky duke."[74] As with "A Vision of the Past," the humor lies in the narrator's foibles, in the gap between his self-conception and material reality "on the ground," where he is a vulnerable body in an inhospitable environment. The element of the ridiculous in the story's second half obscures the disturbing violence of its first half, but it also represents a

[73] Suzanne Keen, *Victorian Renovations of the Novel: Narrative Annexes and the Boundaries of Representation* (Cambridge University Press, 2005), 175.
[74] Wells, *Complete Short Stories*, 61.

carnivalesque take on the "man conquers nature" cliché – a man stuck in a tree, a bird stuck on the ground.

In the most important sense, the colonizer "wins" in this story. Butcher is rescued, returns home, and makes a good deal of money from selling the Aepyornis bones. No lessons are learned. There are hints, however, of a political critique. Wells's ironic distance from the main character, established via the frame structure, the naming, and the absurd humor, suggests that the colonizer who fancies himself lord of the tropics is in reality no more than a butcher, leaving a trail of blood and bones wherever he goes. "Aepyornis Island" is, on one level, a jokey story about the struggle for existence between two apex predators on a small atoll, and on another level, it is a story about the unexamined brutality with which European colonizers responded to the resistance of colonized people. These meanings coexist even if they do not seamlessly cohere.

"In the Avu Observatory" is a similarly structured tale, with a dangerous animal threatening a European man of science in the tropics. Woodhouse, an assistant at an astronomical observatory in Borneo, is watching the stars one night when he realizes that he is not alone in the dark observatory. A flying creature – some bat-like composite of "vast wing," "grey-brown fur," "velvety ear," and "row of keen teeth" – is in the building with him and begins to attack him.[75] Woodhouse is able to fight back with a broken water bottle, and he succeeds in injuring the creature, though he never sees it clearly. He blacks out, and when he awakens the next morning, his Dyak assistant and fellow observer Thaddy are treating his injuries, but the creature is nowhere to be found.

The story includes a few subtle hints that the Dyak people might know more about this creature than they let on. Before Woodhouse is attacked, he overhears one of them sing "a queer chanting song, in which the others joined at intervals," and when he recovers the next morning, he notices "that one of the Dyak servants was looking at him with a curious expression."[76] Thaddy informs Woodhouse that the Dyaks tell stories of "a Big Colugo, a Klang-utang," a nocturnal flying creature.[77] (Real colugos are small gliding mammals, sometimes called flying lemurs.) It is hard to tell whether these references to the Dyaks are merely Wells's attempt to add some ethnographic local color to the story, or whether they suggest some other connection between the Dyaks and the creature.

[75] Ibid., 18–19.
[76] Ibid., 17, 20.
[77] Ibid., 21.

Perhaps the attacking creature is a symbol, or even a supernatural agent, of the Borneo locals who cannot rebel against their English occupiers quite so openly.

"Aepyornis Island" and "In the Avu Observatory" both place representatives of empire and Western science in scenarios that force them to recognize their own animal vulnerability. The moments of bodily vulnerability – the collector sleeping in a tree to escape the predations of the flightless bird, the observer crouching beneath a telescope to protect himself from the swooping colugo – are resolved by the end of each story, however. Butcher makes it off the island, and Woodhouse wakes up the next morning, and neither reconsiders the ideologies of empire and anthropocentrism in any lasting way. Ever the stiff-upper-lip Englishman, Woodhouse pluckily concludes, "On the whole, if the Borneo fauna is going to disgorge any more of its novelties upon me, I should prefer that it did so when I was not occupied in the observatory at night and alone."[78] In the stories of the next decade, however, namely "The Valley of Spiders" (1903) and "The Empire of the Ants" (1905), Wells was ready to embrace an irresolution that issued a more pronounced challenge to those ideologies.

"The Valley of Spiders" is an unusual story in Wells's oeuvre. Unlike "Aepyornis Island" and "In the Avu Observatory," it is not comic in tone. Kelly Hurley classifies it as gothic; I am tempted to call it Symbolist for its evocative, indirect style.[79] There are no proper nouns in it, only three men on horseback – the "master" and two followers, "the little man" and "the gaunt man" – pursuing a "half-caste girl" who has refused the leader's advances and is now fleeing through a mountainous country.[80] Their pursuit is interrupted when, passing through a valley, they come upon a swarm of poisonous spiders, floating on the wind, against whom their swords are useless. The gaunt man is killed by the spiders, and, when the danger passes, the leader kills his remaining companion in order to take his horse. He heads back home, but a plume of smoke in the distance lets him know that the girl has escaped his clutches … for now.

Though it is tonally and stylistically different from Wells's other animal stories of the period, "The Valley of Spiders" nevertheless shares with them a number of themes. One is, of course, the "uncrowning" narrative, in which a small and unlikely predator, the spider, disrupts the plans of

---

[78] Ibid.
[79] Hurley, *The Gothic Body*, 69–72.
[80] Wells, *Complete Short Stories*, 438, 440, 441.

man. Another is the psychological drama of powerful men confronted with rebellion. "[P]eople marvelled," the little man thinks, "when the master was disobeyed even in the wildest things. This half-caste girl seemed to him, seemed to every one, mad – blasphemous almost."[81] But later, when he realizes that the leader has fled from the spiders and left the gaunt man to die, the little man begins to understand disobedience. "You are a coward, like myself," he says. "Why are you our lord?"[82] The question is unthinkable to the leader, who retaliates by killing the little man. The story illustrates, via a symbolist logic, the brutality of the imperialist psyche, which grasps for possession of all things and finds any challenge to its power intolerable. The master is an archetype of power without conscience, one that Butcher also embodies in "Aepyornis Island" at the moment he attacks the fleeing African workers, and that George Ponderevo enacts in *Tono-Bungay* when he goes to collect quap and kills a man.

At the end of "The Valley of Spiders," the master has been defeated for the moment, but in defeat he has learned a lesson that makes him even more dangerous. A swarm of spiders cannot be stopped at the point of a sword. One can only beat a spider by becoming a spider, replacing brute force with cunning. In the final sentences, he notices that "there were many dead spiders on the ground, and those that lived feasted guiltily on their fellows." He looks at them, preying on their own as he has preyed on his own, and then he looks over his shoulder at the smoke, and says to himself, "Spiders. Well, well ... The next time I must spin a web."[83] In a complex, interconnected animal world, being a large apex predator is not the only way to succeed, a lesson the master is ready to transpose to the political realm.

Like "The Valley of Spiders," "The Empire of the Ants" locates resistance to human and European power in small but deadly arthropods who, as the stories' titles suggest, own the land in a way humans cannot. Unlike "Valley," though, "Empire" portrays the animal threat as an enduring one, not a transient phenomenon resulting from a well-timed breeze. Published in *The Strand* in 1905, "The Empire of the Ants" follows a gunboat crew that has been dispatched to the remote Batemo River, a fictional tributary of the Amazon, to deal with a plague of ants. The ants are hyper-intelligent, socially organized, and poisonous, and

[81] Ibid., 441.
[82] Ibid., 445.
[83] Ibid., 446.

they have already claimed multiple human victims. When the crew reaches its destination, they encounter another boat that the ants have commandeered. This vessel's entire crew is dead. The captain, Gerilleau, orders his reluctant lieutenant, da Cunha, to board the ghost ship and investigate. As readers might foresee, things don't turn out so well for the unfortunate da Cunha, who is stung by the ants and dies later that night. Perplexed, Gerilleau undertakes a number of absurd measures – he orders his crew to burn the ghost ship, to "'oot and vissel" (hoot and whistle) at the empty villages, to shoot pistol shots at the ants, and finally to fire the boat's big gun at their tiny adversaries.[84] These measures are about as effective as swords were against the spiders in "The Valley of Spiders" – that is to say, not at all. As Linda Dryden points out, this scene likely owes something to Conrad: "The futility of the attempt to eradicate the swelling army of ants echoes the futility of the French frigate in *Heart of Darkness* firing its useless missiles into the coastline of the vast continent of Africa."[85] Gerilleau and his crew, stymied, turn back, leaving the ants behind. "By 1920 they will be half-way down the Amazon," the narrator says, concluding, "I fix 1950 or '60 at the latest for the discovery of Europe."[86]

"Empire" does not technically take place in the colonies – it is set in Brazil, which had been an independent country since 1822 – but, as Ross G. Forman shows, for Victorians Brazil represented a desirable target for economic imperialism and thus an attractive setting for adventure literature.[87] The story's setting is a "virgin land" of exactly the sort that would have been targeted by colonial powers, though it resembles Conrad's Congo much more than, say, the Kukuanaland of *King Solomon's Mines*. That is to say, it is a dangerous place beyond the edge of human civilization, Thomas H. Huxley's amoral jungle rather than H. Rider Haggard's lush lost world. Dryden observes, "Wells's evocation of the vastness of the Amazon rainforest echoes Marlow's sense of the insignificance of humanity against the expanse of the African jungle in *Heart of Darkness*."[88] As in Conrad's novel, the landscape's fecundity is more grotesque than beautiful, and impossible

---

[84] Ibid., 594.
[85] Dryden, *Joseph Conrad and H. G. Wells*, 92. Dryden also demonstrates how the story's setting, plot structure – a boat moving up a river toward a primeval continental interior – and themes of existential horror parallel *Heart of Darkness* (89–93).
[86] Wells, *Complete Short Stories*, 597.
[87] Ross G. Forman, "When Britons Brave Brazil: British Imperialism and the Adventure Tale in Latin America, 1850–1918," *Victorian Studies* 42.3 (1999): 455–87.
[88] Dryden, *Joseph Conrad and H. G. Wells*, 90.

for a hardheaded English engineer like the protagonist to assimilate — "the waste of it, the headlong waste of it, filled his soul."[89]

The most famous part of the story is a passage in which the protagonist Holroyd, far from home, reflects on the inhospitable environment in which he has found himself: "In England he had come to think of the land as man's. In England it is indeed man's, the wild things live by sufferance, grow on lease, everywhere the roads, the fences, and absolute security runs." By contrast, in the Amazon region the forest is "interminable," "invincible," and indifferent to humans. "[T]he still, silent struggle of giant trees, of strangulating creepers, of assertive flowers, everywhere the alligator, the turtle, and endless varieties of birds and insects seemed at home, dwelt irreplaceably," writes Wells, echoing both Darwin's entangled bank with its "endless forms" and Huxley's "silent but strenuous battle."[90] This is an environment with no room for humans — "man at most held a footing upon resentful clearings, fought weeds, fought beasts and insects for the barest foothold, fell a prey to snake and beast, insect and fever, and was presently carried away." The animals and plants rebuff human attempts at colonizing the Batemo valley, prompting Holroyd to ask, "Who were the real masters?" The answer, as he discovers, is not humans, nor even "the puma, the jaguar," but instead the ants.[91]

The story is not only about the dark Darwinian forest, however, but also about the colonial management that aims to tame it. The crew has been sent by Brazilian military authorities to provide a pest control service. After its failure, the engineer Holroyd is, for his part, concerned that the ants "threaten British Guiana, which cannot be much over a trifle of a thousand miles from their present sphere of activity"; he recommends that "the Colonial Office ought to get to work upon them at once." The narrator likewise declares that "the Brazilian Government is well advised in offering a prize of five hundred pounds for some effectual method of extirpation."[92] In the face of the terrifyingly indifferent forest and the powerful ants, however, these last-ditch attempts to take control through the channels of governmental bureaucracy seem nearly hopeless. In the twentieth century, as we will see, British ecologists marketed themselves as useful public servants whose research could help manage pests and protect economically valuable species throughout the empire. Wells recognized

[89] Wells, *Complete Short Stories*, 586.
[90] Ibid., 589.
[91] Ibid.
[92] Ibid., 596.

that this sort of management would be desirable for European imperial administrations long before he had the vocabulary to describe it as "ecological." But in "Empire," the illusion of colonial control over nature is shattered. As Gerilleau repeats despairingly, "What is one to *do*?"[93]

It's worth noting that while "Empire" features an assortment of imperial types as characters, from the English engineer Holroyd to the Creole captain Gerilleau, the Portuguese lieutenant da Cunha, and, insultingly, a "Sambo" who the Europeans don't bother to mention by name, indigenous people are missing from the story. They are mentioned only once, and very obliquely at that – a rumor that "the people are going," fleeing from the ants.[94] This absence suggests that at least one way of understanding the ants is as an allegorical substitute for the missing Indians, rebelling against those who encroach on their land, driving back the European colonizers. As Charlotte Sleigh points out in her reading of the story, nineteenth- and twentieth-century entomology often posited analogies between colonized people and dangerous insects.[95] From her perspective, "Empire" is a fable of colonial rebellion. Gerilleau and his crew have the big guns – the imperial power – but it's the much smaller ants that rise up and win the day.

For the story's narrator, though, it doesn't end there. It's not just that the ants drive back settlers who try to take over their native territory. It's that the creatures become a colonizing force of their own, one poised to spread over all of South America and, in a few decades, to "discover" Europe. "Empire" thus belongs to a category of Wells's animal stories that, following Stephen Arata, we can call reverse colonization narratives. Arata argues that the reverse colonization plot is "the period's most important and pervasive narrative of decline," featuring prominently in works such as Stoker's *Dracula*, Haggard's *She*, Wells's *War of the Worlds*, and stories by Kipling, Doyle, and others.[96] A close relative of the invasion narratives that gripped British readers at the end of the century, the reverse colonization genre "expresses both fear and guilt" – fear that a Britain in decline is newly vulnerable to attacks from "more vigorous, 'primitive' peoples," guilt that British forces have already committed so many of the genre's most fearful atrocities against indigenous people in

[93] Ibid., 594.
[94] Ibid., 585.
[95] Charlotte Sleigh, "Empire of the Ants: H. G. Wells and Tropical Entomology," *Science as Culture* 10.1 (2001): 33–71.
[96] Stephen D. Arata, "The Occidental Tourist: 'Dracula' and the Anxiety of Reverse Colonization," *Victorian Studies* 33.4 (1990): 621–45, quote on 623.

the colonies.[97] "The Empire of the Ants" draws on the conventions of Victorian invasion literature at the same time that it anticipates the ecological concept of invasive species.

What is interesting about this tale is not only that it revolves around an animal invasion, but also that it is written as a posthoc reconstruction of a historical event assembled from "fragments" of other narratives. It exposes the univocal, authoritative mien of science and journalism as a bricolage of multiple partial perspectives. In so doing, "Empire" shows how important perspective is for understanding both cross-species and cross-cultural interactions. What looks like a disruption of the balance of nature from one perspective looks like business as usual from another; what looks like progressive expansion from one angle looks like an unwarranted invasion from another. The story embraces a topsy-turvy narrative relativity that undergirds a deeper sense of science and politics as relative.

"The Empire of the Ants" initially reads like a straightforward story with a third-person narrator, limited to Holroyd's perspective and possibly that of Gerilleau, who dwells outside the story world – what Gerard Genette would call a heterodiegetic narrator.[98] About halfway through the story, a single sentence, isolated on the page in its own paragraph, changes our perception of the narrator as third person, limited, and heterodiegetic: "He [Holroyd] has described these ants to me very particularly."[99] The sentence is the first use of a first-person pronoun in the story, and set off by itself, it is impossible to miss. It pulls the rug out from under readers, retrospectively recasting everything that came before, for now we recognize that the narrator is not an inherently trustworthy heterodiegetic narrator but instead a character within the story world. In the story's closing paragraphs, we learn that this narrator is an acquaintance of Holroyd's: "I heard this story in a fragmentary state from Holroyd not three weeks ago," he explains.[100] Not only is the story secondhand, it is also a reconstruction of the "fragments" of Holroyd's testimony. What Ian Watt has said of the framing device in *Heart of Darkness* (clearly a major influence on "Empire," as Linda Dryden shows) is true of this story as well: it represents an "ironic consciousness" and a "retreat from the omniscient author."[101] It replaces certainty with irony, knowledge with speculation.

[97] Ibid.
[98] Gerard Genette, *Narrative Discourse: An Essay in Method*, transl. Jane E. Lewin (Cornell University Press, 1983), 244–5.
[99] Wells, *Complete Short Stories*, 591.
[100] Ibid., 596.
[101] Ian Watt, *Conrad in the Nineteenth Century* (University of California Press, 1981), 210–11; Dryden, *Joseph Conrad and H. G. Wells*, 89–93.

The narrative relativity of "Empire," along with its reverse colonization plot, highlights the partiality of Holroyd's account. What looks to Holroyd like a disaster and to the narrator like a management problem is neither from the perspectives of the ants, the indigenous people they symbolize, and nature itself. For the ants, it is success in the struggle for existence; for the indigenous people the ants symbolize, it is a justified recrimination against the European invaders; for nature, chillingly indifferent, it matters not whether humans outcompete ants or vice versa. And for Wells, one suspects, the absurdity of the captain ineffectually firing the big gun at the tiny insects or Holroyd demanding that the Colonial Office "get to work upon them at once" is darkly comic. The reverse colonization plot is satisfying because it turns the tables on the powerful, rendering them powerless in a carnivalesque reversal.

"The Sea Raiders" (1896), a short story about a little-known carnivorous octopus that invades the Devonshire coast, likewise mixes a reverse colonization plot with a bricolaged narrative. The invasive species in question, *Haploteuthis ferox*, kills and eats several boaters and swimmers before returning to the deeps, its retreat as mysterious as its emergence. Like the ants of "Empire," these creatures are intelligent and hunt in packs. The story's main witness, Mr. Fison, observes "the downward bend of the tentacle-surrounded mouth, the curious excrescence at the bend, the tentacles, and the large intelligent eyes, [which] gave the creatures a grotesque suggestion of a face." Before he can observe more, "slowly uncoiling their tentacles, they all began moving towards him--creeping at first deliberately, and making a soft purring sound to each other" – a throwback to the scene in "A Vision of the Past" where the intelligent amphibians encircle the narrator.[102] "The Sea Raiders," along with "The Empire of the Ants" and to some extent "A Vision," falls into a category that Hurley describes as "stories of parallel evolution": stories which assume that, just as humans have undergone progressive evolution, so might other species be evolving new abilities, unbeknownst to us.[103] The results are creatures which appear "monstrous" to humans, but are presented as "logical products of natural processes," i.e. evolution by natural selection.[104]

"The Sea Raiders" is narrated in a documentary style, combining the accounts of eyewitnesses, reports from other towns, and zoological

[102] Wells, *Complete Short Stories*, 172.
[103] Hurley, *The Gothic Body*, 68–70.
[104] Ibid., 70.

details about the creatures. The narrator, who refers to himself as "the writer" and seems to be a scientific journalist of some sort, has interviewed Fison, heard the accounts of other boaters who "told their story in gesticulated fragments," and consulted the zoologist Hemsley, who proposes that the octopuses have surfaced because "a pack or shoal of these creatures may have become enamored of human flesh by the accident of a foundered ship sinking among them, and have wandered in search of it out of their accustomed zone."[105] This narrative technique, which blends a number of seemingly authoritative sources, might, if we follow J. R. Hammond, seem "calculated to lull the reader by its seeming truthfulness." Hammond argues that the story "sets a tone of scientific confirmation which dispels skepticism."[106] Yet there are many cracks in the narrative which invite the reader's skepticism. Like "Empire," the univocal account has been assembled from unconfirmed ecological theories and the "fragments" of traumatized eyewitnesses. All eyewitness testimonies are potentially unreliable, but especially Fison's, whose near-death experience with the octopuses is compared to "an evil dream ... Hill and the monsters, all the stress and tumult of that fierce fight for life, had vanished as though they had never been."[107] The struggle, in other words, leaves behind no material evidence except the absence of evidence – the missing boat, the disappeared people.

Writing about Conrad's *Lord Jim*, which adopts similar narrative techniques, Michael Valdez Moses notes that "our 'final' view of Jim is nevertheless a speculative synthesis, a narrative construction assembled out of multiple, sometimes unreliable, often prejudicial or partial, and frequently contradictory views of the novel's eponymous character."[108] As the "editor" of Jim's life story, Marlow has collected more information about him than anyone, and yet, as he says, "It is impossible to see him clearly."[109] For Moses, this narrative bricolage reflects the uneven traffic of information at the peripheries of empire. The same could be said of Wells's fables – they reflect the patchy, disorienting flow of information that passes for knowledge at the edges of empire, from the translated Dyak legends of the "Big Colugo" to Butcher's tall tales to Holroyd's "fragmentary" testimony to the "gesticulated fragments" of the boaters in

---

[105] Wells, *Complete Short Stories*, 177, 176.
[106] Hammond, *H. G. Wells and the Short Story*, 64.
[107] Wells, *Complete Short Stories*, 175–6.
[108] Michael Valdez Moses, "Disorientalism: Conrad and the Imperial Origins of Modernist Aesthetics," in *Modernism and Colonialism: British and Irish Literature 1899–1939*, ed. Richard Begam and Michael Valdez Moses (Duke University Press, 2007): 43–69, quote on 59.
[109] Joseph Conrad, *Lord Jim* [1899–1900] (Doubleday, 1920), 252.

"The Sea Raiders." At some level, they represent the failure of European colonialism to catalogue the colonies, to subordinate the empire to a rationalized regime of knowledge and management.

For Wells's fables, though, there is one more element to their posthoc, frankensteined narrative form, and that is the absence at its heart, the one testimony that can never be incorporated: the animals' point of view. The colugo, the Aepyornis, the ants, the octopuses, the spiders – they are the agents who drive the stories, and Wells seems to view them as sentient creatures who *have* perspectives. "Suppose presently the ants began to store knowledge, just as men had done by means of books and records, use weapons, form great empires, sustain a planned and organized war?" Holroyd asks himself.[110] But those ant perspectives are irrecoverable. Plagues, competition, predation, and the spread of invasive species were subjects to which both Wells and the scientific ecologists who followed him could speak. But the question of how things look from a niche other than our own ... that was for others to answer.

1.4   Animal Ecology in the Twentieth Century

At the fin de siècle, Wells spun stories about the struggle for existence for an age of decadence. In doing so, he lit on many of the issues which would preoccupy animal ecologists in the twentieth century – the continual "war" against insect pests, mysterious fluctuations in animal population sizes, the unpredictable effects of exotic species introduced in a new environment, disruptions to normal food chains, and so on. When Charles Elton wrote *Animal Ecology* (1927), the first textbook of the new subdiscipline, he too devoted considerable attention to parasitism, population flux, and "plagues" of animals and diseases, as well as other concepts that have become major parts of ecological theory, including the niche and the food cycle. Like Wells's fables, scientific animal ecology is rooted in Darwinian nature. But most early scientific ecologists did not share Wells's sense of humans' cosmic smallness. They believed that with the right expertise, nature could be managed for the benefit of the empire.

Animal ecology grew up in a peculiar moment of environmental history. On one hand, the prospect of nature under man's control seemed more possible, and more desirable, than ever. It was a new century. The American frontier was closed, the scramble for Africa by European

---

[110] Wells, *Complete Short Stories*, 589.

powers complete, and most of the large fauna in Africa, Asia, and North America greatly diminished in number due to hunting, disease, and habitat loss. Nature no longer seemed like a vast, threatening jungle, but like a game preserve in need of intelligent management.[111] Enter the ecologist, the ideal person for such a task. As Peder Anker's *Imperial Ecology* shows, the rise of ecology was deeply entwined with (one might say parasitic upon) colonial administration; young ecologists marketed themselves and their field as one that could be of enormous service to the British Empire in its attempts to settle and sow new territories. The government, Anker explains, "needed people with flexible abilities and interdisciplinary knowledge. The most common task for such ecological entrepreneurs throughout the empire was to transform forests to farmland, deserts to grassland, thus creating environments fit for various colonial interest groups."[112] Julian Huxley was perhaps the best salesman for ecology's usefulness on these grounds. In his introduction to Elton's *Animal Ecology*, he enthused, "Ecology is destined to a great future. The more advanced governments of the world, among which, I am happy to say, our own is coming to be reckoned, are waking up to the fact that the future of plant and animal industry, especially in the tropics, depends upon a proper application of scientific knowledge."[113] It is this attitude that Anker captures when he describes the Oxford school of ecologists (which included Elton, Julian Huxley, Arthur Tansley, and others) as a "Board of Directors" for nature.[114]

On the other hand, ecological study was beginning to uncover just how much scientists still had to learn before intelligent management of the environment was attainable, and just how much damage people might unwittingly do in the process. The tsetse fly is a case study in ecology's limits. Although big-game hunters had reduced the lion population of sub-Saharan Africa, mitigating one threat to humans living in the region, colonial managers found in the tsetse fly a much smaller, yet more intractable enemy. Inhabiting a wide range of middle Africa, the tsetse fly carries parasites that cause sleeping sickness in humans and nagana in

[111] See Harriet Ritvo's "Destroyers and Preservers" for more on this shift, one that is also attested to in Wells's "On Extinction," Huxley's "Man vs. Tsetse Fly," *The Listener* May 31, 1933: 863–5, and Elton's *Animal Ecology*, which points out that "the present numbers of the larger wild animals are mostly much smaller than they used to be" (106).

[112] Anker, *Imperial Ecology*, 80.

[113] Julian Huxley, "Editor's Introduction," in *Animal Ecology*, by Charles Elton (Macmillan, 1927): ix–xvii, quote on xiv.

[114] Anker, *Imperial Ecology*, 110. Worster's *Nature's Economy* takes a similar perspective, arguing that Elton's ecology was dominated by a "management ethos" (314).

farm animals. As Julian Huxley wrote in his 1933 article, "Man vs. Tsetse Fly," "it is really the little creatures that are the most dangerous."[115] He went on to exhort his countrymen to recognize the scale of the problem, in terms that echo Wells's "Empire of the Ants": "as Englishmen we have to remember that ... over many parts of our African colonies, though it is we who claim the sovereignty, the tsetse fly is the real ruler."[116] In Tanganyika, for example, two-thirds of the land is uninhabitable by humans; "the tsetse fly is king. That is bad enough, but it is made worse by the fact that the tsetses, left to themselves, are spreading into new regions, and crowding the natives and their cattle into a smaller area."[117] Ever the optimist, Huxley predicted (wrongly) that within fifteen years scientists would have solved the tsetse fly problem and "banished" the insect from large swathes of Africa.[118] Huxley's sanguine outlook notwithstanding, the tsetse fly appears throughout the early ecological literature as an obdurate antagonist that resists every attempt at control.

At the same time that ecologists were butting up against the problem of the tsetse fly, they were also learning more about the damage that introduced species could do to a biotic community. Elton recognized the problem of invasive species even in the 1920s. His first book discusses a classic case study of invasive species spread by humans – the plant *Lantana* which was introduced to Hawaii, and which spread like wildfire once the (also nonnative) turtle dove was introduced to the islands and began disseminating its seeds.[119] In *The Ecology of Animals* (1933) he pursued the issue, writing, "Originally the world had been split up by natural barriers into fairly well-limited zoogeographical areas. But the invention by man of better and better means of transport has had the unintended result of spreading round the world large numbers of animals whose arrival has often been the start of serious new pests or diseases."[120] Elton was, at the time, cautiously optimistic that biological controls, such as imported parasites, could be found for many invasive species. By the time he wrote *The Ecology of Invasions by Animals and Plants* (1958), however, he was less confident. "The human race has been increasing

---

[115] Julian Huxley, "Man vs. Tsetse Fly," 863.
[116] Ibid.
[117] Ibid.
[118] Ibid., 865. The tsetse fly has not been eradicated even today and still causes disease in humans and livestock. However, some control programs have been moderately successful in reducing harm. See Dietmar Steverding, "The History of African Trypanosomiasis," *Parasites and Vectors* 1.3 (2008) for an account of twentieth-century control programs and their successes and failures.
[119] Elton, *Animal Ecology*, 54–5.
[120] Charles Elton, *The Ecology of Animals* [1933] (Methuen, 1960), 77.

like voles or giant snails," he despaired, "and we have been introducing too many of ourselves into the wrong places."[121] Elton came to believe that biotic communities were too complex for humans to artificially recreate; the best hope for applied ecology lay in "reducing direct power over nature, not increasing it; of letting nature do some of the jobs that engineers and chemists and applied biologists are frantically attempting now."[122] Conservation, in other words, might be a better long-term strategy than micromanagement.

One case of an animal "invasion" that Elton discusses in *Animal Ecology* is worth quoting at length for several reasons. It offers an example of an ecological change that greatly affected humans without us being aware of it. Its narrative technique would not be out of place in a Wells story, as it figures animal dispersal in the language of colonial conquest. And it exemplifies Elton's ability to see complex and dramatic animal worlds where most others see nothing at all. It is the story of why bubonic plague became less common in Europe after the seventeenth century:

> The dying down of the disease coincided with certain interesting events in the rat world. The common rat of Europe had been up to that time the Black or Ship Rat (*R. rattus*), which is a very effective plague-carrier owing to its habit of living in houses in rather close contact with man. Now, in 1727 great hordes of rats belonging to another species, the Brown Rat (*R. norvegicus*), were seen marching westwards into Russia, and swimming across the Volga. This invasion was the prelude to the complete occupation of Europe by brown rats. Furthermore, in most places they have driven out and destroyed the original black rats (which are now chiefly found in ships), and at the same time have adopted habits which do not bring them into such close contact with man as was the case with the black rat ... These important historical events among rats have probably contributed a great deal to the cessation of serious plague epidemics in man in Europe, although they are not the only factors which have caused a dying down of the disease ... We have described this example of the rats at some length, since it shows how events of enormous import to man may take place in the animal world, without any one being aware of them.[123]

Surely few English readers in 1927 realized that they were living in occupied territory, annexed by the brown rat empire, nor that their new occupiers were more benevolent than the old ones. Elton's narrative embellishments – "marching westwards" like an army, "complete

[121] Elton, *The Ecology of Invasions by Animals and Plants*, 144.
[122] Ibid., 145.
[123] Elton, *Animal Ecology*, 53.

occupation of Europe," "historical events among rats" – seem whimsical in their anthropomorphism, but there is a serious element underlying them. He saw the "sociology and economics" and, the above passage suggests, history, of animals as the special province of animal ecology.[124] Nature was no longer the static other to culture, society, and history; for Elton, nature was historical through and through.

Elton was drawn to the study of invasive species like the brown rat and *Lantana* because they were a special case of what Julian Huxley called Elton's "pet subject," fluctuations in the numbers of animals.[125] The questions that most fascinated Elton throughout his career were quantitative ones: how many animals are there in a given biotic community, and how do those numbers change over time? He found that "plagues" of animals, or extreme and rapid population growth followed by a die-off every few years, were not aberrations but instead a normal part of ecology. As he explains in *The Ecology of Animals*,

> One of the most important generalizations that can be made about wild animal populations is that they fluctuate greatly in numbers. Naturalists of the nineteenth century took over without alteration the idea of the balance of life, i.e. constant populations. The earlier religious ideas had included a concept that the world was created in an orderly way, and disturbances in this order were attributed either to the acts of man himself or to the acts of God in punishing man for his presumption in upsetting this order, or perhaps in doing anything new at all. This general concept fitted naturally into the later biological theories of adaptation among animals, since it was supposed (rightly) that animals were closely adapted to their surroundings and (wrongly) that this adaptedness would lead to a state of steady balance between the numbers of different species. Whatever the various theories of adaptation may be found to require we are now in a position to show that wild animals do fluctuate very much and that these fluctuations are not simply the result of developments of human civilization in which man has interfered with natural conditions, as has happened with the introduction of pests into islands or the destruction of predatory animals.[126]

Elton recognized that his claim about population flux would seem unorthodox not only by early nineteenth-century natural theological standards, but even by post-Darwinian biological standards. If "beautiful adaptations" were supposed to limit or mitigate the waste in nature, they were a failure. In fact, for some species (which are now known as

---

[124] Ibid., vii.
[125] Huxley, "Editor's Introduction," xiv.
[126] Elton, *The Ecology of Animals*, 61–2.

r-selected species), a rapid reproductive rate that produces many young, only a few of which make it to adulthood, *is* their adaptation.[127]

Did Elton shudder when he thought about the mice which increase until "epidemic diseases break out and wipe out the major part of the population," or about the "small birds like thrushes, blackbirds, and tits" who die in great numbers each time there is a very cold winter in England?[128] Did he recoil from the wasteful death which is not the exception but the rule in nature? Or did the abstraction of numbers allow him to see these things unemotionally? If he did flinch, there are few signs of it in his writing. When discussing the decimation of the American bison, he declared, "It is not much use mourning the loss of these animals, since it was inevitable that many of them would not survive the close settlement of their countries."[129] And when summing up his own contribution to ecology, he wrote, "failures in regulation of numbers of various animals ... form by far the biggest part of present-day economic problems in the field," and that is why animal numbers should be studied.[130] Population flux thus becomes not an existential horror but an economic issue, one that ecologists can help solve if the species in question is a commercially important one.

Nevertheless, it is not entirely correct to characterize Elton as a management type who perceived value only in economic growth, efficiency, and a rationalized version of nature. He was also a literature lover, one who quoted Robert Browning, Arthur Conan Doyle, and Wells's 1904 novel *The Food of the Gods* in his book on invasion ecology, and who declared that "there is more ecology in the Old Testament or the plays of Shakespeare than in most of the zoological textbooks ever published!"[131] He had a respect for amateurs, writing that that he had "learnt a far greater number of interesting and invaluable ecological facts about the social organization of animals from gamekeepers and private naturalists, and from the writings of men like W. H. Hudson, than from trained zoologists."[132] He also acknowledged and respected non-Western

---

[127] The distinction between *r*-selected species, which produce many young but expend little energy on them, and *K*-selected species, which produce few offspring and care for them during their youth, was first proposed by Edward O. Wilson and Robert MacArthur in *The Theory of Island Biogeography* (Princeton University Press, 1967).

[128] Elton, *Animal Ecology*, 108, 130.

[129] Ibid., 106.

[130] Ibid., 188–9.

[131] Elton, *Ecology of Invasions by Animals and Plants*, 143, 31–2, 109; Elton, *Animal Ecology*, 7; H. G. Wells, *The Food of the Gods* (Charles Scribner's Sons, 1904).

[132] Elton, *Animal Ecology*, 7.

knowledge. His chapter on animal communities presents itself as a gloss on three Chinese proverbs, and he opens *The Ecology of Animals* by citing the ecological expertise not of famous Western scientists, but instead of "[t]he Masai of Central Africa," who knew long before Europeans did that mosquitoes transmitted malaria; "the Eskimo," who first understood that foxes and dogs share diseases; and "the natives of Shansi," who recognized the correlation between periodic increases in sandgrouse and "climate changes."[133]

Finally, Elton's writing has a panache of its own. It plays with scale in disorienting but intriguing ways, as he moves effortlessly from the whole globe as an ecological unit to the parasitic community within a single animal. "[T]he term 'animal community' is really a very elastic one," he explains, "since we can use it to describe on the one hand the fauna of equatorial forest, and on the other hand the fauna of a mouse's caecum."[134] There is something cinematic about his style, as it zooms in and out and all around the world to illustrate different ecological concepts. Like Wells, Elton had a gift for defamiliarizing the familiar, whether he was asking readers to see Europe as an empire of rats or to see mouse intestines as an ecosystem.

The point is that, while scientific ecology like Elton's work needs to be understood as part of the modern culture of instrumental reason, which demands of all things usefulness and quantitative economic value, it is not only that. Even as Elton's writing hawks ecology's promise of controlling nature for capitalism and empire, it also holds contradictory elements which resist professionalization, anthropocentrism, and scientific hegemony. It still has the capacity to disturb and to charm, revealing glimpses of the animal worlds around us, vast and tiny and intricate and unsettling, worlds that most of his readers had no idea were there all along.

1.5   The Struggle Repressed

The themes at stake in Wells's fables – the "uncrowning" of humans, the threats of extinction, invasion, and retrogression, the allegory of imperial relations, the narrative bricolage, the grotesque aesthetics, and above all the struggle for existence – are also at stake in his scientific romances. It would be relatively straightforward to unpack the Morlocks' grotesquerie

---

[133] Ibid., 50; Elton, *The Ecology of Animals*, 1.
[134] Elton, *Animal Ecology*, 17.

in *The Time Machine*, to read the Beast People in *The Island of Doctor Moreau* as allegorical stand-ins for the victims of colonialism, or to identify the parallels between the ants and octopuses of "The Empire of the Ants" and "The Sea Raiders" and the invading Martians in *The War of the Worlds*. The last is an especially interesting case because the narrator of *The War of the Worlds* repeatedly compares the besieged humans to animals – "a flock of sheep," "little frogs hurrying through grass from the advance of a man," "a disturbed hive of bees," and so on.[135] In fact, the experience of being colonized by Martians leads him to identify with these animals and regret the depredations visited upon them by humans: "I touched upon an emotion beyond the common range of men, yet one that the poor brutes we dominate know only too well. I felt as a rabbit might feel returning to his burrow and suddenly confronted by the work of a dozen busy navvies digging the foundations of a house"; "Surely, if we have learned nothing else, this war has taught us pity – pity for those witless souls that suffer our dominion."[136] These sentences, Christina Alt argues, reflect not only "a sense of diminishment or dethronement" for humans, but also "a compensatory empathy for and identification with the animal."[137] They are perhaps the closest Wells ever came to the animal protection movement.

However, those novels are ultimately less about animals in themselves than about the human/animal divide within humans. The real horror of the Morlocks, the Beast People, and the Martians is that they are us. The first two express humans' primitive side, the animal within us that, without the pacifying effects of civilization, we might easily revert to. The latter expresses the threat of the human mind separated from the bodily emotions, the possibility that evolution might make us all brain and no heart. These twin horrors – that we might degrade back into violent animals, that we might progress into hyper-rationalized, unfeeling machines – are extremely significant for literary and intellectual history. But the novels are at once more and less than the short stories. In the longer works Wells further develops his version of the Freudian divides: man/animal, ego/id, civilization/unconscious. But in doing so he leaves behind

---

[135] H. G. Wells, *The War of the Worlds*, [1897] ed. David Y. Hughes and Harry M. Geduld (Indiana University Press, 1993), 70, 100, 117.

[136] Ibid., 164, 169.

[137] Christina Alt, "Extinction, Extermination, and the Ecological Optimism of H. G. Wells," in *Green Planets: Ecology and Science Fiction*, ed. Gerry Canavan (Wesleyan University Press, 2014): 25–39, quote on 30.

zoology for psychology. The material, nonhuman animals that animate the fables are replaced by a system of symbols for different aspects of the human subject. It would not be fruitful to overstate the differences between the novels and the short stories, but nor would it do to collapse the distinctions between them. Studied as a corpus in its own right, the short stories show us something different.

Rather than dwell on the 1890s scientific romances, then, let us conclude by way of a lesser-known work: Wells's 1923 Utopian novel *Men Like Gods*. This might seem a strange text to end on, first because it isn't a very good book, and second because it is in so many respects the polar opposite of his fables. In *Men Like Gods*, the technocratic views that Wells came to embrace in the twentieth century are put on full display. A bumbling but well-meaning journalist finds himself transported to an alternate universe whose inhabitants have created a Utopia on Earth. A key part of their Utopian society is deft ecological management. Indeed, Julian Huxley praised the novel for its vision of nature under the control of scientists, writing,

> Mr. Wells also imagines a purging of the organic world. The triumphs of parasitology and the rise of ecology have set him thinking; and he believes that, given real knowledge of the life-histories and interrelations of organisms, man could successfully proceed to wholesale elimination of a multitude of noxious bacteria, parasitic worms, insects, and carnivores. Here again we have no right to quarrel. Mr. Wells does not need to be reminded of the thistle in California or the rabbits in Australia: his Utopians proceed with exemplary precautions. All this is but an extension of what has already been begun.[138]

Readers of Wells's 1890s scientific romances and fables might well look at *Men Like Gods* and wonder, what on earth happened? How did the author of so many tales that deflated scientific hubris, punctured anthropocentrism, and critiqued the arrogance of imperialism go on to write a Utopian novel that posited technocratic world government and utter subjugation of nature as the way forward? How could we go from the dismal empire of ants and *The Time Machine*'s degenerate posthuman species to this sunny, creepily competent vision of the future?

The shift in Wells's writing after 1900, 1905, or 1908 (depending on how one regards his Edwardian works) is a major preoccupation of Wells criticism. Most scholars agree that Wells's writing changed because of his intensifying conviction that literature ought to do something in

---

[138] Julian Huxley, *Essays in Popular Science* [1926] (Chatto & Windus, 1933), 68.

the world, a conviction that would cause rifts with Joseph Conrad and Henry James.[139] But Julian Huxley may have lit on part of the explanation for the change in his review when he suggested that "the triumphs of parasitology and the rise of ecology have set him thinking." Christina Alt, contrasting the pessimism of *The War of the Worlds* with the optimism of *Men Like Gods*, likewise pinpoints the advent of scientific ecology, which encouraged "a new confidence – even arrogance – in humanity's ability to exert control over the natural world," as a determinative factor.[140] Perhaps the imperial, managerial ecology championed by Julian Huxley and, for a time at least, Charles Elton persuaded Wells that his fin-de-siècle prognostications had been too gloomy. Perhaps the development of applied ecology in the twentieth century gave him hope.

However, within the pages of *Men Like Gods* lurk the same disturbances that haunt stories like "The Empire of the Ants" and "The Sea Raiders." One of the characters from the present universe objects to the Utopians' ecological management, professing that they have meddled with the "Balance of Nature."[141] But the Utopians, like Elton and Wells, do not see nature as existing in balance at all. "Half the species of life in our planet also, half and more than half of all the things alive, were ugly or obnoxious, inane, miserable, wretched, with elaborate diseases, helplessly ill-adjusted to Nature's continually fluctuating conditions, when first we took this old Hag, our Mother, in hand," they explain.[142] It is difficult to look past the misogyny and contempt for "ugly and obnoxious" things in this pronouncement, but if we can, we will see something else – a horror at the animal suffering that is part of nature. Elton must have seen this suffering when he studied fluctuations in animal populations. Thomas H. Huxley had seen it too, and was moved by it to turn away from nature in his study of ethics. If Wells and the early ecologists dreamed of a nature under human mastery, it may not have been motivated purely by greed or lust for power. It may also have reflected a desire to reduce suffering, a desire that for Wells's Utopians did not stop at humans but encompassed all sentient creatures.

An earlier version of this chapter gave Joseph Conrad the last word. It suggested that Wells's turn to Utopian ecology and the early ecologists' enthusiasm for applied work may have been ways of working through a

---

[139] See Dryden's *Joseph Conrad and H. G. Wells* and James's *Maps of Utopia* for useful accounts of this shift.

[140] Alt, "Extinction, Extermination, and the Ecological Optimism of H. G. Wells," 25.

[141] H. G. Wells, *Men Like Gods* (Macmillan, 1923), 91.

[142] Ibid., 107.

repressed horror at the waste and suffering in the animal world, a horror which if laid bare would be, to borrow Conrad's words, "too dark – too dark altogether ..."[143] This version, too, will give Conrad the last word, but in a different way. For if Wells at the fin de siècle looked, unblinking, at an indifferent and wasteful nature, he was never unrelentingly nihilist. The animal world he saw had also its carnivalesque pleasures, its grotesque fecundity as well as its disease and death, its humorous uncrownings and recrownings, its worms and bugs and twisted mud-fish and all that fish's descendants. Conrad saw all of this at once too, and wrote that nature was like a giant knitting machine: "I am horrified at the horrible work and stand appalled. I feel it ought to embroider – but it goes on knitting ... It knits us in and it knits us out. It has knitted time, space, pain, death, corruption, despair and all the illusions – and nothing matters. I'll admit however that to look at the remorseless process is sometimes amusing."[144]

---

[143] Joseph Conrad, *Heart of Darkness* [1899], ed. Ross C. Murfin (Bedford/St. Martin's, 2011), 93.
[144] Joseph Conrad, *The Selected Letters of Joseph Conrad*, ed. Laurence Davies (Cambridge University Press, 2015), 82.

CHAPTER 2

Aldous Huxley, Henry Eliot Howard, and the Observational Ethic

Aldous Huxley has struck many readers through the years as more scientist than novelist. Huxley criticism teems with metaphors of the laboratory and the zoo.[1] His 1920s fiction has "something of the coldness of the vivisectionist"[2]; it "contain[s] much merciless vivisection of the life and classes that Huxley knew"[3]; "he was interested less in how to capture the elusive poetical emotion or intellectual insight alive than in how to dissect it – or vivisect it – and lay it out clear on the anatomical table"[4]; his 1928 novel *Point Counter Point* is "[c]learly ... a zoo"[5]; for the working classes "Huxley has the attention that a scientist has for strange and unforeseen forms of animal life"[6]; he was "as fascinated by human beings as a zoologist at the sight of his first okapi or duck-billed platypus."[7] Like his alter ego Philip Quarles in *Point Counter Point*, Huxley is considered a zoological novelist, detachedly applying a scientific gaze to the people around him and seeing the animal within the human.

Huxley's early fiction is constantly associated with zoology but, strangely, it is always a human zoology. Animals as such rarely receive attention from Huxley scholars. Yet animals *qua* animal appear at pivotal moments within Huxley's novels, and they differ markedly from the animal similes he uses to represent humans. If zoomorphic humans are a key component of Huxley's satire and a target for his cold, "vivisecting" pen, his literal animals escape both. Huxley's animals are neither jokes

---

[1] In this chapter, "Huxley" will refer to Aldous Huxley, and Julian Huxley will be referred to by his full name.

[2] Nicholas Murray, *Aldous Huxley: A Biography* (Thomas Dunne, 2002), 138.

[3] Ibid., 133.

[4] Peter Firchow, *Aldous Huxley: Satirist and Novelist* (University of Minnesota Press, 1972), 31.

[5] Jerome Meckier, "Quarles Among the Monkeys: Huxley's Zoological Novels," *Modern Language Review* 68 (1973): 268–82, quote on 271.

[6] Harold H. Watts, *Aldous Huxley* (Hippocrene, 1972), 42.

[7] Alexander Henderson, *Aldous Huxley* (Chatto & Windus, 1935), 130; quoted in Sanford E. Marovitz, "Aldous Huxley's Intellectual Zoo," *Philological Quarterly* 48.4 (1969): 495–507, quote on 496.

nor scientific objects. They are subjects whose interiority, like that of H. G. Wells's animals, is mysterious and opaque to human observers.

Huxley's biting satire includes among its targets people who refuse to recognize animal subjectivity. His fiction skewers professional vivisectionists. Although he cannot be reckoned an antivivisectionist or proponent of animal rights in any straightforward way – he is too much his grandfather's grandson for that – Huxley does critique the scientific gaze that reduces laboratory animals to inert experimental objects. Characters who are willfully blind to animal suffering in his novels tend to be equally blind to human suffering, especially when it comes to marginalized humans – women, the poor, and people with disabilities. Those who refuse sympathy with animals, Huxley implies, also fail to fully recognize other human subjects.

To recognize animal subjectivity, though, is not necessarily to represent it directly. Unlike his peers D. H. Lawrence and Virginia Woolf, Huxley rarely attempts empathetic representations of animals' subjective experiences. Instead, he makes use of a thin description, based on and mostly limited to external observation, to represent animals. Thin description, as Heather Love (drawing on the philosopher Gilbert Ryle) defines it, encompasses "forms of analysis that describe patterns of behavior and visible activity but that do not traffic in speculation about interiority, meaning, or depth."[8] Thin description does not necessarily preclude a "thick" understanding of behavior that makes recourse to subjectivity, intent, or social meaning. Instead, it offers an empirical foundation for such an understanding. It puts the observer or describer in the position of a recording device; "by turning oneself into a camera, one could – at least ideally – pay equal attention to every aspect of a scene that is available to the senses and record it faithfully."[9] Thin description is a method common in the sciences and social sciences, and it became an important tool for zoology in the work of classical ethologists Konrad Lorenz and Niko Tinbergen, who eschewed laboratory experimentation in favor of observing, recording, and describing animal behavior in the wild.[10]

This chapter argues that even before Lorenz and Tinbergen established their ethological idiom, writers like Aldous Huxley and naturalists like Henry Eliot Howard were already gravitating toward thin description

---

[8] Heather Love, "Close Reading and Thin Description," *Public Culture* 25.3 (2013): 401–34, quote on 404. It is worth noting that Love's central interest in this essay is in thin description as a method for literary criticism, rather than thin description as a feature of literature.

[9] Ibid., 407.

[10] Ibid., 416.

in their writing about animals. They found in thin description a way of deferring, without denying, claims about animals' subjective experience. Their animal descriptions expressed an ethos of careful, attentive observation, a humble form of empiricism that acknowledges the limitations of the observer's knowledge. Howard, a British ornithologist who is best known for describing territoriality in birds, was an important figure in the transition from natural history to scientific ethology, as the historian Richard W. Burkhardt, Jr. shows.[11] Though Howard believed that his objects of study were conscious subjects, he warned his fellow observers against slipping into a thick, emotionally laden description too easily. If a bird's behavior "is to be understood aright; if, that is to say, the exact position it occupies in the drama of bird life is to be properly determined, and its biological significance estimated at its true value," he cautioned, "it is above all things necessary to refrain from appealing to any one of the emotions which we are accustomed to associate with ourselves, unless our ground for doing so is more than ordinarily secure."[12] To understand territoriality, he continued, we must avoid an overly anthropomorphic vocabulary that would frame a bird's relationship to a location "in terms of one or other of the emotions which centre round the human home."[13] For Howard as for Huxley, thin description reflects not a disbelief in animal subjectivity but a commitment not to misrepresent "the drama of [animal] life."

Huxley's use of thin description aligns him not just with Howard and the ethologists, but also with a cadre of modernist writers who pushed back against subjective, psychological density in their writings. Modernist fiction is often seen as practically synonymous with explorations of psychological depth, as evidenced by the centrality of stream-of-consciousness writing in discussions of modernist narrative. But in the last two decades critics have begun to call attention to the ways in which many modernists rejected subjectivist aesthetics. Joshua Gang, for example, identifies in Samuel Beckett and others a "mindless modernism" influenced by behaviorist psychology, while Martin Jay argues that "anti-psychologism" forms an important strand of modernist thought

[11] Richard W. Burkhardt, Jr., *Patterns of Behavior: Konrad Lorenz, Niko Tinbergen, and the Founding of Ethology* (University of Chicago Press, 2005), 92–8. Burkhardt cites Edmund Selous, Henry Eliot Howard, and Frederick B. Kirkman as the three British ornithologists whose work contributed most to the development of scientific ethology. Not only did they study bird behavior in the field, they also spoke to evolutionary theory, especially the issue of sexual selection (70).
[12] H. Eliot Howard, *Territory in Bird Life* (John Murray, 1920), 21.
[13] Ibid.

(one that includes T. S. Eliot's doctrine of impersonality).[14] Douglas Mao, meanwhile, claims that even for writers like Virginia Woolf, who seems to be the paragon of subjectivist modernism, the world of nonhuman objects represented an alluring respite from a domineering subjectivity; one important thread of modernism, in his reading, is an attempt to escape from consciousness.[15] Adding behaviorism, antipsychologism, and object aesthetics/politics to the spectrum of modernist contexts has enriched our understanding of the literary debates that produced such different effects in the works of Beckett, Woolf, and other writers we place under the umbrella of modernism.

It has become clear that psychological depth is not the *sine qua non* of modernism that it was once reputed to be, but scholars have not yet fully registered how the study of animals informed modernist thinking about literary methods. Modernist writers turned to animals to test the limits of subjectivist and objectivist approaches to fiction. Each writer had to make decisions about whether to make animals characters or scenery, knowable or unknowable subjects, thinking selves or mere bodily behaviors. These decisions offer insight into their positions on several important literary questions. Should literary description be empirical or introspective? Should character-building rely more on surface appearances and behaviors or psychological depth? Does a true self even exist separable from our animal bodies and external behaviors? Huxley's ethological thin description, like Beckett's behaviorism, Eliot's impersonality, and Woolf's objects, belongs in the new canon of nonsubjectivist modernist techniques. It reflects his writerly commitment to empiricism, and it aligns with his attention to surfaces (both physical and social) as well as his deep sense that humans are ourselves animals.

For Huxley as for Howard, observation and thin description have both epistemological and ethical implications. Epistemologically, they reflect a modest form of empiricism that acknowledges animals' subjective experience, but does not pretend to have access to it. Ethically, they offer a nonviolent alternative to what Christina Alt characterizes as "the

[14] Joshua Gang, "Mindless Modernism," *NOVEL* 46.1 (2013): 116–32; Martin Jay, "Modernism and the Specter of Psychologism," *Modernism/Modernity* 3.2 (1996): 93–111. See also Paul Scott Stanfield, "'This Implacable Doctrine': Behaviorism in Wyndham Lewis's *Snooty Baronet*," *Twentieth Century Literature* 47.2 (2001): 241–67, and Ella Zohar Ophir, "Toward a Pitiless Fiction: Abstraction, Comedy, and Modernist AntiHumanism," *Modern Fiction Studies* 52.1 (2006): 92–120 for explorations of antisubjectivist characterization in Wyndham Lewis and Laura Riding.
[15] Douglas Mao, *Solid Objects: Modernism and the Test of Production* (Princeton University Press, 1998), 8–9.

new biology." This experimental, lab-based approach to the life sciences gained traction in the early twentieth century, but it did not always demonstrate concern for animal suffering. As Alt explains, "practitioners of the new biology regarded the antivivisection movement as a challenge to their newly attained authority and combated this threat by dismissing protectionist views as the irrational sentimentality of unqualified amateurs."[16] Huxley was closely connected to a number of scientists involved in the new biology, but his fictional representations of scientists and laboratories register a serious discomfort with animal experimentation. This unease reaches its climax in *Brave New World*, in which the techniques that Pavlov and other scientists developed through animal experimentation are applied to humans. Against the backdrop of the new biology, observation becomes not just a method in Huxley's 1920s fiction but also a keystone in his ethics of nonviolence.

2.1   Huxley as Zoological Novelist

What does it mean to say that Huxley is a zoological novelist? For Huxley scholars like Sanford E. Marovitz and Jerome Meckier, it means two things. First, the animal simile is one of the sharpest tools of Huxley's satire. Born into a family of Darwinians, Huxley knew that all humans were animals first, and his imagery reminds readers that even the most intellectually ambitious of his characters are still animals, "lizard-like or leonine, dog-like, ape-like, 'ferret-faced' or aquiline human animals who indulge in exactly the same fundamental natural processes as the beasts called forth to represent them."[17] His 1920s novels constitute an "intellectual zoo"; they put on display their characters, often the toast of English society, so that readers may see them scratching, biting, and otherwise embarrassing themselves.[18] Second, animality as embodiment forms a key part of Huxley's "amphibious" philosophy. As Mark Rampion, purportedly the wisest character in *Point Counter Point*, thinks, "To be a perfect animal *and* a perfect human – that was the ideal."[19]

Zoological satire and the amphibious ideal are both useful tools for unpacking Huxley's fiction, but neither can fully explain Huxley's animal

[16] Alt, *Virginia Woolf and the Study of Nature*, 48. Alt attributes the development of the new biology to Thomas H. Huxley, who promoted laboratories and experimentation over the Victorian practices of taxonomy centered in the natural history museum (42–3).
[17] Marovitz, "Aldous Huxley's Intellectual Zoo," 496.
[18] Ibid., title; see also Meckier, "Quarles Among the Monkeys," 271.
[19] Huxley, *Point Counter Point* [1928] (Dalkey Archive Press, 2009), 111.

representations. They speak to a familiar desire to reconcile the mind/ body divide but say little about animals as such. The successful amphibian is equally at home in the human world of the intellect and the animal world of emotions and physical desires; the targets of Huxley's zoological satire, on the other hand, fail on at least one of these counts. Yet Huxley's fiction also undercuts the position of the zoological satirist. Characters who are good at identifying the foolish animal within others are bad at being animals themselves. Such characters make it clear that while Huxley may at times imitate the detached scientist observing the human zoo, he ultimately rejects the lacerating scientific gaze as a model for authorship.

Huxley is a zoological novelist in a third sense as well. His narrative method, as Daniel Aureliano Newman demonstrates, draws on biological research. Analyzing *Eyeless in Gaza* (1936), a novel known for its anachrony – each chapter set in a different year in the life of the protagonist, ordered seemingly at random – Newman argues that Huxley was actually creating a new kind of Bildungsroman modeled on the life history of the axolotl. The axolotl is a salamander which fascinated developmental biologists, including Julian Huxley, because it remained in its juvenile form its entire life, unlike other amphibians, which undergo metamorphosis from their aquatic juvenile form to their air-breathing adult one. Julian Huxley had discovered that axolotls, if fed sheep thyroid, will metamorphose, a discovery that, Newman suggests, inspired novelists like Aldous Huxley to rethink the linear narrative of development typical to the Bildungsroman.[20] This chapter makes a related argument about Huxley's 1920s fiction: that it sketches out a narrative method in response to contemporary biological science. In this case, the science is not developmental biology but ethology.

Philip Quarles, the novelist character of *Point Counter Point*, comes close to exemplifying this ethological method but ultimately falls short. His approach to literature is usually seen as, if not identical with Huxley's, at least closely related to it.[21] Quarles records in his writing journal,

---

[20] Daniel Aureliano Newman, "'Education of an Amphibian': Anachrony, Neoteny, and *Bildung* in Huxley's *Eyeless in Gaza*," *Twentieth Century Literature* 62.4 (2016): 403–28.

[21] See, for example, Peter Bowering's *Aldous Huxley: A Study of the Major Novels* (Oxford University Press, 1969), 85–6, which describes Philip Quarles's characterization as a piece of "self-criticism" on Huxley's part; Keith M. May, *Aldous Huxley* (Elek, 1972), 79–80, 91, 93; and Firchow, *Aldous Huxley*, 112. All of these critics agree that Quarles is to some extent an autobiographical representation of Huxley himself.

Since reading Alverdes and Wheeler I have quite decided that my novelist must be an amateur zoologist. Or, better still, a professional zoologist who is writing a novel in his spare time. His approach will be strictly biological. He will be constantly passing from the termitary to the drawing room and the factory, and back again. He will illustrate human vices by those of the ants, which neglect their young for the sake of the intoxicating liquor exuded by the parasites that invade their nests. His hero and heroine will spend their honeymoon by a lake, where the grebes and ducks illustrate all the aspects of courtship and matrimony.[22]

Philip's satirical comparative zoology diminishes his human characters. He plans to address meaningful experiences like parenthood, love, and work not through a description of individuated emotions, but through a disinterested ethological analysis. His animal analogies, like Huxley's, work to expose his characters' foolishness.

Quarles's references to ants, grebes, and ducks no doubt reflect the influence of Huxley's brother Julian. Julian Huxley's studies of courtship in the great crested grebe and the wild duck were some of the earliest works of ethology in England, and he published a popular science book entitled *Ants* in 1929. For Julian Huxley, grebes represented an egalitarian form of marriage because of their mutual courtship displays (as Chapter 3 discusses in greater detail). Ducks, meanwhile, conduct a more violent and unequal form of mating, in which females are sometimes trampled and drowned, something he found appalling.[23] From Julian Huxley's anthropomorphic language of "courtship" and "marriage," and his moralizing comments on the "disharmony" of ducks' mating rituals and the superiority of the grebes' mutual, monogamous pairings, it is hardly a leap to Philip Quarles's idea that grebes and ducks might illustrate the virtues and vices of human romantic relationships.

But there is one vital difference between Julian Huxley's zoology and Philip Quarles's. For Philip, the ants, ducks, and grebes are unimportant in themselves; they are merely tools to illustrate the biological underpinnings of human behavior. The animals, in other words, are entirely subordinated to the human story. As an ethologist, however, Julian Huxley found the animals interesting in themselves. The parallels between human and animal behaviors were clearly visible to Julian Huxley, but

---

[22] Huxley, *Point Counter Point*, 315. Alverdes and Wheeler are Friedrich Alverdes, author of the 1927 *Social Life in the Animal World*, and William Morton Wheeler, an entomologist who studied social insects.

[23] See Julian Huxley, "The Courtship-Habits of the Great Crested Grebe," *Proceedings of the Zoological Society of London* 35 (1914): 491–562; and Julian Huxley, "A 'Disharmony' in the Reproductive Habits of the Wild Duck," *Biologisches Zentralblatt* 32 (1912): 621–3.

neither was reducible to the other. For Quarles, the grebes are hollow symbols for people; for Julian Huxley, the grebes may have had symbolic import but never lost their essential grebe-ness. In other words, Quarles's zoology devalues both people and grebes, while Julian Huxley's aimed to elevate both (albeit at the expense of the ducks).

Quarles is usually read as an intelligent and sympathetic character with one tragic flaw: he is coldly unemotional. His intellect flourishes while his relationships, especially his marriage, wither. He fails to meet Rampion's ideal because he is incapable of being "a perfect animal." Quarles's zoological gaze may produce good satire, and it may allow him to perceive his friends' problems in ways that they cannot, but it also has blind spots. "Like Quarles himself, the zoological perspective is incomplete," as Meckier says.[24] Incomplete because it fails to account for the observer's own animality; but also, I would add, because it is uninterested in animals in themselves. In contrast, Aldous Huxley's own representations of animals, at their best, move beyond the hollow structures of simile and metaphor to express a genuine, respectful curiosity, akin to the curiosity of the ethologist. It is not just that he mimics the observational methods of ethology; he also internalizes the ethos underlying them.

2.2 Vivisection and Its Discontents

It is perhaps unfair that Huxley has been cast as a literary vivisector, a vivisector of men, because his fiction expresses unease with the actual practice of vivisecting animals. Within his fiction, characters' support for animal experimentation is a shorthand for their social and ethical failings. This is not to say that Huxley aligns himself in any straightforward way with the animal protection movement; such an alignment would risk accusations of sentimentality or antiscientific belief. Instead he passes judgment on the vivisectors through a rhetorical strategy that borrows a few tactics from the antivivisection movement's playbook and adapts them to his own satirical style. This strategy allows Huxley to critique animal experimentation while dodging the extremism and feminine irrationality that were commonly attributed to the antivivisection movement. Huxley does not roundly condemn science, nor does he adopt sentimental Victorian modes of representing animal subjectivity. But his fiction does suggest that animal experimentation degrades the experimenter, rendering him (and it is pretty much always a him) morally

[24] Meckier, "Quarles Among the Monkeys," 273.

callous even outside the laboratory. The novels also imply that pro-vivisectionist thinking is infected by a misogynistic strain which devalues women because of their emotional ties to animals.

The animal protection debates intersect with modernist literary debates because both were fought on the terrain of sentimentality. Antivivisection was part of a larger change in attitudes toward animals in the nineteenth century, as Christina Alt explains. The 1824 establishment of the Society for the Prevention of Cruelty to Animals, the 1869 passage of the Sea Birds Preservation Act, the 1880s activism against the plumage trade – these events, Alt suggests, index a growing concern about the treatment of animals in Victorian Britain.[25] But not everyone was on board with the new humane outlook. Philip J. Armstrong argues that both scientists and many modernist writers came to despise "sentimentalism, especially as associated with compassionate identification between humans and animals."[26] Armstrong's account of this backlash offers important context for understanding why Aldous Huxley would not simply tap into existing antivivisection discourses:

> [A] thoroughgoing devaluation of sentimental feeling began in the lat-ter part of the nineteenth century, as demonstrated by the writings of H. G. Wells, largely because of the increasing authority of industrial capitalism and scientific positivism ... Accepting, indeed embracing, the new social organization of taste and sensibility, modernism attempted to regain for art some of the cultural authority lost to science and industry by thoroughly repudiating all forms of sentimental narrative and affect ... The modernists presented sentimentalism not just as a symptom of the Victorian complacency they sought to disturb, or the mass culture from which they wished to distinguish themselves, but also an ideological ruse, an affective opiate, by which bourgeois consciousness was manipulated, flattered and politically neutralized.[27]

"Inevitably," Armstrong concludes, "sentimental attachment to animals became a particular target of modernist suspicion."[28] For Aldous Huxley, allied with the scientists in his family and the modernist writers in his circle of friends, sentimentality was bound to be a bête noire. His critique of vivisection would have to find grounding elsewhere.

The most famous literary response to the vivisection debate is not by Huxley, of course; it is H. G. Wells's 1896 novel *The Island of Doctor*

[25] Alt, *Virginia Woolf and the Study of Nature*, 46–7.
[26] Armstrong, *What Animals Mean in the Fiction of Modernity*, 165.
[27] Ibid.
[28] Ibid., 166.

Moreau. This novel struck many readers as one of the most horrifying and scathing condemnations of vivisection in print. The fiendish Moreau experiments on live animals, using surgical methods to turn them into "Beast People" who live in dread of his laboratory, which they call the "House of Pain." The rhetoric Moreau uses to justify his experiments, as Mason Harris shows, echoes that of real physiologists like Claude Bernard. Moreau declares that he is motivated by a scientific love of knowledge, which makes "the thing before you ... no longer an animal, a fellow-creature, but a problem."[29] Such passages struck readers as chillingly inhumane. Yet Wells did not personally oppose vivisection; as Harris points out, he actually defends the practice in his essay "Popular Feeling and the Advancement of Science."[30] And, as Armstrong argues, Moreau's conviction that humans are already animalistic aligns closely with Wells's own views.[31] How do we make sense of the apparent contradictions between Wells's stance and his novel's import – and, by extension, between Huxley's close ties to physiologists and his novels' import?

The answer lies in satire, a literary method that tends to exceed its authors' intentions. In Armstrong's reading, *Island* is better understood not as a straightforward horror story about the evils of scientific hubris, but as a satire in the Swiftian vein. As such, he cautions against the assumption that either Moreau, the voice of heartless scientism, or Prendick, the voice of antivivisection, is a spokesman for the author. Instead, the novel "critique[s] both positions by taking them to their satirical extremes."[32] However, "satire is a dangerous beast, likely to bite the hand that unleashes it," Armstrong quips, and Wells's satire accidentally bites back at the pro-vivisectionist stance that he elsewhere adopted as his own.[33] To read *Island* as an antivivisectionist screed is, then, in Armstrong's view, an ahistorical misinterpretation that nevertheless gets at something true about the novel. Likewise, as Jay Clayton argues, to read Huxley's *Brave New World* as a jeremiad against science is an understandable misinterpretation of its author's intentions that requires more historicism to correct.[34] Huxley, too, found that satire's "sharp edges cut

---

[29] H. G. Wells, *The Island of Doctor Moreau* (Signet, 1996), 115; quoted in Mason Harris, "Vivisection, the Culture of Science, and Intellectual Uncertainty in *The Island of Doctor Moreau*," *Gothic Studies* 4.2 (2002): 99–115, quote on 103.

[30] Ibid., 101.

[31] Armstrong, *What Animals Mean in the Fiction of Modernity*, 81.

[32] Ibid., 80.

[33] Ibid., 81.

[34] Jay Clayton, "The Modern Synthesis: Genetics and Dystopia in the Huxley Circle," *Modernism/Modernity* 23.4 (2016): 875–96.

in many directions" (to quote Clayton) and undercut his own intentions. *Brave New World's* dystopia "narrowed the options it presented to two choices," heartless science or passionate primitivism, "neither of which [Huxley] meant to be acceptable."[35] I want to argue that something similar is going on with Huxley's pre-*Brave New World* representations of scientists. He probably did not set out to denounce vivisection specifically, but it is as if his satirical pen could not help but puncture and anatomize the provivisectionist viewpoint along with everything else it wandered across.

Huxley would have been familiar with the vivisection debates that began in the 1870s and continued into the twentieth century because many of his intellectual influences, including his grandfather Thomas H. Huxley, Charles Darwin, H. G. Wells, and his friend J. B. S. Haldane participated in them. A number of issues were at stake in this dispute: animal welfare, of course, but also the autonomy of scientific research, the role of ethics and emotions in scientific practice, and the place of women in public life. This history can help us better understand Huxley's choices in writing about vivisection. From his forebears Huxley inherited a respect for biological science, but also a sense of apprehension about what happens when science is divorced from sympathy.

Divided loyalties like Huxley's were common in the vivisection debates. For example, Darwin, an animal lover who never practiced vivisection and wrote that it made him "sick with horror," nevertheless grudgingly defended the practice as sometimes necessary for the advancement of physiology.[36] Yet he also argued strenuously, in *Descent of Man*, that animals have consciousness, emotions, and intelligence – and thus, to answer Jeremy Bentham's famous question, that they can indeed suffer. One example Darwin adduces to demonstrate the existence of animal emotions seems overtly damning of vivisection. He writes, "every one has heard of the dog suffering under vivisection, who licked the hand of the operator; this man, unless he had a heart of stone, must have felt remorse to the last hour of his life."[37] Such a claim implies that for Darwin, sympathy is, and should be, a part of scientific studies on animals. Thomas H. Huxley, like Darwin, "had his own horror of experiments on *conscious* animals."[38] But he worried that antivivisectionists were antiscience and

[35] Ibid., 891.
[36] Quoted in Janet Browne, *Charles Darwin: The Power of Place* (Princeton University Press, 2003), 421.
[37] Darwin, *Descent of Man*, 40.
[38] Adrian Desmond, *Huxley: From Devil's Disciple to Evolution's High Priest* (Perseus, 1999), 457.

would interfere with progress in physiology, and he supported the physiologists during the Royal Commission hearings on vivisection in 1875, hearings that led to the passage of the Cruelty to Animals bill in 1876.[39]

The next generation of science commentators was similarly ambivalent on the issue. Perhaps the most immediate sources for Aldous Huxley's understanding of vivisection were his brother Julian Huxley and his friend J. B. S. Haldane. Julian Huxley practiced vivisection in the teens and twenties, experimenting on marine invertebrates and tadpoles to learn about the processes of development in experiments clearly related to those of the *Point Counter Point* character Lord Edward Tantamount.[40] But in 1934, in response to antivivisectionist concerns, he gave up his vivisector's license and upheld the ban on vivisection at the London Zoo, where he served as secretary.[41] J. B. S. Haldane, meanwhile, publicly argued in favor of vivisection but privately had reservations. In 1927, when an animal protection bill was before Parliament, Haldane declared it unnecessary, claiming that he had witnessed many animal experiments, "but none which, so far as pain is concerned, I should object to having performed on myself."[42] (Those familiar with Haldane's predilection for experimenting on himself might find this claim less than reassuring.) But, as biographer Ronald Clark points out, Haldane was more ambivalent about animal experimentation than he let on, and later in his life, under the influence of Gandhi, recommended that people avoid using dogs and rats in experiments because one should "avoid causing suffering to others unless they volunteer for it."[43]

One tactic of the Victorian antivivisection movement was to claim that, in the words of historian Craig Buettinger, vivisection "morally brutalized the vivisectors themselves."[44] This accusation targeted some of the most notorious practitioners of vivisection in the nineteenth century,

[39] Susan Hamilton, "Introduction," in *Animal Welfare and Anti-Vivisection 1870–1910: Nineteenth-Century Woman's Mission*, ed. Susan Hamilton (Routledge, 2004): xiv–xlvii.
[40] See J. A. Witkowski's "Julian Huxley in the Laboratory: Embracing Inquisitiveness and Widespread Curiosity," in *Julian Huxley: Biologist and Statesman of Science*, ed. C. Kenneth Waters and Albert Van Helden (Rice University Press, 1992): 79–103 for an account of Huxley's laboratory research.
[41] Joe Cain, "Julian Huxley, General Biology and the London Zoo, 1935–1942," *Notes and Records of the Royal Society* 64 (2010): 359–78.
[42] Quoted in Ronald Clark, *J. B. S.: The Life and Work of J. B. S. Haldane* [1968] (Bloomsbury, 2011), 67. Haldane was almost certainly the inspiration for James Shearwater's auto-experimentation in Huxley's *Antic Hay*.
[43] Ibid.
[44] Craig Buettinger, "Women and Antivivisection in Late Nineteenth-Century America," *Journal of Social History* 30.4 (1997): 857–72, quote on 862.

including Claude Bernard, John Burdon Sanderson, and Emanuel Klein, who shocked many antivivisectionists with their seeming indifference to animal suffering. Bernard, a French physiologist, published *Introduction to the Study of Experimental Medicine* in 1865, a book that described and defended vivisection. Bernard argued that "[t]o learn how man and animals live, we cannot avoid seeing great numbers of them die, because the mechanisms of life can be unveiled and proved only by knowledge of the mechanisms of death."[45] He also characterized the scientist's view as one unburdened by sympathy, pursuing pure knowledge: "A physiologist ... no longer hears the cry of animals, he no longer sees the blood that flows, he sees only his idea and perceives only organisms concealing problems which he intends to solve."[46] According to the historian of science Anita Guerrini, Bernard often used dogs in his experiments, and he paid little attention to anesthesia in his book, despite being familiar with its uses.[47]

The English physiologist John Burdon Sanderson, J. S. Haldane's uncle and J. B. S.'s great-uncle, studied with Bernard in Paris in the 1850s. He published his own *Handbook for the Physiological Laboratory* in 1873, a textbook that enraged antivivisectionists for neglecting to discuss anesthesia.[48] Sanderson claimed that he did not mention anesthesia in his handbook because it was "a thing taken for granted" among physiologists, a claim that rang hollow to many opponents since the *Handbook* was, in Sanderson's own words, "intended for beginners in physiological work."[49] To many activists, Bernard and Sanderson's books reflected a cavalier attitude toward animal pain – they were familiar with the uses of anesthesia yet did not seem to consider pain prevention a central part of animal research.

Emanuel Klein's testimony before the Royal Commission investigating vivisection seemed to confirm this cavalier attitude. Klein stated that he did not use anesthetics during his experiments "except for convenience sake." When the chairman asked if this mean Klein "[had] no regard at all to the sufferings of the animals," Klein responded, "No regard at all for such little suffering as is in my operations. A man who

---

[45] Claude Bernard, *Introduction to the Study of Experimental Medicine* [1865], transl. Henry Copley Greene (Dover, 1957), 99.
[46] Ibid., 103.
[47] Anita Guerrini, *Experimenting with Humans and Animals: From Galen to Animal Rights* (Johns Hopkins University Press, 2003), 86.
[48] Ibid., 89; Deborah Rudacille, *The Scalpel and the Butterfly: The Conflict Between Animal Research and Animal Protection* (University of California Press, 2001), 26.
[49] John Burdon Sanderson, ed. *Handbook for the Physiological Laboratory* (Lindsay and Blakiston, 1873), vii; quoted in Hamilton, "Introduction," xix, xviii.

conducts special research and performs an experiment has no time, so to speak, for thinking about what the animal will feel or suffer."[50] Klein described, as an example of an experiment that would not require anesthesia, "bleed[ing] a young dog to death by opening a vessel."[51] Deborah Rudacille pinpoints Klein's testimony as a major factor in the passage of the Cruelty to Animals Act of 1876 – most of his listeners were so horrified by his cold testimony and indifference to animal pain that they became convinced something had to be done.[52] Thomas H. Huxley declared, after hearing about Klein's testimony, "It is not [the antivivisectionist] Hutton who has beaten me, but Klein. He has done more for our enemies than they could have done by their joint efforts, without him, by his wantonly and mischievously brutal talk."[53]

Aldous Huxley's fictional physiologists bear out a less morally serious version of the argument that vivisection desensitizes scientists and cultivates a general hardheartedness. His scientist characters Lord Edward Tantamount, in *Point Counter Point*, and James Shearwater, in *Antic Hay*, are not exactly sociopathic fiends in the mold of Dr. Moreau. But their characters are in some sense deformed by their experiments. Both are portrayed as child-like and naïve; both are cuckolds who fail to understand their wives; and both are callously indifferent to the social and economic injustices that preoccupy their associates. As Robert S. Baker argues, "Huxley's novelistic treatment of the scientist is an index to his increasingly disapproving critique of the socio-economic applications of science as well as its charismatic status in the early twentieth century."[54] For Baker, Huxley's scientist characters reveal the author's emerging dissatisfaction with the technocratic scientific ideology which "reduced everything to measurement, efficiency, instrumentality, and a rationalism bent on exploiting and controlling the natural world."[55] Shearwater and Lord Edward are cases in point: they are so wrapped up in their animal experiments that they lose sight of important swathes of human life.

In *Point Counter Point*, Huxley makes this point through a faintly satirical scene. Early in the novel, as party guests fill the lower levels of

[50] Royal Commission, *Report of the Royal Commission on the Practice of Subjecting Live Animals to Experiments for Scientific Purposes* (George Edward Eyre and William Spottiswoode, 1876), 328.
[51] Ibid.
[52] Rudacille, The *Scalpel and the Butterfly*, 39–40.
[53] Quoted in Hamilton, "Introduction," xxvi. The quote is originally from a letter dated May 25, 1876 from Huxley to Michael Foster, in the Huxley Papers, 4.120.
[54] Robert S. Baker, "Science and Modernity in Aldous Huxley's Interwar Essays and Novels," in *Aldous Huxley: Between East and West*, ed. C. C. Barfoot (Rodopi, 2001): 35–58, quote on 39.
[55] Ibid., 41.

Tantamount House, Lord Edward (reportedly based on J. S. Haldane), and his assistant Frank Illidge tuck themselves away in an attic laboratory to conduct experiments on a newt.[56] The two are studying development and regeneration by surgically exchanging the newt's leg for a tail bud. If the tail bud is young enough, it will grow into a leg; if not, it will produce "a monster with a tail where an arm should have been."[57] Huxley's language in this laboratory scene is carefully neutral, avoiding any verbiage that would too obviously register as pathos and excite sympathy for the mutilated newt. But there are hints that such experiments might deform the experimenter as much as the test subject. For example, Lord Edward is described as "one of those monsters which haunt the palaces of only the best and most aristocratic families," comparable to the "Beastie of Glamis" or the Minotaur.[58] The repetition of the word "monster" connects the scientist and the animal in a kind of sympathetic magic; as he damages the newt, so he damages himself.

Although Huxley lampoons Lord Edward, who is as knowledgeable about developmental biology as he is clueless about his wife's private life or his assistant's Marxist activism, the character is not altogether a joke. Take, for example, the story of how Lord Edward fell in love with science. Reading Claude Bernard is the catalyst that inspires a young Edward Tantamount to pursue a career in physiology. Bernard writes that "the life of the animal ... is only a fragment of the total life of the universe," and for Lord Edward, this phrase triggers an epiphany about the interrelatedness and malleability of all matter.[59] The description of Lord Edward's revelation is not satirical like the description of his newts. It suggests that Huxley is not castigating physiology altogether, but recognizes within physiology a kind of materialist philosophy that is spiritually meaningful, at least to Lord Edward, who "suddenly and for the first time ... realize[s] his solidarity with the world."[60] It is also important to note that Lord Edward is more conscientious about animal pain than his inspiration Claude Bernard – he takes care to anesthetize his newts before cutting them.[61] These details suggest that while Lord Edward may be an underdeveloped person, he is no Moreau, nor even a Klein.

---

[56] Firchow, *Aldous Huxley*, 212.
[57] Huxley, *Point Counter Point*, 31.
[58] Ibid., 33.
[59] Ibid., 28–9.
[60] Ibid., 29.
[61] Ibid., 30.

Huxley reserves much more serious moral censure for another pro-vivisectionist character, Philip Elver of *Those Barren Leaves*. When one of the main characters in the novel, the impecunious intellectual Mr. Cardan, gets lost in the Italian countryside, he meets a brother and sister pair, Philip and Grace Elver. Grace has an intellectual disability. The Elvers invite Mr. Cardan to stay the night with them, and after Grace goes to bed, a drunken Philip Elver reveals a devious plan to Mr. Cardan. "[D]o you believe in vivisection?" he asks. Cardan responds that he does not think vivisection is wrong "if the cutting serves some useful human purpose."[62] Pressing him, Elver leads Mr. Cardan to disclose that he does not believe in animal rights. "I'm not one of those fools who think that one life is as good as another, simply because it *is* a life," Mr. Cardan declares. "You must recognize a hierarchy of existences."[63] Elver latches onto this claim, and pursues it further. "Then you'll admit," Elver says, "that an intelligent man is worth more than an imbecile, a moron."[64] Bit by bit, Elver confesses that he is plotting to kill his "imbecile" sister in order to get her inheritance.

Mr. Cardan, of course, recognizes the immorality of Philip Elver's plan. But he is no saint either; he immediately begins scheming to marry Grace Elver in order to get her inheritance for himself. Marriage is presumably better than murder, but neither Elver nor Cardan respect Grace's own subjectivity. For both, she is merely a means to an end. The conversation between Elver and Mr. Cardan, however, demonstrates the slippery slope of pro-vivisection arguments. The arguments that Mr. Cardan uses to justify vivisection – that "a hierarchy of existences" renders a human more valuable than a dog, a dog more valuable than a grasshopper, and a genius like Archimedes more valuable than "the soldier who killed Archimedes" – Elver takes up in order to justify his belief that his own life is worth more than his sister's.

It is now an axiom within animal studies that this hierarchy of existences has, throughout Western history, been used to rationalize a hierarchy within the human species, in which some people are considered more human than others. Giorgio Agamben, for example, uses the term "anthropological machine" to describe philosophy's perpetual attempts to draw a hard line between humans and animals, and between the "human" part of a person and the "animal" part of him or her.

---

[62] Aldous Huxley, *Those Barren Leaves* [1925] (Dalkey Archive Press, 1998), 193.
[63] Ibid., 194.
[64] Ibid., 195.

Agamben argues that this philosophical trend is complicit in fascism, which rendered Jews as animals, and he calls for a stop to the anthropological machine.[65] Cary Wolfe links this hierarchy of existences explicitly to the dehumanization of people with disabilities. He points out that twentieth-century philosophers who believe that language is the foundation of human subjectivity would deny that autistic people like Temple Grandin, who "thinks in pictures," are thinking subjects.[66]

Even in the Victorian era, it was clear to antivivisectionists that the hierarchy which sanctioned animal experimentation could also be deployed against oppressed people, including people with disabilities. Frances Power Cobbe asked in 1875, "If it be proper to torture a hundred affectionate dogs or intelligent chimpanzees to settle some curious problem about their brains, will they advocate doing the same to a score of Bosjemen, to the idiots in our asylums, to criminals, to infants, to women?"[67] It was not merely a hypothetical question; human beings deemed less than human due to their class, sex, or race were in fact subjected to cruel medical experiments in the nineteenth and twentieth centuries.[68]

Mr. Cardan himself begins to backtrack on his answer as he meditates on the question, moving from the moral certainty of the "hierarchy of existences" to a relativism that calls that hierarchy into question. After declaring that Archimedes' life is worth more than the soldier's, Mr. Cardan begins to hedge: "One has no justifying reason for saying so, but only one's instinctive taste ... If, like Tolstoy, your tastes run to good fatherhood, left cheeks and agriculture, then you'll say that the life of the soldier is worth just as much as the life of Archimedes – much more, indeed ... But I can't speak for others."[69] In this monologue, Cardan begins to realize that the hierarchies people believe in are deeply influenced by their social contexts, and that his own valuation of intellectual ability is no absolute standard, but rather a reflection of his own tastes and education. It is a characteristically modernist moment of doubt.

---

[65] Agamben, *The Open*, 33–8.

[66] Cary Wolfe, *What is Posthumanism?* (University of Minnesota Press, 2009), 129.

[67] Frances Power Cobbe, "The Moral Aspects of Vivisection," *The New Quarterly Magazine*, vol. 4 (Ward, Lock, and Tyler, 1875): 222–37, quote on 227; quoted in Hamilton, "Introduction," xlii.

[68] See Coral Lansbury's *The Old Brown Dog: Women, Workers, and Vivisection in Edwardian England* (University of Wisconsin Press, 1985), 83–95, for an account of gynecological experimentation on poor women in Victorian England. Unethical and nonconsensual human experiments did not end in the nineteenth century; one need only think of sterilization programs in the US, Nazi human experiments, and the Tuskegee syphilis study to realize how widespread they were in the history of medicine.

[69] Huxley, *Those Barren Leaves*, 194.

The values that once seemed stable and objective, under further analysis, begin to seem relative and changeable. Cardan's hesitation does not lead to a radical overhauling of his beliefs – his plot to marry Grace Elver for the money shows that he still considers himself more valuable than her by way of his intellectual superiority. But it does suggest that Huxley was skeptical about notions like the "hierarchy of existences," which serve more to justify unjust social structures than to objectively describe the world.

Mr. Cardan's initial argument that vivisection is morally acceptable "if the cutting serves some human purpose" echoes one of the chief defenses of Victorian pro-vivisectionists: that animal experimentation could alleviate human suffering, and that antivivisectionists who loved animals did not care about human beings.[70] Thomas H. Huxley captured this feeling when he noted sarcastically that antivivisectionists "are ready to let disease torture hecatombs of men as long as poodles are happy."[71] This is an argument not easily shrugged off, and one that Aldous Huxley took seriously. One pivotal moment in *Antic Hay*, known to critics as the coffee stall scene, addresses the link between human suffering and animal suffering. The scene critiques the Cruelty to Animals Act that was passed to regulate vivisection by showing a poor man who has been disadvantaged by the law. At the same time, it demonstrates a link between indifference to animal suffering and indifference to human suffering, implying that it is vivisectionists like Shearwater who do not care sufficiently for humans.

The coffee stall scene begins when Shearwater and Theodore Gumbril, the protagonist of *Antic Hay*, are walking down a London street with some friends after dinner. While Shearwater speaks about his physiological researches, Gumbril overhears a conversation between some poor people at a coffee stand. A man's horse has been euthanized under the Cruelty to Animals law because it was old and limping; the loss of his horse has put the man out of work. He and his wife, who is pregnant, have walked all the way to Portsmouth and back without food in search of a job that did not pan out. Gumbril, horrified by what he hears, alerts his friends to their plight, and they collect five pounds to give the unfortunate couple. The friends then disperse, and Shearwater and Gumbril walk home together.

---

[70] Craig Buettinger, "Antivivisection and the Charge of Zoophil-psychosis in the Early Twentieth Century," *The Historian* 55.2 (1993): 277–88.
[71] Desmond, *Huxley*, 461.

Though Shearwater and Gumbril have a conversation on their walk home, they are really speaking past one another. Shearwater is still preoccupied with his science, planning an experiment to dehydrate a person and find out the effects on his blood composition, and Gumbril is still meditating on the poor couple:

> "Those poor people at the coffee stall," Gumbril answered. "It's appalling that human beings should have to live like that. Worse than dogs."
> "Dogs have nothing to complain of." Shearwater went off at a tangent. "Nor guinea-pigs, nor rats. It's these blasted anti-vivisection maniacs who make all the fuss."
> "But think," cried Gumbril, "what these wretched people have had to suffer! [...] One has no idea of it until one has actually been treated that way oneself. In the war, for example, when one went to have one's mitral murmurs listened to by the medical board [...] One felt like a cow being got into a train. And to think that the majority of one's fellow beings pass their whole lives being shoved about like maltreated animals!"
> "H'm," said Shearwater. If you went on sweating indefinitely, he supposed, you would end by dying.[72]

Shearwater, his mind still in his laboratory, declares himself indifferent to the suffering of experimental animals. Gumbril, meanwhile, is indignant that the poor couple is forced to live "like animals," without the care and dignity that human beings deserve. No one holds an explicit animal welfare agenda in this scene. Gumbril does not express concern with the plight of actual animals, whether laboratory rats or stray dogs or cattle on trains, but only with people who are treated like animals. And, indeed, the policeman who confiscates the poor man's horse under the Cruelty to Animals Act seems like the villain in this story, since it is his actions that put the man out of work. The horse's euthanization seems to confirm the Victorian vivisectionists' charge that animal welfare activists lacked sympathy for human beings.

It would be easy, then, to read the scene as one that pits compassion for animals against compassion for human beings in a zero-sum game. But the scene's contrapuntal technique suggests that the two might be mutually reinforcing, not mutually exclusive. Shearwater's professed indifference toward laboratory animals betrays his implicit indifference toward suffering humans – he is not really listening to Gumbril, and does not spare a thought for the couple at the coffee stand. It is the same line – "Dogs have nothing to complain of" – that evinces both kinds of callousness. He is speaking about actual laboratory dogs, but

[72] Aldous Huxley, *Antic Hay* (George H. Doran, 1923), 92–3.

in doing so reveals his lack of interest in the poor couple's complaints as well. Gumbril, meanwhile, implicitly links the suffering of the couple to the suffering of the old horse with the phrase "maltreated animals." He means it as a simile for the people, but it also rings back to their narrative, and to the literal animal whose euthanization triggered their problems. There is a kind of symmetry at work in these phrases – Shearwater intends his words to be literal and overlooks their metaphorical signification, while Gumbril intends his words to be metaphorical and overlooks their literal signification. Neither character fully recognizes the connection between animal suffering and human suffering, but the audience, reading between the lines, can put it together.

Another aspect of the vivisection debate that resonates in Huxley's fiction is its gendered nature. The antivivisection movement in England was mostly spearheaded by women, including Frances Power Cobbe, Mona Caird, and Anna Kingsford. The movement deployed traditional gender roles strategically by suggesting that women could prevail upon male scientists to be more compassionate. At the same time, it flouted those roles by insisting that women have a voice in public life.[73] Further, as Coral Lansbury argues, many Victorian women found it easy to empathize with laboratory animals because they too were treated as objects of scientific and medical inquiry, with little regard for their subjectivity or agency.[74] Fighting for animal rights, then, meant indirectly fighting for women's rights.

Pro-vivisectionists, meanwhile, latched onto the largely female demographic of the antivivisection movement for their own purposes, using sexist language and ideas to criticize their opponents. The *Pall Mall Gazette* editorialized against the Cruelty to Animals bill in 1876, decrying the notion that "sentimental feminine agitators" might influence law.[75] Many scientists appealed to the stereotype of the irrational woman in framing their defenses of vivisection. Elie de Cyon, in an article for the *Contemporary Review*, asked rhetorically, "Is it necessary to repeat that women – or rather, old maids – form the most numerous contingent of this group [antivivisectionists]? Let my adversaries contradict me, if they can show among the leaders of the agitation one young girl, rich, beautiful, and beloved, or one young wife who has found in her home the full

[73] Rudacille, *The Scalpel and the Butterfly*, 51.
[74] Lansbury, *The Old Brown Dog*, x, 83–95.
[75] Quoted in Sally Mitchell, *Frances Power Cobbe: Victorian Feminist, Journalist, Reformer* (University of Virginia Press, 2004), 244. The quote is originally from a 22 June 1876 *Pall Mall Gazette* editorial.

satisfaction of her affections!"[76] The misogyny behind Cyon's words is palpable. Another scientist, the American neurologist Charles Loomis Dana, even claimed that a deep concern for animal welfare constituted a mental illness called "zoophil-psychosis," a kind of neurosis especially likely to befall idle women.[77] He recommended that one "zoophil-psychotic" undergo gynecological surgery to treat her illness.[78] Pro-vivisectionists portrayed their opponents as, at best, overly soft-hearted and unreasonable, and at worst as hysterical lunatics.

Huxley's response to these gendered debates is mixed. His representations of laboratory animals clearly eschew the kind of sentimentality that antivivisectionists embraced in their publications. There are many reasons why Huxley would resist writing about animal subjectivity from the inside, but one of them is probably because doing so might strike readers as mawkish, feminine, and unscientific, and Huxley did not wish to be seen as any of those things. Meanwhile, one passage in *Point Counter Point* echoes the pro-vivisectionist claim that women were irrational about vivisection and did not really understand the science behind it. One young woman at the Tantamount party reports that Lord Edward "[c]uts up toads and salamanders and all that … And he takes guinea pigs and makes them breed with serpents."[79] This misrepresents Lord Edward's work, making it seem more witchery than science.

Predominantly, though, Huxley's writing about vivisection works to expose rather than to reinforce the latent sexism in the scientific camp. For example, *Antic Hay* correlates Shearwater's animal experiments to his neglect of his wife Rosie, a Madame Bovary-esque character who longs for a more romantic life. Shearwater alternately patronizes and ignores Rosie, refusing to see her as an intellectual equal, and she consequently feels unsatisfied with their relationship. She begins an affair with Gumbril in a case of mistaken identities: Gumbril does not know that she is his friend's wife, and she does not know that Gumbril is her husband's friend. Rosie's marital unhappiness is hardly surprising when one considers that her husband has publicly declared that he finds kidneys much more interesting than romantic love.[80]

---

[76] Elie de Cyon, "The Anti-Vivisectionist Agitation" [1883], in *Animal Welfare and Anti-Vivisection 1870–1910*, vol. 3, ed. Susan Hamilton (Routledge, 2004): 223–35, quote on 232.
[77] Buettinger, "Antivivisection and the Charge of Zoophil-psychosis," 280.
[78] Ibid., 284.
[79] Huxley, *Point Counter Point*, 35.
[80] Huxley, *Antic Hay*, 86–7.

One scene makes especially clear the way Shearwater's physiological pursuits exclude Rosie, intimating a connection between his indifference to her inner life and his indifference to the laboratory animals' inner lives. As Gumbril, outfitted in a fake beard, is scrambling to leave the Shearwater house after an afternoon tryst, Shearwater is returning home and conversing with another young scientist:

> "I take my rabbit and I inject into it the solution of eyes, pulped eyes of another dead rabbit. You see? ... The rabbit," continued the young man, and with his bright eyes and staring, sniffing nose, he looked like a poacher's terrier ready to go barking after the first white tail that passed his way; "the rabbit naturally develops a specific anti-eye to protect itself. I then take some of its anti-eye serum and inject it into my female rabbit, I then immediately breed from her." He paused.
>
> "Well?" asked Shearwater, in his slow, ponderous way. He lifted his great round head enquiringly and looked at the doggy young man from under his bushy eyebrows....
>
> "[T]he young ones are born with defective sight ... We seem to be affecting the germ plasm directly. We have found a way of making acquired characteristics ..."
>
> "Pardon me," said Gumbril. He had decided that it was time to be gone. He ran down the stairs and across the tiled hall, he pushed his way firmly but politely between the talkers.
>
> "... heritable," continued the young man.[81]

When the other scientist, later identified as Lancing (a rather Dickensian moniker for an experimental biologist), leaves, Shearwater goes inside, greets Rosie, and reflects on her recent changes in behavior: "Rosie was getting much better, Shearwater reflected, as he washed his hands before supper, about not interrupting him when he was busy. This evening she had really not disturbed him at all, or at most only once, and that not seriously."[82] Shearwater remembers, with relief, that Rosie has given up trying to learn about physiology, and thinks that she should instead "go in for stenciling patterns on Government linen. Such pretty curtains and things one could make like that. But she hadn't taken very kindly to the idea."[83]

The conversation shines an unflattering light on Shearwater and Lancing's brand of science. Partly this is because of their naïve belief in Lamarckian evolution – the inheritance of acquired characteristics – which, as Jay Clayton points out, Huxley casts in parodic terms.

[81] Ibid., 152–3.
[82] Ibid., 155.
[83] Ibid.

"Everything in this scene," Clayton observes, "underlines how bogus Huxley finds such pseudo-science."[84] I would argue that neo-Lamarckism is not the only scientific trend being condemned in this scene. Huxley also indirectly indicts animal experimentation, at least in its more reckless guises. The conversation between Shearwater and Lancing reveals a rather disturbing process of "pulp[ing] eyes," "injecting" healthy rabbits, and producing congenitally ill rabbits. Neither man concerns himself with the test animals' suffering. What makes the conversation even stranger is that both scientists are themselves coded as animals, one a dog who sees the rabbits as his prey, the other a cow. (Here, as elsewhere in the novel, Shearwater's "ponderous" manner seems bovine; when readers first meet him, he is directly compared to a cow.)[85] In the earlier street scene, Gumbril had invoked both dogs and cows as examples of "maltreated animals," using them to illustrate the extent of the poor couple's suffering. In this scene, on the other hand, no character mentions or even thinks of the rabbits' distress in the laboratory – neither "dog" nor "cow" feel sympathy with the rabbits – but the images faintly echo the coffee stall scene, issuing a subtle challenge to the instrumental reason that makes dogs, cattle, and human beings into objects to be tested, shuffled, and sorted.

Juxtaposing the rabbit conversation with Gumbril's disguised exit and Shearwater's delusive thoughts about Rosie, the scene invites us to think about how these three threads of the narrative comment on each other. The scene highlights Shearwater's self-centered obliviousness in general, not just to animal suffering but also to Gumbril's accidental betrayal and Rosie's unhappiness. Shearwater sees Rosie not as an equal partner but as a child-like figure in need of guidance. He urges her away from physiology, a more masculine field of study, and toward a stereotypically feminine activity instead – decorating curtains. He does not understand her frustration with this kind of enforced femininity, nor does he understand the true cause of her behavioral changes: that she is preoccupied with her new lover Gumbril. Shearwater neither comprehends nor cares about the inner lives of either his wife or his test subjects. Yet Rosie's inner life indisputably exists. So, readers might conclude, do the animals'.

---

[84] Jay Clayton, "Genome Time: Post-Darwinism Then and Now," *Critical Quarterly* 55.1 (2013): 57–74, quote on 68. Even though Lancing's experiments sound ridiculous, they may be loosely inspired by the real experiments of Louis Pasteur. To create a vaccine, Pasteur would infect rabbits with rabies, then kill the infected animals and transplant tissue from their brain into the brains of healthy rabbits. Then he made an inoculation from the spinal cords of the second group of rabbits and injected it into dogs, who were then able to ward off rabies. See Rudacille, *The Scalpel and the Butterfly*, 23–4.
[85] Huxley, *Antic Hay*, 62.

In *Those Barren Leaves*, meanwhile, Huxley offers a sympathetic portrait of an animal-loving woman who it would have been easy to satirize, had he chosen to do so. This portrait suggests a subtle sympathy with the female-driven antivivisection movement. Mrs. Chelifer is a saintly person who takes in and cares for stray dogs and stray people. She is a vegetarian, and at her former home in Oxford, she had surrounded herself with "troops of derelict dogs," "moth-eaten cats," and "poor children" who came for a bite to eat.[86] Her son Francis has persuaded her to move to Italy, where she joins the Aldwinkle party at the center of the novel and promptly befriends Grace Elver. Mr. Cardan decides this is because "poor Grace was the nearest thing to a stray dog or cat that Mrs. Chelifer could find," and another character concludes that Mrs. Chelifer is "one of Nature's Quakeresses."[87] Visiting Rome with Mr. Cardan and Grace, Mrs. Chelifer sees a group of abandoned cats trapped in a sunken forum, and the sight elicits her characteristic sympathy.

Weeks later, her son Francis Chelifer sees something strange while driving through Rome:

> The lady in grey was leaning over the railings, lowering very carefully at the end of a string, to which it was ingeniously attached by four subsidiary strings passed through holes bored in the rim, a large aluminum pannikin filled with milk. Slowly revolving as it went down, the pannikin was lowered to the floor of the sunken forum. Hardly had it touched the ground when, with simultaneous mewings and purrings, half a dozen thirsty cats came running to it and began to lap at the white milk.[88]

Chelifer quickly recognizes the woman as his mother. There is, to be sure, something faintly ridiculous about the scene, with the "ingenious" contraption and "street boys whoop[ing] with delight" at the strange woman.[89] But Huxley declines to exaggerate the silliness. Instead, Mrs. Chelifer appears almost as a modern-day St. Francis. The parallel comes readily to readers' minds because she has named her son Francis, and because the group has recently driven through Assisi.[90] St. Francis-like, Mrs. Chelifer joins in communion with the hungry cats. It would have been easy for Huxley to mock Mrs. Chelifer as a sentimental old woman, or a stereotype of femininity and motherhood; she might even resemble the Victorian antivivisectionist animal lovers who were accused of

[86] Huxley, *Those Barren Leaves*, 96.
[87] Ibid., 211, 210.
[88] Ibid., 271.
[89] Ibid., 271–2.
[90] Ibid., 235–6.

zoophil-psychosis. But in the face of the other characters' insincerity and selfishness, she appears instead to be the real moral center of the novel. Indeed, her cat-feeding device renders her not only a maternal figure, but also a benevolent amateur engineer, one who devotes her experimental energies to helping animals. She is in this respect the opposite of vivisectionist figures like Shearwater and Lord Edward.

Huxley was likely modeling Mrs. Chelifer on real women he saw or heard about in Italy. Feral cats have long populated Roman ruins. At Torre Argentina, an ancient temple, a colony of cats lives under the protection of *gattari*, or "cat ladies." Jenny Diski writes that in 1929, when the excavation of Torre Argentina was completed, the cats moved in, and the *gattari* followed them. Today, she reports, it is a well-run cat sanctuary, where volunteers feed the cats and veterinarians give them medical care *pro bono*.[91] Since *Those Barren Leaves* was published in 1925 and Torre Argentina was not fully excavated until 1929, it is not likely that Torre Argentina was the particular ruin Huxley had in mind. But Mrs. Chelifer nevertheless seems like a prototype for the many real *gattari* who have taken care of Rome's homeless cats over the years.

Another reason to take Mrs. Chelifer seriously is that her guiding philosophy represents, in embryonic form, the philosophy Huxley would himself come to embrace in the 1930s. For if the young Huxley is known as a too-clever satirist who believed in nothing, in middle age he turned quite seriously to the study of ethics. Huxley became a vegetarian around the time he embraced Eastern philosophy under the guidance of the mystic Gerald Heard.[92] The guru Dr. Miller of Huxley's 1936 novel *Eyeless in Gaza* recommends that the protagonist "eat like a Buddhist," linking a vegetarian diet to a pacifist philosophy.[93] Miller's vegetarianism reflects his belief in a mysterious connection between animal protein in the intestine and "skepticism and despair" in the mind, whereas Mrs. Chelifer's arises from a more straightforward sympathy with animals.[94] But both Dr. Miller and Mrs. Chelifer offer an alternative to the other characters' disaffected, shallow, self-centered outlooks; and in both novels, a key part of this alternative outlook is nonviolence toward animals.

[91] Jenny Diski, *What I Don't Know About Animals* (Yale University Press, 2011), 179–82.
[92] Peggy Kiskadden, interview with David K. Dunaway, in *Aldous Huxley Recollected: An Oral History* by David K. Dunaway (AltaMira, 1999): 32–4; see also Murray, *Aldous Huxley*, 344.
[93] Huxley, *Eyeless in Gaza*, 424.
[94] Ibid., 425.

2.3 Thin Description and the Observational Ethic

The vivisectionist's gaze was not the only viewpoint available to zoologists in the twentieth century. Another kind of scientific gaze was being cultivated in other quarters: that of the ethologist. Ethology avoided the violent penetrations of physiology in favor of a noninvasive, observational approach to animals. Unlike many Victorian naturalists, ethologists did not kill the animals they studied in order to furnish museums. And unlike comparative psychologists, they studied animals in their natural habitats rather than in laboratories. The great English field naturalist Edmund Selous, whose work on bird behavior was an important precursor to classical ethology, was emphatic about the link between observation of, and nonviolence towards, animals. "Now that I have watched birds closely," he wrote in 1901, "the killing of them seems to me as something monstrous and horrible."[95] Other twentieth-century naturalists came to frown upon specimen collection as well, as Christina Alt shows. They recognized that collecting threatened the survival of rare species, and Freud's psychoanalytic theory pathologized the collecting impulse as a perversion.[96] Meanwhile, the spread of technologies like field glasses, cameras, and mist nets "further enabled naturalists to study animals without killing them."[97]

Even Julian Huxley seems to have had some sympathy for nonviolent science, despite his dabbling in animal experimentation. His 1917 poem, "The Captive Shrew," asks the titular creature, "Is it a sin to prison you?" The poem concludes that "Tis not by holding in the hand / That one can hope to understand," and that the better course of action is not to imprison the animal in a laboratory or cage, but instead to "pursue you with my mind."[98] To pursue with the mind rather than the net, to shoot with the camera rather than the gun, to capture in the frames of binoculars or photographs rather than in cages or specimen cabinets – the replacement of old practices with nonviolent alternatives was a key trend in early-twentieth-century natural history. And in a late twentieth-century return to Selous's outlook, ethology became the branch of zoology most amenable to animal welfare discourses. Jane Goodall and Marc

[95] Edmund Selous, *Bird Watching* (J. M. Dent and Co., 1901), 335; quoted in Burkhardt, *Patterns of Behavior*, 81. Burkhardt names Selous as one of three amateur English ornithologists whose behavior studies helped pave the way for the development of classical ethology.

[96] Alt, *Virginia Woolf and the Study of Nature*, 49–52.

[97] Ibid., 53.

[98] Julian Huxley, *The Captive Shrew and Other Poems of a Biologist* (Basil Blackwell, 1932), 3, lines 2, 17–8, 28.

Bekoff, a primatologist and a canid ethologist, are leading voices of the animal protection movement today. Their forms of research are compatible with a philosophy of nonviolence toward animals, and their studies of animal behavior have led them to conclude that animals are conscious subjects in need of protection.[99]

Ethology, however, has not always been comfortable talking about animals as subjects. When Goodall began working with the chimpanzees of Gombe in 1960, a different style was de rigueur. Under the sway of the classical ethologists Konrad Lorenz and Niko Tinbergen, the discipline had, at midcentury, adopted an "objectivist" language of reflexes and reactions. It aimed to describe animal behaviors without recourse to consciousness. Ethology was still a young science at the time, and thin description helped to legitimate it by giving it a scientific air, distinguishing it from the anthropomorphic styles of Victorian natural history. These efforts at professionalization help explain why Goodall's methods, which involved naming chimpanzees and attributing personalities to them, prompted angry reactions from the establishment in the 1960s. Animal personalities did not fit into the objectivist trend.[100]

Classical ethologists like Tinbergen and Lorenz, as Richard W. Burkhardt explains, aimed to distinguish their work not only from natural history, but also from two rival approaches to animal behavior, animal psychology and behaviorism.[101] Tinbergen was direct about his disdain for animal psychology. He believed that animal psychologists were pursuing a dead end trying to make scientific claims about animals' subjective experience, and he thought that ethology's "objectivist" methods were the wave of the future.[102] In a 1979 letter, Tinbergen recalled that when he first met Lorenz in 1936, "we were very much concerned with defending our 'objectivist' approach against the then prevailing notion that the aim of animal psychology was to find out what animals experience subjectively."[103] This was not because Tinbergen did not believe in animal subjectivity, but because he considered it beyond the bounds of science.

---

[99] Bekoff and Goodall are cofounders of Ethologists for the Ethical Treatment of Animals, which promotes ethical and noninvasive methods for zoological research; see www.ethologicalethics.org.

[100] See Jane Goodall's "Learning from the Chimpanzees: A Message Humans Can Understand," *Science* 282.5397 (1998): 2184–5, which describes how 1960s ethology considered any discussion of animals' minds unscientific. Goodall says that editors criticized her first scientific paper for referring to chimpanzees as "he" and "she" rather than "it." She also caught flak for assigning the chimpanzees names and explaining their behaviors "in terms of motivation or purpose."

[101] Burkhardt, *Patterns of Behavior*, 8.

[102] Ibid., 225.

[103] Quoted in ibid., 187. The quote is originally from a letter dated June 6, 1979 to Burkhardt.

His objectivist methods had "nothing to do with whether I think that animals experience something. I do think that, but it is in my opinion totally irrelevant. Experiences are not perceivable, and thereby not usable in animal ethology."[104]

Lorenz, for his part, was open about his dislike of behaviorism. One might expect behaviorism to appeal to the classical ethologists because it too rejected introspection and subjectivist speculation, preferring instead dispassionate, external observations of behavior. As Eileen Crist points out, ethology shares with behaviorism an objectivist idiom and external viewpoint.[105] But both Tinbergen and Lorenz held that animals should be studied in their natural environment, not in the artificial setting of a laboratory. Behaviorists, in their view, taught animals how to run mazes but neglected their instinctive behaviors and the environmental context that had selected for those instincts. Lorenz argued in a 1936 lecture that research in animal psychology thus far had not been sufficiently attentive to the evolutionary significance of animal behavior patterns. Burkhardt explains that Lorenz believed instincts (as opposed to subjective experience or learned behaviors) should be the primary study of scientists interested in animal behavior because instincts, which are inherited and unchanging, hold a key to the animal's evolutionary history.[106]

Tinbergen and Lorenz's objectivist, observational approach to animals required a new language, one shorn of subjectivity, a language Eileen Crist describes as "mechanomorphic." Classical ethology's idiom made animals sound more like machines than like subjects. For example, Tinbergen describes a falcon hunting in the following way: "A peregrine falcon in which the hunting drive becomes active, searches for prey until it is found. The sight of prey releases the motor response of catching, killing and eating, which is a chain of simple, relatively rigid, responses."[107] With the passive voice and vocabulary of "drives," "releases," and "motor responses," the passage may seem like a circuitous and bizarre way to describe a bird's behavior. But, Crist observes, these forms are designed to describe the bird's actions while bracketing off questions about its psychology. As she acknowledges, even though "neither Tinbergen nor Lorenz wanted to 'desubjectify' animals," desubjectification was nevertheless the effect of their

---

[104] Quoted in ibid., 435. The quote is originally from a letter dated July 4, 1952 to Otto Koehler, in the Koehler Papers at Universitätsarchiv Freiburg im Breisgau.
[105] Crist, *Images of Animals*, 79.
[106] Burkhardt, *Patterns of Behavior*, 185.
[107] Niko Tinbergen, "The Hierarchical Organization of Nervous Mechanisms Underlying Instinctive Behaviour," *Symposia of the Society for Experimental Biology* 4 (1950): 305–12, quote on 307; quoted in Crist, *Images of Animals*, 93–4.

technical language. "Mechanomorphism was the price of the idiom that ethologists opted for," she writes.[108] This was the disciplinary environment that Goodall found herself chafing against in 1960.

It would be naïve to take at face value Tinbergen's claim that animals' subjective experience is "totally irrelevant" to ethology. It is not at all irrelevant to questions of animal welfare, and ethology has never in its history been divorced from such questions. Darwin and Selous, two forerunners of classical ethology, developed a deep concern for animal welfare partly through their studies of animal behavior. And many contemporary ethologists are invested in animal welfare too; witness, for example, environmental enrichment programs in laboratories and zoos, which are designed to improve animals' quality of life based on ethological research.[109] In the face of this longer history, the classical ethologists' conclusion that animals' subjective experiences are "irrelevant" seems to reflect a narrow view of science and an old-fashioned desire for science to be pure, objective, and detached, unsullied by any murky ethical quandaries.

But if we follow Heather Love, we might see ethological thin description in another light: not as a way of foreclosing animals' interior experiences, but as a way of building the empirical basis for them. Thin description can serve as the bottom layer of a better thick description in the future, one that would explore the subjective meanings of animals' behaviors without merely projecting anthropomorphic patterns onto them. It is this more generous understanding of thin description that the following pages apply to Henry Eliot Howard and Aldous Huxley, two writers who hesitated to make definitive claims about animals' subjective lives yet retained a constant faith in the existence of those lives.

Usually, it is Julian Huxley who is regarded as the most influential transitional figure between natural history and ethology. Both Burkhardt and Crist position him as a leader who helped make the study of behavior scientific, and simultaneously a committed subjectivist whose language of "courtship rituals," "penguin dances," and "mutual selection" implied that behaviors are meaningful from the animals' point of view (as Chapter 3 discusses in greater depth).[110] But Howard's ornithological writing, which also stems from the transitional period between natural

---

[108] Ibid., 89.
[109] See, for example, Angélica da Silva Vasconellos and César Ades' "Possible Limits and Advances of Environmental Enrichment for Wild Animals," *Revista de Etologia* 11.1 (2012): 37–45, which reviews a number of studies on environmental enrichment and urges researchers to examine multiple indicators of animal welfare, including behavior and physiological changes, when studying and managing captive animals.
[110] Burkhardt, *Patterns of Behavior*, 124; Crist, *Images of Animals*, 172–9.

history and classical ethology, is even more clearly than Julian Huxley's a transitional form between the subjectivist and objectivist registers. Howard's work aims to make the mechanistic language that would come to dominate classical ethology compatible with his belief in the animal mind. His work earned the respect of fellow biologists including Lorenz, Tinbergen, and Julian Huxley, especially his contributions to the study of territoriality. In his 1935 book *The Nature of a Bird's World*, Howard argued that each bird inhabits multiple "worlds" in its life – "a territory world, a sexual world, a nesting world, a brooding world" – all of which structure its changeable behaviors.[111] Howard shared Lorenz and Tinbergen's interests in birds' instincts and behavioral patterns, and he used the notions of stimulus and response to describe these behaviors. But he also insisted that a bird could not be reduced to a stimulus-response machine. On the contrary, he declared, "[a] bird is free."[112]

Howard's ornithological writing shifts deliberately back and forth between the storytelling register of the naturalist and the mechanistic language of the ethologist. *The Nature of a Bird's World* begins with what Howard calls "the sexual story of a Waterhen." His protagonist "lives on a pond about a third of an acre in size," and, it being spring, soon "he has a mate."[113] Over a period of weeks, Howard narrates their courtship, nest-building, and brooding of the eggs; eventually, the babies are born. In one suspenseful moment, "[a] rat lounges to the edge of the pond beside the young," whereupon the male waterhen "rushes at it and a whirlwind of action follows; wings beat, feet strike, beak pecks; the rat runs and he chases it up the bank ... then returns with slow and stately walk calling loudly – a triumphant defense."[114] Howard clearly knew and valued the narrative forms and stock characters of natural history – the protective father, the villain, and the innocent young all are represented here.

But Howard also knew the objectivist idiom then coming into vogue in behaviorist psychology and ethology, an idiom which was more cautious about attributing emotions or even causation to animals' actions. He catalogued the male waterhen's behaviors into six categories: "sings, fights, claims a territory, is excited sexually, builds, broods," a list that seems surprisingly reductive (only six?).[115] And Howard often translated his observations into the sterile passive voice that Crist calls mechanomorphic;

---

[111] Howard, *The Nature of a Bird's World*, 55.
[112] Ibid., 88.
[113] Ibid., 2–3.
[114] Ibid., 8.
[115] Ibid., 16.

witness the following passage on "false reactions," or moments when a bird's behavior seems contextually inappropriate:

> A study of false reaction suggests a biological inference. Birds respond to appropriate stimulation with different intensity, and the range of difference is wide. Reaction lies somewhere in the body, and the range of its intensity depends upon changes in the body and upon the way the body functions; its activity depends upon stimulation of appropriate intensity which lies somewhere in the total organization. Stimulation and response are forms of activity which can only function in association; and it is difficult for them to synchronize when the activity of one depends upon the independent activity of the other.[116]

Thus, sometimes birds do inexplicable and seemingly stupid things, like performing a sexual display for their mate even when another male bird is present and ready to fight, or collecting nest material long before it is nest-building season, or after the nest is complete. Birds are instinct-driven animals, and sometimes those instinctive behaviors get triggered at the wrong time. By making nominalizations such as "reaction," "activity," "stimulation and response" the subjects of his sentences, Howard emphasizes the birds' lack of agency when it comes to activating these instinctive behaviors – fight, display, build, and so on.

On the whole, though, Howard seems to prefer the bird-centric language of natural history to the behavior-centric language of classical ethology. While he finds the latter useful for describing bird life without making unwarranted assumptions about the animals' conscious intent, he worries that it obscures a bird's unified subjectivity. "So long as I perceive two orders of control and refer one to mechanisms in the body and one to acts of mind," he reflects, "I lose sight of the bird who loses its identity neither in physical process nor in fragments of mental process nor in change. And in thus losing sight of the bird I lose sight of the continuity."[117] Channeling William James, who argued that consciousness is "personal," ever-changing, and yet "continuous," Howard argues that a bird subject, too, is a single, continuous unit.[118] To divide bird life into discrete behaviors or even discrete "worlds," as Howard does, is a convenience for the ethologist, but it does not quite capture the holistic view he is after. "How difficult it is to think of these forms of behavior as a unitary whole," he muses. "[A]s I write they are detached in my thoughts, each with an element of structure peculiar

[116] Ibid., 21.
[117] Ibid., 94.
[118] James, *The Principles of Psychology*, vol. 1, 225.

to it; yet that I wish to avoid for somehow the many are one, and it is the one not the many, the bird not its parts, with which the changes deal."[119] Ultimately, Howard's quandary is irresolvable. As he declares in the preface to *The Nature of a Bird's World*, "a bird is the mystery ... I would not change it."[120]

Aldous Huxley's descriptions of animals reflect the same inclination to observe without overinterpreting that motivated Howard. He did not use the same language of reflexes and mechanisms as the ethologists, but his descriptions remain rooted in the external position of the observer, saying little about the animals' inner experiences. They do not imply that such inner experience is nonexistent, only that it is mostly inaccessible. In Huxley's fiction, this thin description of animals undergirds an observational ethic that counters the ethical failures of vivisection. While vivisection violently penetrates the animal body, thin description declines to penetrate the animal mind.

Antic Hay offers special insight into Huxley's use of thin description as a way of respecting animals' mysterious difference. The protagonist's father, Gumbril Sr., has a respectful, wondering relationship with the flock of starlings that takes shelter in his garden. An architect and throwback to the eighteenth-century ideals of proportion and beauty, Gumbril Sr. is out of place in the modern age. But when he is in his garden, watching the birds, he comes close to realizing the Good Life. At the end of the novel, when Theodore Gumbril and Myra Viveash visit him, they find him in his garden, where the starlings are sleeping:

> There was no sound but the rustling of the leaves. But sometimes, every hour or so, the birds would wake up. Something – perhaps it might be a stronger gust of wind, perhaps some happy dream of worms, some nightmare of cats simultaneously dreamed by all the flock together – would suddenly rouse them. And then they would all start to talk at once, at the tops of their shrill voices – for perhaps half a minute. Then in an instant they all went to sleep again and there was once more no sound but the rustling of the shaken leaves. At these moments Mr. Gumbril would lean forward, would strain his eyes and his ears in the hope of seeing, of hearing something – something significant, explanatory, satisfying. He never did, of course; but that in no way diminished his happiness.[121]

While Gumbril Sr. can imagine what goes on inside the birds' heads – perhaps they have a dream in common – he does not pretend to

[119] Howard, *The Nature of a Bird's World*, 25.
[120] Ibid., vii.
[121] Huxley, *Antic Hay*, 336.

know. This lingering mystery means that his observations are nearly inexhaustible – he can watch the starlings night after night, mentally cataloguing their behaviors. Though he is not privy to the "something significant, explanatory, satisfying" that would make sense of the starlings' strange behavior, he retains faith that that something exists.

Gumbril Sr. tells Myra that he believes the starlings have some kind of telepathic connection allowing them to all wake together and sing together. He further speculates that perhaps humans could access that telepathy too, if only they could get in touch with their animal consciousness – "It's a faculty ... we all possess, I believe. All we animals."[122] Then he announces that he has a feeling the starlings are about to burst into song at that moment. The three characters become quiet, and listen. And ... nothing happens. Gumbril Sr. "burst[s] out happily laughing" and says, "Completely wrong!" Perhaps someday telepathy will be possible, but for the present, even sensitive people like Gumbril Sr. cannot penetrate the starling mind. It remains an enigma, one that he is content to accept; he simply feels honored that the starlings have graced his garden with their presence.

Gumbril Sr.'s belief in animal telepathy resembles that of Edmund Selous, whose 1931 book *Thought-Transference (or What?) in Birds* posited some "supernormal" mechanism through which flocks of birds were able to think and move as a single unit. Selous records an observation of a flock of starlings which "turned, wheeled, reversed the order of their flight, changed in one shimmer from brown to grey, from dark to light, as though all the individuals composing them had been component parts of one individual organism." Witnessing this collective behavior, Selous is moved to ask "how, without some process of thought-transference so rapid as to amount practically to simultaneous collective thinking, are these things to be explained?"[123] Like Gumbril Sr., Selous is unable to predict the birds' immediate, collective movements or to perceive any external stimulus prompting them to rise together, change direction together, or otherwise act as one. And like Gumbril Sr., Selous is fascinated by these observations, and wonders why others do not find the birds' behavior as extraordinary as he does. In the postscript to *Thought-Transference (or What?)*, he laments that "what is familiar is not commonly paid much attention to as being no novelty." Anthropocentrism is partially responsible for this lack of curiosity about animals; it "place[s]

122 Ibid., 337.
123 Edmund Selous, *Thought-Transference (or What?) in Birds* (Constable, 1931), 10.

man in a fancied position of overwhelming importance, so that, separately and collectively, the lives and actions of all other species [are] to be explained" only in reference to man, "a mode of envisaging things which shifted the wonder, where called for, from the means to the supposed object of them."[124] From Selous's perspective, Gumbril Sr.'s curiosity about and love for the starlings would reflect both a mindset proper to a naturalist and a moral sense of humility.

When, in *Antic Hay*, Gumbril Jr. and Myra leave his father's house, they make a final stop at Shearwater's laboratory, a space which provides an illustrative contrast to Gumbril Sr.'s garden. There, they find Shearwater pedaling away on a stationary bicycle, performing on himself the experiment in dehydration he had been planning during the coffee stall scene. (Shearwater is pedaling not just for science, but also in an attempt to free himself of his infatuation with Myra.) After peeking in on him, Gumbril and Myra visit the other laboratory animals:

> In the annex of the laboratory the animals devoted to the service of physiology were woken by the sudden opening of the door, the sudden irruption of light. The albino guinea-pigs peered through the meshes of their hutch and their red eyes were like the rear lights of bicycles. The pregnant she-rabbits lollopped out and shook their ears and pointed their tremulous noses towards the door. The cock into which Shearwater had engrafted an ovary came out, not knowing whether to crow or cluck ... The rats who were being fed on milk from a London dairy came tumbling from their nest with an anxious hungry squeaking. They were getting thinner and thinner every day; in a few days they would be dead. But the old rat, whose diet was Grade A milk from the country, hardly took the trouble to move. He was fat and sleek as a brown furry fruit, ripe to bursting. No skim and chalky water, no dried dung and tubercle bacilli for him. He was in clover. Next week, however, the fates were plotting to give him diabetes artificially.[125]

The passage offers little or no comment on the animals' subjective experience. It resolutely avoids the language of pathos that antivivisectionists would have used to describe the scene. Other than the rooster, who does not know "whether to crow or cluck," Huxley makes no claims about the creatures' inner lives. The narrator's perspective remains external, describing only those things that are empirically observable: the guinea pigs' eyes, the rabbits' ears and noses, the rats' squeaking. The last is described as "anxious" and "hungry," a clue to their feelings; but even here, those

---

[124] Ibid., 244.
[125] Huxley, *Antic Hay*, 348.

adjectives modify the *sounds* the rats make, not the rats themselves. The narrator has more access to the minds of the scientists than the minds of the animals. He knows that Shearwater and Lancing intend to give the old rat diabetes, but not what it is like to be that rat.

Yet the passage operates under the assumption that the animals do have subjective experience, even if it cannot be directly known or described. The animals' empirically observable features – their eyes, ears, noses, and voices – point to the modes by which they sense and respond to the world around them. They react to the presence of Gumbril and Myra, moving to the fronts of their cages to better apprehend the people who have just entered and turned the light on. The thin rats' squeaking communicates something – perhaps hunger, perhaps anxiety, perhaps something entirely different. But it functions as an ethical demand to be recognized as feeling, aware subjects.

One reader who probably heard the demand of the lab rats was Virginia Woolf. In *A Room of One's Own*, Woolf discusses the same experiment, suggesting that the rats fed low-quality milk are analogous to women writers:

> For surely it is time that the effect of discouragement upon the mind of the artist should be measured, as I have seen a dairy company measure the effect of ordinary milk and Grade A milk upon the body of the rat. They set two rats in cages side by side, and of the two one was furtive, timid and small, and the other was glossy, bold and big. Now what food do we feed women as artists upon?[126]

Woolf does not credit Huxley with introducing her to the experiment, and it is possible that she learned about it elsewhere. But considering that Woolf knew Huxley and had already reviewed *Limbo* (1920), it seems probable that she read *Antic Hay* and there encountered Huxley's description of the rats. Her prose transforms them into a simile for male and female artists, who receive encouragement or discouragement and in turn grow big or small, "bold" or "timid." Like Huxley, she makes little or no claim about the subjective experience of the rats themselves. But, like Huxley's thin description, Woolf's analogy opens the possibility that readers will recognize and relate to their suffering.

This recognition of other species, which does not require definitive knowledge about the substance of their inner lives, forms the backbone of Huxley's most ambitious prose in *Antic Hay*. As Gumbril and Myra listen to Shearwater's assistant Lancing explain the "secrets" of the

---

[126] Virginia Woolf, *A Room of One's Own* [1929] (Harcourt, 1989), 53.

laboratory, the interconnectedness of all life forms becomes visible to them. "The vast, unbelievable, fantastic world opened out as [Lancing] spoke," Huxley writes:

> There were tropics, there were cold seas busy with living beings, there were forests full of horrible trees, silence and darkness. There were ferments and infinitesimal poisons floating in the air. There were leviathans suckling their young, there were flies and worms, there were men, living in cities, thinking, knowing good and evil. And all were changing continuously, moment by moment, and each remained all the time itself by virtue of some unimaginable enchantment. They were all alive. And on the other side of the courtyard beyond the shed in which the animals slept or uneasily stirred, in the huge hospital that went up sheer like a windowed cliff into the air, men and women were ceasing to be themselves, or were struggling to remain themselves. They were dying, they were struggling to live.[127]

Juxtaposing "men" with sea creatures, "trees," "leviathans," "flies," and "worms," the first three sentences put them syntactically on the same level, none grammatically subordinate to the others. They are all related, "all alive." The second half of the paragraph juxtaposes the laboratory animals with people in the hospital. When Huxley writes, "They were dying, they were struggling to live," the "they" immediately refers to the hospitalized people, but could equally well describe Shearwater's lab rats. The lab and the hospital alike are antiseptic places where animal life battles to endure, and Huxley need not make recourse to the language of mind or internal experience to capture the profoundness of this battle.

Huxley's ecological vision in this passage is hardly the stuff of a Sierra Club calendar, it's worth noting. It is a vision of disease – "infinitesimal poisons" – and decay – "flies and worms" – a vision of monsters and "horrible trees" and death. Like H. G. Wells, Huxley recognized the horror and violence of the organic world as well as the strange wonder of it. The narrator's voice here achieves distance without detachment or irony, a distance that does not preclude feeling for the animal and human bodies living and dying in its field of vision. At the end of the novel, the narrative eye zooms out to a level where all life looks equally sized, equally miraculous, and equally vulnerable.

Animals appear not only in the climactic closing moments of *Antic Hay*, but also the end of *Those Barren Leaves*. In the latter novel, the appearance of goats inspires characters to reflect on otherness and

---

[127] Huxley, *Antic Hay*, 349.

recognition. Calamy, one of the guests at the palace Cybo Malaspina, decides to stay in Italy when the Aldwinkle party disperses. He wishes to live a solitary, meditative life in the Italian Alps, at least for a while, in order to find himself. Mr. Cardan and Francis Chelifer go to the mountains to bid him farewell, and the trio sees a goatherd bringing in his goats for the night. Chelifer, the former editor of *The Rabbit Fanciers' Gazette* and author of an article entitled "Symbology of the Goat," observes, "I believe those are the first goats I have seen, or smelt, in the flesh since I took to writing about them in my paper. Most interesting. One tends to forget that the creatures really exist." And Mr. Cardan responds, "One tends to forget that anything or anyone really exists, outside oneself ... It's always a bit of a shock to find that they do."[128]

Like Huxley's other thin descriptions, this scene makes no claims about the animals' subjective experience. Neither the characters nor the narrator speculate about what the goats are thinking or feeling. Yet the goats seem to demand recognition from the men, as physical beings rather than symbols of the sort Chelifer is used to analyzing. At stake in the scene is an ethical imperative to acknowledge that others "really [exist], outside oneself." *Those Barren Leaves* is a novel about the self-centered solipsism of intellectual society, a culture in which people talk past each other, objectify each other, and fail to communicate in any meaningful sense. Yet this final scene foregrounds the need to recognize others as subjects, even when that subjectivity is opaque. The goats are present, they exist materially, outside the human mind. Look at them, Huxley exhorts his readers. To see others, without projecting, without abstracting, just seeing, is the first step in Calamy's quest to be a better person.

What Huxley's animal representations show is that thin description does not have to represent an absolute retreat from questions of animal consciousness and animal ethics. It can also indicate a respect for animals' otherness, and an epistemological modesty that acknowledges the limitations of knowledge when it comes to other species. Recent animal studies theory recognizes the anthropomorphism present in many representations of animal subjectivity. Rather than projecting our own feelings onto animals, perhaps we need more representations that accept the unknown aspects of animal minds. As Kari Weil argues, animal ethics emerges from "a concern with and for alterity," a recognition that an animal is "an other whom we cannot presume to know" and yet are bound to care

---

[128] Huxley, *Those Barren Leaves*, 309.

for.[129] At some point, this care requires us to try to get to know animals by empathizing with them, but a too-quick empathy "risks becoming a form of narcissistic projection that erases boundaries of difference."[130] From this perspective, Aldous Huxley and Eliot Howard model attentive observation and nonhubristic epistemology as ways of recognizing animal otherness without trampling it.

2.4 What to Do About Nightingales

In *Brave New World* (1932), the only one of his novels that is still widely read today, Huxley imagines a dystopian society in which the techniques perfected on laboratory animals come home to roost. The classical conditioning methods that behaviorist psychologist Ivan Pavlov had developed on dogs are applied to humans in *Brave New World*. In the "Neo-Pavlovian Conditioning Rooms," babies are trained to associate books and flowers with loud noises and electric shocks. "They'll grow up with what the psychologists used to call an 'instinctive' hatred of books and flowers," one character explains.[131] Older children are exposed, via "sleep-teaching," to the aphorisms that constitute the future state's ideology: "Everyone belongs to everyone else"; "Ending is better than mending"; "Everybody's happy now."[132] Behaviorist conditioning comes to replace liberal education, as humans are made into lab rats. Pavlov, who in real life performed cruel surgeries called esophagotomies on dogs in order to measure their gastric secretions at the sight of food, is perhaps the most insidious of the vivisectionists mentioned in Huxley's fiction.[133]

Brave New World implies that the problem with the behaviorist laboratory is not that its conditioning techniques do not work, but that it cannot account for the better parts of human life. In the future state, behaviorism creates an impoverished intellectual and artistic climate. The people of Huxley's dystopia live in a controlled environment only slightly richer than that of Shearwater's laboratory animals. Huxley's critique of laboratory biology, which began in *Antic Hay*, *Those Barren Leaves*, and *Point Counter Point*, reaches its apex in *Brave New World*. The laboratory in Huxley's fiction represents the limited outlooks of the vivisectionist

---

[129] Weil, *Thinking Animals*, 17.
[130] Ibid., 19.
[131] Aldous Huxley, *Brave New World* [1932] (TriadGrafton, 1977), 36.
[132] Ibid., 56, 62, 85.
[133] Daniel P. Todes, *Ivan Pavlov: A Russian Life in Science* (Oxford University Press, 2014), 154–5.

and the behaviorist. It is a prison where instrumental reason renders humans and animals into countable, controllable objects.

Huxley's resistance to vivisection and behaviorism, though, should not be understood as a rejection of science in general. He saw in ecology and ethology a different ethic at play. In the 1963 essay *Literature and Science*, the last work he wrote before his death, Huxley argued that modern literature had not paid enough attention to developments in modern science. Like *Antic Hay* and *Those Barren Leaves*, *Literature and Science* turns to animals in its final pages. Discussing how the science of ecology has changed human thought, Huxley calls for an awareness of ecological ethics in literature. "Animals, said the theologians of Catholic orthodoxy, are without souls and may therefore be used as though they were things," Huxley writes. "For the ecologist," he continues, "man's inhumanity to Nature deserves almost as strong a condemnation as man's inhumanity to man. Not only is it profoundly wicked, and profoundly stupid, to treat animals as though they were things, it is also wicked and stupid to treat things as though they were *mere* things."[134] At the end of his career, Huxley explicitly brought together Buddhist philosophy, modern science, and animal ethics, calling for a greater respect for animals and other parts of the "planetary whole." Animals are not things, but subjects of an undefined sort.[135]

After discussing ecology's contribution to philosophy, in the second-to-last section of *Literature and Science*, Huxley turns to ethology, specifically Howard's work on bird territory. He contends that modernist poets have not paid enough attention to ethology. "In this second half of the twentieth century," Huxley asks, "what should a literary artist, writing in the English language, do about nightingales?"[136] He argues that a poet should be aware of ethologists' insights into why birds sing:

> Howard and his fellow ethologists had discovered what Philomel's outpourings signified, what was their purpose. Man is the measure of all things. How true – for us! But for nightingales, the measure of the nightingale universe is nightingales; the measure of a tiger's world is, for tigers, simply tigers. That the ethologists have been able to recognize this triumph and to act upon it represents a major triumph of the scientific method. Philomel, it turns out, is not Philomel, but her mate. And when

[134] Aldous Huxley, *Literature and Science* [1963] (Ox Bow, 1991), 109–10.
[135] For an extended discussion of Huxley's views on nature, especially as they intersect with Buddhist thought, see Lambert Schmithausen, "Aldous Huxley's View of Nature," in *Aldous Huxley: Between East and West*, ed. C. C. Barfoot (Rodopi, 2001): 151–74.
[136] Huxley, *Literature and Science*, 112.

the cock nightingale sings, it is not in pain, not in passion, not in ecstasy, but simply in order to proclaim to other cock nightingales that he has staked out a territory and is prepared to defend it against all comers.[137]

Modern poets *should* be aware of these things; but, says Huxley, poems like T. S. Eliot's *The Waste Land*, which refers to a female nightingale singing, fail to take any of this ethological knowledge into account, opting instead for naïve anthropomorphism. "[O]ne would never suspect that Mr. Eliot is a contemporary of Eliot Howard and Konrad Lorenz," Huxley complains.[138]

Huxley's objection to Eliot's representation of the nightingale might strike readers as a reminder of the gulf between Huxley's realist aesthetic and Eliot's modernist one. How typical that the unmodernist Huxley would want poems to be more like science, we might think; the great poet Eliot was after something different altogether. Yet Huxley is proposing something more aesthetically radical here than a casual reading registers. What would it mean for a poet to assimilate the idea that nightingales are the measure of nightingales, tigers the measure of tigers? It would mean recognition of, and respect for, the animal's otherness, one that would lead to a nonhuman presence in literature as uncharted and alienating as anything that Eliot or Pound ever wrote. It would mean a literary experimentation and innovation in conjunction with, not opposed to, modern science.

Huxley's own representations of animals, as interesting as they are, do not quite realize this vision of a literature that could represent the nightingale universe or the tiger's world. His thin description demurs on this point. Yet his 1920s fiction successfully evades the errors he would later identify in Eliot's poem; in writing about animals, Huxley avoided making humans the measure of their world. I think *Literature and Science* is wrong about one thing, however. If it is hard to believe that T. S. Eliot was a contemporary of Howard and Lorenz, it is much easier to believe that D. H. Lawrence and Virginia Woolf were. Lawrence and Woolf's animal representations begin to build upon the empirical foundations that Huxley, Howard, and others laid down in their thin descriptions. They attempt to envision animal worlds beyond the measure of humans.

[137] Ibid., 116.
[138] Ibid., 115.

CHAPTER 3

Romantic Ethologies: D. H. Lawrence and Julian Huxley

In 1928 Aldous Huxley, his brother Julian, and his friend D. H. Lawrence spent several weeks together in neighboring chalets in the Swiss Alps. Lawrence, despite his struggle with tuberculosis, was working on several projects, including an edition of his collected poems. Julian Huxley, meanwhile, was working on *The Science of Life*, a multi-volume treatise on biology coauthored with H. G. Wells and G. P. Wells.[1] Other than their mutual connection with Aldous, Julian Huxley and Lawrence had little in common. Lawrence had cultivated a reputation for intuitive vitalism, while Huxley espoused scientific rationalism.[2] Julian Huxley later recalled the heated debates that surfaced that winter:

> Lawrence often exploded with a snort of impotent rage when we talked about scientific matters. Aldous and I discussed evolutionary and physiological ideas, including the possibility of mankind's genetic improvement. This particularly infuriated Lawrence, who believed that more power exercised by 'the dark loins of man,' greater freedom for our instincts and our intuitions, would solve the world's troubles.[3]

Aldous Huxley corroborated his brother's impression of Lawrence's attitude toward science, later recollecting a "long and violent argument on evolution, in the reality of which Lawrence always passionately disbelieved." Aldous tried to persuade Lawrence with evidence, but Lawrence reportedly responded, "'I don't care about evidence. Evidence doesn't mean anything to me. I don't feel it *here*.' And he pressed his hands on

---

[1] See David Ellis's *D. H. Lawrence: Dying Game, 1922–1930* (Cambridge University Press, 1998), 398–401, for an account of this holiday.
[2] Throughout this chapter, "Huxley" will refer to Julian Huxley, and Aldous Huxley will be referred to by his full name.
[3] Julian Huxley, *Memories*, vol. 1 (George Allen and Unwin, 1970), 160.

his solar plexus."[4] Even with Aldous as mediator, it is hard to imagine how things remained civil during the shared holiday.

This meeting between Lawrence and Huxley warrants a place in intellectual history because they were perhaps the two most important thinkers on animals in early twentieth-century Britain. Lawrence wrote about animals more frequently than any other major modernist figure. Many of his poems, especially in *Birds, Beasts and Flowers* (1923) and *Pansies* (1929), describe particular animals, and many of his novels feature pivotal human-animal encounters. As critics including Carrie Rohman and Philip J. Armstrong have explored, Lawrence saw animal life as a promising alternative to modernity, industrial capitalism, and Enlightenment reason.[5] Huxley, meanwhile, was trained as a zoologist. Between 1912 and 1930 he published a series of papers on bird courtship, and he also wrote books and essays about animal behavior for popular audiences. These texts helped found the field of ethology, which aimed to create a science of animal behavior.

Despite their philosophical differences – and they are legion – Lawrence and Huxley found one point of common ground. They shared an essentially Romantic understanding of animal subjectivity. Like the Romanticism which emerged among poets and philosophers of the late eighteenth and early nineteenth centuries, Lawrence and Huxley's approach to animals embraced intuition, assumed that nature is meaningful, and emphasized emotional expression over rational intellect.[6] As Rohman says of Lawrence, "his work serves as a classic 'romantic' response to the 'official' version of Enlightenment subjectivity that imagines the human as perfectible through reason."[7] Most importantly, the "Romantics" of this chapter resist mechanistic reductionism in their studies of life. As Maurizio Esposito argues in *Romantic Biology, 1890–1945*, many twentieth-century scientists drew from Romantic predecessors like Kant, Goethe, and Schelling a belief that "in the organic realm the

---

[4] Aldous Huxley, "Introduction," in *The Letters of D. H. Lawrence*, ed. Aldous Huxley (Heinemann, 1956): ix–xxxiv, quote on xv.

[5] Armstrong, *What Animals Mean in the Fiction of Modernity*, 144–50; Rohman, *Stalking the Subject*, 100–1.

[6] Michael Ferber, *Romanticism: A Very Short Introduction* (Oxford University Press, 2010). Describing Schelling's Romantic philosophy, Ferber emphasizes the role of intuition, writing that Schelling viewed nature as an organism and believed that humans have "an intuitive grasp of nature in its unity and infinitude" (122). Ferber also discusses how many Romantics imagined nature as speaking or as giving voice to God – think Baudelaire's "forests of symbols" in "Correspondences" (100–3). Finally, Ferber acknowledges the influence of the Age of Sensibility on Romantic literature, quoting Wordsworth's definition of poetry as "the spontaneous overflow of powerful feelings" (56).

[7] Rohman, *Stalking the Subject*, 101.

whole had a priority over the constituent parts; the parts were explained, shaped, and organized according to the properties of the entire organism during its development."[8] An animal is one such whole which, Romantic poets and organicist biologists would agree, must be understood *as* a whole and not reduced to its material parts.

Lawrence and Huxley's Romantic ethologies contested mechanistic explanations for animal behaviors. The two saw animal life as emotional and instinctive, not rational, and they sought to understand it through empathy and intuition, not solely empirical evidence. This empathy led them to project their own, dissimilar values onto animals – Lawrence saw in animals an individualism he admired, while Huxley saw cooperative, progressive forms of sociality. Yet both Lawrence and Huxley perceived animals as subjects, and they shared a vision of the animal subject as a being ruled by passions and instincts. For Lawrence especially, animals were expressive beings akin to poets.

This chapter compares Lawrence and Huxley's representations of several different forms of animal behavior, from social and sexual behaviors to play. It aims to show that Lawrence was more scientifically literate, and a more attentive observer of animals, than he usually gets credit for. Likewise, Huxley was more of a Romantic than most readers realize. An element of empiricism adulterates Lawrence's intuitive epistemology, and a streak of intuition runs through Huxley's scientific practice. What results are forms of ethology that reveal the inextricable blend of zoological fact with the observer's subjectivity. Aldous Huxley was reluctant to represent animals' inner lives because he knew empathy always shades into projection, especially when the other cannot speak for itself. Lawrence and Julian Huxley, on the other hand, accepted that risk as they entered the thicket of animal subjectivity and dared to write thick descriptions of animal behavior.

3.1 Lawrence's Animal Philosophy

Scholars have long recognized animality as an important axis of Lawrence's writing, and the recent "animal turn" in literary criticism has swung Lawrence back into the spotlight.[9] His work pivots on a primitivist critique of modern civilization, suggesting that humans need to get back to their animalistic roots. What this means is a matter of debate,

---

[8] Maurizio Esposito, *Romantic Biology, 1890–1945* (Routledge, 2016), 2.
[9] I borrow the phrase "animal turn" from Weil's *Thinking Animals*.

but in works like *Women in Love* and *Lady Chatterley's Lover*, it involves greater sexual freedom and less intellectualizing. Lawrence thus makes animality a symbol for humans' primitive essence, a more authentic way of being than modern civilization allows.

But this primitivist symbolism lies in tension with another Lawrentian value, the desire to have an unmediated encounter with the animal other. Many critics argue that in animal-centric works like *Birds, Beasts and Flowers* and *St. Mawr*, a novella about a horse, Lawrence registers the otherness of animal life, seeing animals not as symbols or anthropomorphic projections, but as real and strange beings. "How stupid anthropomorphism is!" Ursula Brangwen exclaims in *Women in Love*.[10] Stupid, perhaps, but not always avoidable. As Carrie Rohman puts it, when Lawrence "uses humanity as a poem's ultimate reference point, the poetry usually becomes symbolic and trite"; his animal representations succeed, however, when "Lawrence resists anthropocentric symbolism as he confronts the alterity of the animal other."[11]

Critics like Jeff Wallace and Ross C. Murfin argue that this tension surrounding anthropomorphism is the central theme of Lawrence's animal poetry. Wallace reads Lawrence's animal poems not as attempts to capture the animal in its otherness, but as meditations on how anthropomorphism is the inescapable condition governing human encounters with animals.[12] Murfin, meanwhile, suggests that the poems reveal the impossibility of fresh, unmediated perception. The "voices of education," according to Murfin, always stand between the poet and his animal subject.[13] Amit Chaudhuri takes this perspective even further, claiming that *Birds, Beasts and Flowers* "does not describe animals or beasts at all, but describes their imitations."[14]

---

[10] D. H. Lawrence, *Women in Love* [1920] (Thomas Seltzer, 1922), 301.

[11] Rohman, *Stalking the Subject*, 91. Other works which posit that Lawrence's animal poems (or at least his *good* animal poems) are about encountering otherness rather than cloaking it in symbolism include Sandra Gilbert, *Acts of Attention: The Poems of D. H. Lawrence* (Cornell University Press, 1972), and Helen Sword, "Lawrence's Poetry," in *The Cambridge Companion to D. H. Lawrence*, ed. Anne Fernihough (Cambridge University Press, 2001): 119–35. Kenneth Inniss, in *D. H. Lawrence's Bestiary: A Study of His Animal Trope and Symbol* (Mouton, 1971), also draws a distinction between those works that try to "express the essential fishness of fish, horseness of horse, rabbitness of rabbit" and works that treat the animal as "emblem or archetype," although he does not make a value judgment about this difference (14).

[12] Jeff Wallace, *D. H. Lawrence, Science and the Posthuman* (Palgrave Macmillan, 2005), 119–51.

[13] Ross C. Murfin, *The Poetry of D. H. Lawrence: Texts & Contexts* (University of Nebraska Press, 1983), 106–21. "Voices of education" is a phrase borrowed from Lawrence's poem "Snake."

[14] Amit Chaudhuri, *D. H. Lawrence and 'Difference'* (Clarendon Press, 2003), 60.

"Snake," perhaps Lawrence's most famous animal poem, affords multiple and contradictory readings from these different critical perspectives. The poem describes an encounter between the speaker and a snake at his water trough. The speaker feels "honoured" by the snake's presence, comparing him to "a king in exile."[15] But the "voice of [his] education" insists that the speaker ought to kill the snake because it is venomous.[16] Overcome by this voice, the speaker throws a log at the snake. Instantly he regrets his "pettiness."[17] The poem is full of mythic overtones, echoing and revising the Garden of Eden story. And it is full of sexual symbolism: the speaker describes his horror at seeing the snake "withdrawing into [a] horrid black hole," an image that suggests a feeling of disgust at sexual penetration.[18] Carrie Rohman argues that the poem is best read as a critique of Western humanism, which tends "to reject and destroy the animal [and] in turn impoverishes humanity's own animality."[19]

All of these interpretations are persuasive, but "Snake" also remains firmly grounded in the literal, its vivid descriptions worthy of a naturalist. The snake, the speaker relates,

> trailed his yellow-brown slackness soft-bellied down,
> over the edge of the stone trough
> And rested his throat upon the stone bottom
> And where the water had dripped from the tap, in a small clearness,
> He sipped with his straight mouth,
> Softly drank through his straight gums, into his slack long body,
> Silently.[20]

The observation here is as acute, and almost as literal, as an ethologist might record. The poem is also tagged at the end with "Taormina," a reference to the place of its composition and, one suspects, the snake encounter that inspired it. The tag helps ground the poem in a specific location: it is not only a mythical narrative that takes place in a mythical garden, but also a particular description of a particular snake in a particular place. While deconstruction-minded critics keep busy unpacking the layers of symbolism and intertextuality in "Snake," other readers

---

[15] Lawrence, *Complete Poems*, 350–51, lines 34, 69.
[16] Ibid., 350, line 22.
[17] Ibid., 351, line 74.
[18] Ibid., line 52.
[19] Rohman, *Stalking the Subject*, 93.
[20] Lawrence, *Complete Poems*, 349, lines 8–13.

are drawn to the seeming immediacy of the snake itself, seeing it as, in Sandra Gilbert's words, a "pure [example] of living otherness."[21]

A note in passing: it may seem stilted or overly fussy to refer to the *speaker* of "Snake," rather than to Lawrence, because the poems of *Birds, Beasts and Flowers* are highly autobiographical. Lawrence really did visit Italy, Australia, and the American Southwest while writing these poems, and it is easy to map out which poems correspond to which locales. ("Snake" and "The Ass" are Sicilian poems; "Bat" and "Man and Bat" belong to Florence; "Kangaroo" is obviously Australian, and "Mountain Lion" and "The Red Wolf" American.)[22] Lawrence even included a poem about his real-life dog Bibbles. (W. H. Auden called this "the best poem about a dog ever written, but it makes it clear that Lawrence was no person to be entrusted with the care of a dog."[23]) His aesthetics of immediacy and self-expression further suggest that he was not particularly interested in cultivating a distinction between himself and the speakers of his poems. Nevertheless, I will refer to the poetic speaker rather than to Lawrence throughout this chapter in order to make space for readings in which the poems cast doubt on their speakers' reliability. It should be recognized, though, that Lawrence's speakers are usually a version of his own poetic persona.

"Snake" combines the perspicacious observation of natural history with the allusive density of modernist poetry, but Lawrence would never have described his poetic method as empirical or scientific. He scorned the rational, intellectual stance of science, preferring instead a more intuitive, embodied way of knowing that he dubbed "blood-consciousness." In a 1915 letter to Bertrand Russell, Lawrence explained his concept of blood-consciousness, writing, "One lives, knows, and has one's being in the blood, without any reference to nerves or brain. This is one half of life, belonging to the darkness." Sexuality seems to be an access point for blood-consciousness, "with the sexual connection holding the same relation as the eye, in seeing, holds to the mental consciousness." Lawrence went on to lament that modern life crushes blood-consciousness, subordinating it to the mental consciousness.[24] Although

---

[21] Gilbert, *Acts of Attention*, 164.

[22] See Mark Kinkead-Weekes's *D. H. Lawrence: Triumph to Exile, 1912–1922* (Cambridge University Press, 1996) and David Ellis's *D. H. Lawrence: Dying Game, 1922–1930* for accounts of Lawrence's travels during the early 1920s.

[23] Auden, *The Dyer's Hand*, 289–90.

[24] D. H. Lawrence, *The Letters of D. H. Lawrence, Volume II: June 1913–October 1916*, ed. George J. Zytaruk and James T. Boulton (Cambridge University Press, 1981), 470.

in works like *Psychoanalysis of the Unconscious* (1921) and *Fantasia of the Unconscious* (1922) Lawrence takes pains to distinguish his philosophy from Freud's, it is obvious that his notions of mental consciousness and blood-consciousness roughly parallel Freud's notions of superego and id. Like Freud, Lawrence believed that modern people were bundles of conflict between their animalistic unconscious and their socialized consciousness, which Lawrence describes in "Snake" as "the voices of my accursed human education."[25]

Lawrence's aversion to scientific epistemology is well documented, and he reserved particular contempt for modern biology, despising its evolutionary underpinning and mechanistic approach to life. In *Mornings in Mexico* he declares, "I don't believe in evolution, like a long string hooked on to a First Cause, and being slowly twisted in unbroken continuity through the ages."[26] In *The Rainbow*, meanwhile, Ursula revolts against the mechanistic physics professor Dr. Frankstone, who says, "I don't see why we should attribute some special mystery to life – do you?" In response, Ursula doubles down on her vitalistic beliefs; she "only knew that [life] was not limited mechanical energy, not mere purpose of self-preservation and self-assertion."[27] Lawrence's hostility to evolution and mechanism arises not from religious doctrine but from a secular distrust of science's reductionist, determinist tendencies.

It would be misguided to attribute Lawrence's hatred of science to ignorance. On the contrary, he was well versed in science, particularly the works of the Victorian sages. In his youth, he read Darwin's *Origin of Species*, Thomas H. Huxley's *Man's Place in Nature*, Herbert Spencer's *First Principles*, and Ernst Haeckel's *Riddle of the Universe*. These works had a great impact upon him and, for a time at least, he seems to have accepted the tenets of evolution.[28] In later years, after establishing his antiscientific philosophy, he engaged in debates about science with the Huxley brothers, and he also seems to have been familiar with H. G. Wells's evolutionary *Outline of History*, first published in 1919.[29] Jeff Wallace, drawing on Aldous Huxley's appraisal of his friend, argues that

[25] Lawrence, *Complete Poems*, 351, line 65.
[26] D. H. Lawrence, *Mornings in Mexico* [1927], ed. Virginia Crosswhite Hyde (Cambridge University Press, 1989), 14.
[27] D. H. Lawrence, *The Rainbow* [1915], ed. Mark Kinkead-Weekes (Cambridge University Press, 1989) 408–9.
[28] Roger Ebbatson, *Lawrence and the Nature Tradition: A Theme in English Fiction, 1859–1914* (Harvester, 1980), 32; Wallace, *D. H. Lawrence, Science and the Posthuman*, 16.
[29] Anne Fernihough, *D. H. Lawrence: Aesthetics and Ideology* (Oxford University Press, 1993), 174.

"Lawrence had a profound engagement with science, and … his 'rejection' of it was a position of critical intelligence."[30]

Lawrence's fraught relationship to evolutionary theory is familiar, but his engagement with twentieth-century applications of evolutionary theory, especially ethology, remains mostly unexplored.[31] Ethology offers a new and useful set of terms for understanding Lawrence's animal representations, beyond Lawrence's own vocabulary of blood-consciousness. Zoologists like Huxley wrote about animals' courtship, social behaviors, communication, and play. Lawrence describes the same kinds of animal behaviors, but uses a different descriptive language that reveals the ideological biases saturating ethological language. Most notably, Lawrence replaces zoologists' euphemistic "courtship" with sexually frank descriptions, and he ironizes the animal family life that zoologists perceived in moralized terms. His dislike of evolutionary theory also led him to challenge the zoological understanding of sexual selection in many of his animal poems. Lawrence's poetry creates an alternative form of ethology grounded not in evolutionary theory, but in his understanding of animals as feeling, expressive beings.

3.2   Huxley's Animal Studies

The most prominent British zoologist of the 1920s, Julian Huxley serves as an instructive foil for Lawrence. As a scientist, Huxley was more invested than Lawrence in clear, unbiased, and accurate representations of animals, but like all science, his animal behavior studies reflect the cultural assumptions of his time and place. Huxley identified as a scientific humanist and regarded science and society as necessarily intertwined.

---

[30] Wallace, *D. H. Lawrence, Science, and the Posthuman*, 18.

[31] For examples of critical works that address Lawrence's engagement with evolutionary theory, see Ebbatson's *Lawrence and the Nature Tradition* and *The Evolutionary Self: Hardy, Forster, Lawrence* (Harvester, 1982), and Ronald Granofsky's *D. H. Lawrence and Survival: Darwinism in the Fiction of the Transitional Period* (McGill-Queen's University Press, 2003), which argue that despite Lawrence's ostensible rejection of evolutionary theory, his novels are saturated with evolutionary ideas and narratives. Ebbatson links Lawrence's work to evolutionary theory's recognition of flux and change where people had once seen stability; Granofsky, meanwhile, reads Lawrence as performing acts of selection on his own characters and concepts. Other critics who address evolutionary theory in Lawrence include Rick Rylance, who claims, in "Ideas, Histories, Generations and Beliefs: The Early Novels to *Sons and Lovers*," in *The Cambridge Companion to D. H. Lawrence*, ed. Anne Fernihough (Cambridge University Press, 2001): 15–31, that Lawrence's relationship to evolutionary materialism was a complex one that cannot be "captured by an 'either-for-it-or-against-it' paradigm" (19); and Christopher Heywood, whose "*Birds, Beasts and Flowers*: The Evolutionary Context and Lawrence's African Literary Source," *The D. H. Lawrence Review* 15 (1982): 87–105 links the poems to a Haeckelian evolutionary view of life.

Not content with his grandfather Thomas H. Huxley's proclamation that "the ethical progress of society depends, not on imitating the cosmic process, still less in running away from it, but in combating it," Julian Huxley believed in an intimate connection between science and human progress.[32] He found progress, though not purpose, in evolution; believed that the study of evolution could teach us ethics; and considered humans to have a special place in nature, at the apex of evolution.[33] Unlike Aldous Huxley's fictional scientists, who cloister themselves in laboratories and exhibit sociopolitical ignorance, Julian Huxley was a public intellectual who used his authority as a scientist to advocate for eugenics and birth control, better living conditions for the poor, and liberal politics.

These political beliefs inflected Huxley's ethological work, as historians have demonstrated. "The good of the species," Richard W. Burkhardt, Jr. shows, is a constant feature within Huxley's behavior studies. When he observed animal behaviors that did not seem to promote the good of the species, such as male mallard ducks trampling and drowning female ducks during courtship, he felt repulsed by the "disharmony" he had witnessed.[34] John R. Durant explains the problem: "As a Darwinist, Huxley was well aware of the fact that natural selection did not necessarily produce biological improvement … As a humanist, however, Huxley was anxious to show that as a matter of empirical fact selection does bring about the good of the species at least often enough to secure overall improvement in the long term."[35] Huxley also found the ducks repellent because of his progressive (for the time) gender politics. As Mary M. Bartley argues, his ethological interests centered on bird species that are sexually monomorphic (i.e. species in which males and females look alike) and that exhibit mutual courtship. Huxley admired the monogamy, equality, and cooperative parenting in these species.[36]

Despite his scientific credentials, Huxley's methods for understanding animal behavior were not always strictly scientific. Unlike Lorenz and

---

[32] Thomas H. Huxley, *Evolution and Ethics*, 83.

[33] William B. Provine, "Progress in Evolution and Meaning in Life," in *Julian Huxley: Biologist and Statesman of Science*, ed. C. Kenneth Waters and Albert Van Helden (Rice University Press, 1992): 165–80.

[34] Richard W. Burkhardt, Jr., "Huxley and the Rise of Ethology," in *Julian Huxley: Biologist and Statesman of Science*, ed. C. Kenneth Waters and Albert Van Helden (Rice University Press, 1992): 127–49.

[35] John R. Durant, "The Tension at the Heart of Huxley's Evolutionary Ethology," in *Julian Huxley: Biologist and Statesman of Science*, ed. C. Kenneth Waters and Albert Van Helden (Rice University Press, 1992): 150–60, quote on 156.

[36] Mary M. Bartley, "Courtship and Continued Progress: Julian Huxley's Studies on Bird Behavior," *Journal of the History of Biology* 28 (1995): 91–108.

Tinbergen, fellow pioneers of ethology, Huxley believed that zoologists could make reliable inferences about animals' subjective experiences.[37] In his 1914 paper "The Courtship-Habits of the Great Crested Grebe," Huxley makes his stance clear:

> [B]y comparing the actions of the birds with our own in circumstances as similar as possible, we can deduce the bird's emotions with much more probability of accuracy than we can possibly have about their nervous processes: that is to say, we can interpret the facts psychologically better than we can physiologically. I shall therefore (without begging any questions whatever) interpret processes of cause and effect in terms of mind whenever it suits my purpose so to do – which, as I just said, will be more often than not.[38]

Huxley is making a somewhat remarkable claim here. Not only is empathizing with animals a legitimate scientific method, it is in his view *more scientific* than trying to explain animal behaviors physiologically (at least within the current state of physiological knowledge).[39] Even experts do not know enough about the brain, nervous system, and endocrine system to accurately explain behaviors in those terms, but anyone can "[compare] the actions of the birds with our own in circumstances as similar as possible." Huxley thus advocates an intuitive mode of knowing that differs from Lawrence's more in degree than in kind.

Huxley also draws surprisingly close to Lawrence in his position on a major debate within early twentieth-century biology: vitalism versus mechanism. Vitalists like Ursula Brangwen believed that living matter fundamentally differs from inorganic matter in possessing some mysterious vital spark. Mechanists like Dr. Frankstone, meanwhile, believed that life consists of ordinary physiochemical processes. The theory of vitalism is an old one, but it had renewed popularity in the early twentieth century thanks to Henri Bergson, who posited an "*élan vital*" as the life force

---

[37] See Richard W. Burkhardt, Jr., "The Founders of Ethology and the Problem of Animal Subjective Experience," in *Animal Consciousness and Animal Ethics; Perspectives from the Netherlands*, ed. Marcel Dol (Van Gorcum, 1997): 1–15, and Crist's *Images of Animals* for accounts of this debate.

[38] Huxley, "The Courtship-Habits of the Great Crested Grebe," 510.

[39] See Durant's "The Tension at the Heart of Huxley's Evolutionary Ethology" and Crist's *Images of Animals* for further discussion of Huxley's use of empathy in his ethological studies. Durant writes that Huxley "was willing to exploit his considerable feelings of empathy toward his subjects in order to gain greater insight into both the causes and the consequences of their behavior" (151); Crist, meanwhile, describes Huxley's writing as "lyrical," "replete with human analogies," and indicative of "an empathic connection between the birds and their human observers" (*Images of Animals*, 172, 179).

that drives evolution.[40] Huxley had no truck with Bergsonian vitalism, writing in one essay that the concept of the *élan vital* is about as useful as explaining a train's motion by positing an "*élan locomotif.*"[41]

Why, then, would one of Huxley's colleagues, Solly Zuckerman, call him a vitalist?[42] It is a surprising claim from a fellow biologist, but one that makes sense upon further examination. Though in theory Huxley had no use for the *élan vital,* in practice he could not bear to think of animals as "mere machines," reducible to physiochemical reactions. "Machines they may be: it is the qualification that does not fit," he wrote in a 1923 essay. "They are mechanisms, because their mode of operation is regular; but they differ from any other type of mechanism known to us in that their working is – to put it in the most non-committal way – accompanied by emotion."[43] (His claim echoes his grandfather's assertion in 1874 that animals are automata, but "more or less conscious, sensitive automata."[44]) Emotion, for Huxley, functions as the vital spark, the something extra that makes animals subjects. Technically, emotion is not a vitalist concept; it can theoretically be reduced to physiochemical processes. But its function in Huxley's writing is analogous to the *élan vital* in vitalist writing. It is the currently inexplicable, unprovable supplement to biological mechanism, the thing that makes animals more than mere machines, and the thing that reconciles Huxley to biology's otherwise reductionist tendencies.

Huxley's understanding of animal subjectivity begins from a very different place than Lawrence's – he was a Darwinian through and through – but it arrives at similar conclusions. He resisted the trend of reducing animal behaviors to mindless reflexes, insisting instead

---

[40] Peter J. Bowler, in *Reconciling Science and Religion: The Debate in Early Twentieth-Century Britain* (University of Chicago Press, 2001), offers an account of the debate between neo-vitalists and mechanists in twentieth-century Britain. Bowler explains that new forms of vitalism (holism, organicism, emergence, etc.) were common even among biologists (166–78). Maeia de Issekutz Wolsky and Alexander A. Wolsky, in "Bergson's Vitalism in the Light of Modern Biology," in *The Crisis in Modernism: Bergson and the Vitalist Controversy*, ed. Frederick Burwick and Paul Douglass (Cambridge University Press, 1992): 153–70, suggest that Bergson's own form of vitalism is actually much closer to the view of mainstream biologists than other forms of vitalism. Bergson considered the role of the *élan vital* to be allowing for indeterminacy and "enabling the living matter to change," and Wolsky and Wolsky identify a parallel between this belief and modern biologists' inclusion of constant adjustment in response to the environment in their criteria for life (162–3).

[41] Julian Huxley, *Essays of a Biologist* [1923] (Penguin, 1939), 39.

[42] Solly Zuckerman, "Comments and Recollections," in *Julian Huxley: Biologist and Statesman of Science*, ed. C. Kenneth Waters and Albert Van Helden (Houston: Rice University Press, 1992): 161–4, quote on 163.

[43] Huxley, *Essays of a Biologist*, 93–4.

[44] Thomas H. Huxley, "On the Hypothesis that Animals Are Automata," 239.

that these behaviors were psychologically meaningful for the animals. "[I]t is a very foolhardy 'behaviorist' indeed," he maintained, "who denies the existence of emotion and conscious process!"[45] And he believed that scientists could more or less understand the subjective meanings of animal behaviors by using a little imagination, picturing themselves in the animal's place. This empathic epistemology is not so far removed from Lawrence's intuitive methods for trying to understand animals. Huxley even shared Lawrence's conviction that animal life is emotional rather than rational, writing bluntly that "[b]irds in general are stupid ... but their lives are often emotional, and their emotions are richly and finely expressed."[46]

These similarities should not obscure the real intellectual disagreements between the two men. Rather, they point to the wide range and versatility of the Romantic understanding of animal subjectivity, which was adaptable to scientific and antiscientific worldviews, primitivist and progressive philosophies.

3.3   Courtship, Sex, and Sexual Selection

Both Huxley and Lawrence placed sexuality at the center of animal life, and both assumed that animal sexuality has something to teach us about humans' sexual practices. Huxley viewed the courtship habits of certain birds as a higher, more civilized form of romantic partnership that people would do well to imitate. Lawrence, meanwhile, explored animal sexuality in the 1923 volume *Birds, Beasts and Flowers* to work through anxieties about human sex and individuality; by the late 1920s, with the publication of *Pansies*, he came to portray animal sex as a more primal, authentic expression of "blood-consciousness" and a corrective to people's tendency to over-intellectualize sex. For the former, animal courtship was admirable because highly evolved; the latter came to see it as admirable because primitive.

Huxley and Lawrence's writings also intervene in early twentieth-century debates over sexual selection, Darwin's notion that certain traits, such as brightly colored plumage or large antlers, offer individuals an advantage when it comes to attracting mates. Sexual selection triggered discomfort among scientists and laypeople because it implied that females have sexual agency, animals have minds, and evolution is not

---

[45] Huxley, *Essays of a Biologist*, 94.
[46] Ibid., 96.

always progressive. While Huxley amended the theory of sexual selection to reconcile his Darwinism with his social beliefs, Lawrence alluded
to the controversy in poems that challenge the evolutionary outlook on
animal life.

The two were by no means unusual in portraying animals' mating
behaviors as virtuous examples for humans. Nineteenth- and twentieth-
century natural history was full of what we might today call family
values narratives, cloaking animals' sexual behaviors in the language of
matrimony and domesticity. Animal pairs were routinely referred to as
"husbands" and "wives," females as "coy," intercourse as "marriage." One
popular nature film, *The Cuckoo's Secret* (1922), censures the cuckoo as
a "homewrecker" for laying her eggs in the nests of other birds; another
film labels a pond as a "honeymoon home" for newts.[47] Huxley's ornithological work uses the same language as this moralistic natural history,
discussing the "courtship," "engagement," and "marriage" of birds. But
to more progressive ideological ends: his studies praise egalitarian gender
roles. Lawrence, meanwhile, dispensed with natural history's euphemistic
language of romance altogether, replacing it with a franker sexual idiom
that prefigures his controversial portrayals of sex in novels like *Lady
Chatterley's Lover*.

Huxley's 1914 paper "The Courtship-Habits of the Great Crested
Grebe *(Podiceps cristatus)*; with an Addition to the Theory of Sexual
Selection" begins modestly, with a promise to divulge some new information about grebes. But historians have come to view it as a landmark
paper in the history of ethology. The paper is notable for several reasons.
It establishes Huxley's view that zoological writing should represent
animals as subjects rather than mechanisms. It appropriates natural history's domestic romance plot, twisting it into a more progressive form.
And it introduces the notion of mutual sexual selection (also called
mutual selection), a way of explaining courtship rituals in birds which
Huxley found more compelling than female choice for scientific and
ideological reasons.

The grebe paper portrays the species as evolutionarily advanced, even
civilized, because of its courtship and reproductive behaviors. Early in
the discussion section of the essay, Huxley describes "the act of pairing"
in grebes, including the fact – evidently astonishing to Huxley – that
either the male or the female may be on top during coition. (Although

---

[47] British Instructional Films, *The Cuckoo's Secret*, 1922, British Film Institute National Archive; and
British Instructional Films, *Romance in a Pond*, 1932, British Film Institute National Archive.

he does not explicitly explain this, readers should know that male grebes, like most male birds other than ducks, geese, and swans, do not have penises. Instead, both males and female have cloacae, openings through which sperm can pass from male to female.) Huxley draws a contrast between birds like the chicken, wild duck, and mute swan, in which males are "often rather forcible in [their] methods," and the grebe, in which "the female has the upper hand" and must be willing to initiate copulation.[48] It is obvious that Huxley considers the grebes' way a higher form of sexual behavior from a moral standpoint and an evolutionary one. Not only is grebe intercourse consensual but, Huxley speculates, it also probably developed from the more primitive scenario of male force through a long, complicated process of selection in which "the characters of one sex might be or tended to be transferred to the other, and *vice versa*."[49]

But the primary reason the grebes are highly civilized birds, for Huxley, is not their reproductive behavior. It is that the grebes court each other even when intercourse is off the table. "I have started with the subject of coition," Huxley explains, "because the first thing I want to make clear about the courtship-actions is their total lack of connection with the act of pairing itself."[50] Their courtship rituals are not just foreplay; they are, in Huxley's terms, "*self-exhausting* and not *excitatory*."[51] Indeed, Huxley observes in a footnote on the article's first page that they would be better described as "love-habits" than "courtship-habits" because they are not primarily about securing a mate or initiating coition.[52] Instead, the essay argues, they are about the birds' feelings, feelings which are evolutionarily useful because they keep pairs together long enough to raise their young. Huxley writes that after observation and analysis, "I was thus – much against my preconceived ideas – driven to think of all the complicated postures and evolutions of courtship in the Grebes as being merely *an expression of emotion*."[53] The implication is clear. The grebes aren't just in it for sex, they are in it for love.

The grebe romance of "Courtship-Habits" might initially seem to share the same "family values" as other natural history fables of the time. The birds, Huxley emphasizes, are monogamous and constant to each

---

[48] Huxley, "The Courtship-Habits of the Great Crested Grebe," 507–8.
[49] Ibid., 508.
[50] Ibid.
[51] Ibid., 509.
[52] Ibid., 491.
[53] Ibid., 509.

other – though he has witnessed "flirtations" outside the bonded pair, he thinks "'adultery' ... very improbable in this species."[54] And the insistence that grebe displays are not just acts of sexual desire, but self-exhausting expressions of emotion, seems bound up with a sexual conservatism that privileges chaste romance over sexual relationships. Huxley was no radical when it came to sexual norms. But, as Mary M. Bartley argues, his interest in the grebes dovetails with his support of equal rights for women. Male and female grebes look alike, display identical courtship behaviors, and cooperatively build nests and raise the young. Huxley believed humans should strive for the same kind of gender equality.[55] In a 1916 lecture series, he directly compares humans to grebes, arguing that if women are guaranteed equal rights, women and men will become more similar via the same process of mutual selection. They will transfer the best of masculine and feminine qualities to each other "so that each again, as in the Grebe, will be richer than before."[56]

Huxley, then, adopted and reshaped natural history's marriage plot. Lawrence, meanwhile, rejected its veneer of respectability altogether. After reading Huxley's muted discussion of "pairing" or "coition," it is even today a bit shocking to read Lawrence's descriptions of animal sex. "He-Goat," for example, describes the male goat's frustrated attempt at intercourse in language that is metaphorical but in no way euphemistic:

And as for love:
With a needle of long red flint he stabs in the dark
At the living rock he is up against;
While she with her goaty mouth stands smiling the while as he strikes, since sure
He will never *quite* strike home, on the target-quick, for her quick
Is just beyond range of the arrow he shoots[57]

Lest any inattentive reader fail to notice that the "needle of long red flint" is the goat's penis, Lawrence clarifies in the first line of the next stanza: "Orgasm after orgasm after orgasm."[58] The description seems especially explicit when one recalls that Huxley was too squeamish to even mention the grebes' genitals.

---

[54] Ibid., 522.
[55] Bartley, "Courtship and Continued Progress," 96–101.
[56] Quoted in ibid., 98. The original quote is from a series of lectures entitled "Biology and Man" that Huxley gave at Rice University in 1916; they are in the Julian S. Huxley Archive at Rice, Box 57: 1910–1916, Rice Lectures.
[57] Lawrence, *Complete Poems*, 382, lines 50–5.
[58] Ibid., line 59.

"He-Goat" dispenses with the sense of propriety that led even biologists like Huxley to mask animal sex in the language of marriage and consumption. But this does not make Lawrence a sex-positive feminist; the poem's gender politics are much more regressive than Huxley's. Sex here is figured as violence upon the female goat, an attempt to "stab" her with a "needle" or "arrow" while she resists. Though she succeeds, the poem's sympathies are all on the side of the male goat. The speaker urges him to "find an enemy," to "forget the female herd for a bit, / And fight to be boss of the world."[59] In the poem's logic, the goat is libidinous because, through domestication, "they've taken his enemy from him" and he no longer has a proper outlet for his violent desires.[60] The goat's attempts at sex are merely the last, degenerate expressions of its ancestral desire to fight. Lawrence's natural history of the goat thus reverses Darwin's explanation of sexual selection. Darwin argued that male animals fight each other for access to females; for Lawrence in "He-Goat," fighting is the true primal urge, sex its secondary, degraded manifestation.

Other poems from *Birds, Beasts and Flowers* echo "He-Goat" in presenting sex as something that male animals desire and females withhold. "Tortoise Gallantry," for example, describes the travails of the male tortoise, coopting the chivalrous language of natural history to show that tortoise sex is anything but chivalrous. Unlike Huxley's grebes, who are in love, Lawrence's tortoises are indifferent to each other: "Making his advances / He does not look at her, nor sniff at her, / No, not even sniff at her, his nose is blank," while "she moves eternally slowly away."[61] Only the male's blind "need to add himself on to her" brings the two together.[62] This is "grim, gruesome gallantry," which is to say, no sort of gallantry at all.[63] "Little gentleman," the speaker calls the male tortoise, a phrase that might be ripped straight from a Victorian natural history tome or an early nature film, but that here can only read as ironic.[64] Unlike the he-goat, the male tortoise succeeds in his advances in the next poem in the Tortoises sequence, "Tortoise Shout" (the title referring to the male's scream upon orgasm). But the gender dynamic remains the same – only the male feels desire,

[59] Ibid., 382, lines 77, 79–80.
[60] Ibid., 381, line 39.
[61] Ibid., 362–3, lines 1–3, 27.
[62] Ibid., 362, line 20.
[63] Ibid., line 15.
[64] Ibid., 363, line 37.

while the female is a blank, a "living rock" or "window" against which the male pitches himself, an "apathetic" lump.[65]

While "Tortoise Gallantry" mocks the marriage plot of natural history, the equally ironic "Tortoise Family Connections" challenges its family narrative. Huxley's grebes formed a nuclear family in which mother and father cooperatively raised the young, but the "family connections" of Lawrence's tortoises are non-existent:

> Father and mother,
> And three little brothers,
> And all rambling aimless, like little perambulating
> pebbles scattered in the garden,
> Not knowing each other from bits of earth or old tins.[66]

Lawrence concludes that the baby tortoise is "[f]atherless, motherless, brotherless, sisterless," alone in the world.[67] This lack of family feeling is, in the poem's framework, no lack at all, but a special gift:

> To be a tortoise!
> Think of it, in a garden of inert clods
> A brisk, brindled little tortoise, all to himself—
> Adam![68]

Unencumbered by family, each young tortoise is the first of its kind. To put it in psychoanalytic terms, the baby tortoise is an object of envy for the poem's speaker because it need not go through the painful stages of human psychosexual development in order to establish itself as an individual, separate from its parents. The baby tortoise thus embodies Lawrence's individualistic beliefs.

The adult male tortoise, "He-Goat," and "Ass" of *Birds, Beasts and Flowers* all experience sexual desire as a fall from a higher form of individualism. For the tortoise, it is the fragmentation of the autonomous wholeness he embodied as a juvenile; for the goat, it is the degradation of his ancestral impulse to be "king of the castle"; for the ass, "Somehow, alas, he fell in love, / And was sold into slavery."[69] These poems should be seen as part of the larger constellation of Lawrence's mid-career work, which simultaneously celebrates and reviles sexuality. For if Lawrence could not endorse Victorian sexual puritanism, his mid-career work

---

[65] Ibid., 382, line 52; 363, line 28; 361, line 48.
[66] Ibid., 357, lines 25–8.
[67] Ibid., line 31.
[68] Ibid., 358, lines 46–9.
[69] Ibid., 382, line 62; 378, lines 36–7.

nevertheless reveals anxiety that sex compromises the integrity of the individual. In the cases of the goat and ass, the problem is linked to domestication. The civilizing influence of humans robbed them of their former glory and left them with sex as the only outlet for primal urges. In the tortoise's case, the problem is more elemental. The "cross" of sexuality, "which breaks up our integrity, our single inviolability," is biologically innate, etched on its very shell.[70]

The horror of sexuality in *Birds, Beasts and Flowers* extends to Lawrence's human-centered novels of the period as well. Rupert Birkin in *Women in Love* (1920) faces the same problem as the tortoise, goat, and ass. Birkin, widely considered a fictionalized version of Lawrence himself, has a generally good relationship with Ursula Brangwen (a character supposedly inspired by Frieda Lawrence), but he still harbors sexual resentment toward her because he sees female sexuality as "horrible and clutching" in its possessiveness.[71] Begrudging the tendency to see men and women "as broken fragments of one whole" (a line echoed in the Tortoises sequence with its recurrent image of sex as a cross), Birkin dreams of a day when "[t]he man is pure man, the woman pure woman, they are perfectly polarized ... each one free from any contamination of the other."[72] Birkin's thoughts here are precisely the inverse of Huxley's on gender. While Huxley believed that men and women needed to become more similar, transferring masculine and feminine qualities to each other via mutual sexual selection, Birkin longs instead for absolute difference.

Lawrence seems to have largely worked these anxieties out by the time of his 1928 meeting with Huxley. *Lady Chatterley's Lover*, published later that year, is much more sex-positive than his earlier work (although it has hang-ups of its own, particularly around the female clitoral orgasm). Correspondingly, Lawrence's 1929 poetry volume *Pansies* offers a second look at animal sex that is less tormented than *Birds, Beasts and Flowers*. "The Elephant is Slow to Mate," unlike Lawrence's earlier animal poems, offers an image of animal pairing that is mutually satisfactory and, in its own way, as romantic as Huxley's portrayal of the grebes. The male and female wait

> for the sympathy in their vast shy hearts
> slowly, slowly to rouse
> as they loiter along the river-beds
> and drink and browse
> ....

---

[70] Ibid., 366, line 80.
[71] Lawrence, *Women in Love*, 200.
[72] Ibid., 200–1.

So slowly the great hot elephant hearts
grow full of desire,
and the great beasts mate in secret at last,
hiding their fire.[73]

The elephants' patience seems reflected in the very form of the poem, which is rhymed and organized into visually similar four-line stanzas, without any of the breathless long lines of the free verse in *Birds, Beasts and Flowers*. The greater formal regularity of "The Elephant is Slow to Mate" suggests an image of the poet as one who sits, thinks, and patiently revises, rather than feverishly pouring words out onto the page.

"The Elephant is Slow to Mate" praises the elephants' wisdom in waiting until the right time for sex, but it should not be interpreted as an endorsement of conservative sexual values, an early twentieth-century version of the "true love waits" abstinence movement. The elephants' waiting is not repression, and Lawrence studiously avoids the language of "marriage" that permeated moralistic natural history. The poem is also framed between "Sex Isn't Sin," a frankly didactic poem, and "Sex and Trust," an eight-line poem that functions as Lawrence's explication of "The Elephant is Slow to Mate." "If you want to have sex," the speaker explains, "you've got to trust / at the core of your heart, the other creature ... [N]ot merely the personal upstart; / but the creature there, that has come to meet you."[74] This framing makes it clear that the elephants' romance is a fable, a virtuous example for humans to follow. Sex is a meeting of "creatures" whether they are humans or elephants, and the speaker advises against letting "the personal upstart," or the egoistic mental consciousness, come between them. Lawrence's version of sexual morality here is not puritanical, but it is in its own way just as stringent.

Pansies thus reflects Lawrence's shifting perspective on sexuality, but it also demonstrates his continued dislike of science, and particularly evolutionary theory. The poem "Self-Protection," which I suspect was written partly in response to Lawrence's debates with the Huxley brothers, expresses overt disgust with the theory of natural selection and launches a subtler attack on sexual selection. Objecting to the Darwinian notion that "self-preservation and self-protection" are "the first law of existence," "Self-Protection" proposes a different theory of what makes animals survive and thrive: their capacity for expressing themselves, for giving off vital energy through song, color, or play.[75]

[73] Lawrence, *Complete Poems*, 465, lines 5–8, 13–6.
[74] Ibid., 466, lines 1–2, 4–5.
[75] Ibid., 523, line 3.

> As a matter of fact, the only creatures that seem to survive
> Are those that give themselves away in flash and sparkle
> And gay flicker of joyful life;
> Those that go glittering abroad
> With a bit of splendour.

Lawrence enumerates several examples to support his insistence that self-protection through camouflage, inconspicuousness, and silence is not an adequate explanation for why some animals flourish and others die out. "A nightingale singing at the top of his voice," he writes, "is neither hiding himself nor preserving himself nor propagating his species."[76] Rather, he sings because "it is the culminating point of his existence." Along the same lines,

> A tiger is striped and golden for his own glory.
> He would certainly be much more invisible if he were grey-green.

> And I don't suppose the ichthyosaurus sparkled like the humming-bird,
> no doubt he was khaki-coloured with muddy protective coloration,
> so why didn't he survive?[77]

It is probably no coincidence that some of the species Lawrence lists, including the nightingale, tiger, and hummingbird, are icons of the Romantic tradition, recalling famous poems by Keats, Coleridge, Blake, and Dickinson. These echoes suggest that, in Lawrence's view, poets understand these animals better than evolutionary biologists ever can.

But, the reader of "Self-Protection" may object, Lawrence is simply misunderstanding evolutionary theory. The nightingale's song arose not for its protective function but for its beauty, via sexual selection. Likewise the hummingbird's bright colors. And the tiger's stripes, which seem so vivid to our imagination, *do* offer camouflage in certain environments such as grasslands. As Huxley himself explained in a 1936 letter to *The Field*, there are lots of different types of coloration among animals, some protective, others "whose function is warning, mimicry, sexual stimulation, threat against rivals, recognition between members of the species, etc."[78] Bright, conspicuous colors and natural selection are thus not always at odds with one another.

It is certainly possible that Lawrence's poem merely reflects ignorance of evolutionary theory. But given his familiarity with Darwin, Huxley,

---

[76] Ibid., lines 6–9.
[77] Ibid., lines 10–4.
[78] Julian Huxley, "Protective Colouring," *The Field*, 8 February 1936, 187.

and other evolutionary thinkers, this explanation seems unlikely. Rather, "Self-Protection" may allude to a facet of sexual selection theory that greatly troubled Huxley and other zoologists. That is, how can seemingly maladaptive traits, like ostentatious plumage in male birds, be selected? How does the female preference for conspicuous ruffs or loud singing come to be, and how can it override the tendency of natural selection to promote safe, inconspicuous appearances and habits? The problem with sexual selection, as historians including Bartley, Durant, and Burkhardt have pointed out, is that it does not necessarily lead to evolutionary progress. Sometimes, for example in the peacock with its excessively large and bright tail, sexual selection can work against the good of the species. Huxley responded to this problem by inventing the concept of "mutual sexual selection," which he described as "a blend between Sexual and Natural Selection."[79] Mutual selection, according to Huxley, promoted monogamy, family life, and sexual monomorphism – i.e. traits that were "good" and benefitted the species – and thus was more palatable than Darwinian sexual selection (i.e. female choice), which often promoted "bad" traits such as polygamy, sexual dimorphism, and impractical courtship displays. Mutual selection was a compromise, albeit an uneasy one.[80]

Huxley's worry that sexual selection might be a form of evolution without progress also intersects with eugenicist thought. Many biologists understood sexual selection as a psychological phenomenon in which animals have differential emotional reactions to prospective mates. As Huxley puts it, sexual selection is a way for "the mind of the species" to influence "the future development of colour, structure, and behaviour in the race."[81] Sexual selection, in other words, might be seen as a primitive, unconscious precursor to eugenics. Huxley hoped that sexual selection would tend to operate for the good of the species. But in some cases, the psychological preferences guiding sexual selection might be contrary to a species' best interests, causing the species to dwindle or even die out. The geneticist R. A. Fisher invented the term "runaway selection" to describe cases, such as that of the peacock, in which "plumage development in

---

[79] Huxley, "Courtship-Habits of the Great Crested Grebe," 524.

[80] See Bartley, "Courtship and Continued Progress," 103–4; Durant, "The Tension at the Heart of Huxley's Evolutionary Ethology," 157; and Burkhardt, *Patterns of Behavior*, 121–2, for further elaboration of Huxley's discomfort with sexual selection and his desire to believe that evolution operated for the good of the species.

[81] Julian Huxley, "Courtship Activities in the Red-throated Diver (*Colymbus stellatus Pontopp*); Together with a Discussion of the Evolution of Courtship in Birds," *Journal of the Linnean Society of London, Zoology* 35 (1923): 253–92, quoted in Burkhardt, "Huxley and the Rise of Ethology," 141.

the male, and sexual preference for such developments in the female ...
advance together" until some check is imposed.[82] The result is secondary
sexual traits, and *preferences* for such traits, that continue to be selected
despite disadvantaging the species. Eugenicists worried that something
similar could happen in humans, that sexual selection could lead to
degeneration if it were not directed toward eugenic ends. To put it simply, they were afraid that if women made bad mate choices, the human
species would decline. Fisher wrote in 1930, "[S]exual selection must be
judged to intensify the speed of whichever process, constructive or degen-
erative, is in action," a statement that he applied to both animals and
humans.[83] The specter of degeneration through sexual selection thus cast
doubts on Huxley's optimistic evolutionary theory.

"Self-Protection" alludes to these concerns by playing natural and
sexual selection against one another, then suggesting that neither offers
sufficient explanation for the exuberant overflow of vitality in the nightingale's song and the hummingbird's flittering. Animal traits that might
appear degenerate to a biologist, the poem argues, look dazzling to a
poet. "Self-Protection" and neighboring poems in *Pansies* imply that
these seemingly maladaptive behaviors are aesthetically valuable forms of
self-expression, and thus that poets have a special, empathic understanding of them. In a sequence of poems that includes "Self-Protection,"
"A Man," "Lizard," "Peacock," and "Paltry-Looking People," Lawrence
contrasts the shimmery energy of animal life with the dreariness of modern human life, which crushes people's natural animal spark and turns
them into "wage-slaves." "If men were as much men as lizards are lizards,"
the speaker says ruefully, "they'd be worth looking at."[84] But poets, we
might gather, are an exception. Writing poetry may be a maladaptive
behavior within the gritty ecology of modern industrial capitalism, but
nevertheless poetry survives.

Huxley's wife Juliette once referred to the grebe as "Julian's seraphic
symbol," implying that Huxley's interest in them was not just scientific,
it was spiritual.[85] The vibrant, vital animals of *Pansies* might equally well
be considered Lawrence's seraphic symbol. Evolutionary explanations of
their behaviors and appearances were intolerable to Lawrence because,

[82] R. A. Fisher, *The Genetical Theory of Natural Selection: A Complete Variorum Edition* [1930], ed.
Henry Bennett (Oxford University Press, 1999), 137.
[83] Ibid., 252.
[84] Lawrence, *Complete Poems*, 524, lines 5–6.
[85] Juliette Huxley, *Leaves of the Tulip Tree* (John Murray, 1986), 75, quoted in Bartley, "Courtship
and Continued Progress," 102.

for him, they were not just animals; they were primitive expressionist poets themselves, and their natural poetry, like his own, could not be reduced to a series of calculations about survival and propagation rates. Lawrence's expressionist poetics aim for the same spontaneity, vitality, and natural spark that he sees in the animals. In his essay "Poetry of the Present" (1918), Lawrence elaborates his theory of poetics, writing,

> We can be in ourselves spontaneous and flexible as flame, we can see that utterance rushes out without artificial foam or artificial smoothness. But we cannot positively prescribe any motion, any rhythm. All the laws we invent or discover – it amounts to pretty much the same – will fail to apply to free verse. They will only apply to some form of restricted, limited unfree verse.[86]

The poetry of the present is about the natural, not the artificial, about "direct utterance from the instant, whole man."[87] It is about the same kind of unfettered self-expression that Lawrence sees in the nightingale and the tiger. Even the simile of "flame" in "Poetry of the Present" has its imagistic echo in the "flicker" and "sparkle" of the animals in "Self-Protection." Carrie Rohman argues that "Tortoise Shout," too, reflects Lawrence's larger belief that "becoming-artistic" is a creaturely process, not a rational one. The artistic impulse, Lawrence's work implies, originates not in the human consciousness, but in animal being.[88]

No doubt Lawrence would hate the evolutionary psychology that has become popular today. Many evolutionary psychologists consider art-making in humans a form of sexual display akin to birdsong, functioning to attract mates and perpetuated through sexual selection.[89] Lawrence would despise this notion not because he thought humans so much *above* other animals, but because he considered even birds, elephants, and lizards as expressive selves whose behaviors are not reducible to the genetic calculus of sexual selection. If animals are akin to poets in Lawrence's worldview, it is not because poets are *mere* animals, but because animals are not mere animals either.

---

[86] Lawrence, *Complete Poems*, 184.
[87] Ibid.
[88] Carrie Rohman, "The Voice of the Living: Becoming-Artistic and the Creaturely Refrain in D. H. Lawrence's 'Tortoise Shout,'" in *Experiencing Animal Minds: An Anthology of Animal-Human Encounters*, ed. Julie A. Smith and Robert W. Mitchell (Columbia University Press, 2012): 170–85.
[89] See, for example, Geoffrey Miller's *The Mating Mind: How Sexual Choice Shaped the Evolution of Human Nature* (Anchor, 2001), 258–91, and Denis Dutton's "Aesthetics and Evolutionary Psychology," in *The Oxford Handbook of Aesthetics*, ed. Jerrold Levinson (Oxford University Press, 2005): 693–705.

Huxley and Lawrence were not the first to suppose that we might find guidelines for human sexual behavior by looking to the animals, and they were not the last either. In a curious way, theorists of queer animal studies might be seen as Huxley and Lawrence's heirs.[90] Ethology over the past several decades has revealed an abundance of nonheterosexual behavior in animals. Gay penguins appear regularly in zoos, the news, and children's books; bonobos have captured the popular imagination as the peaceful, free-love, hippie counterpart to their patriarchal chimp cousins; seahorses have become symbols of sexual diversity in nature because it is the males who give birth. Sometimes activists invoke these queer animals as a counterpoint to the argument that anything other than heterosexual desire is "unnatural." Beyond this strategic rhetoric, as Stacy Alaimo argues, the study of queer animals can also teach us about the diversity, flexibility, and pleasure-seeking of animal life. Once, zoologists had to ignore queer animal behaviors, but today, queer culture has given them a framework to see and explain what used to be unseeable or unsayable.[91]

Queer animal studies faces criticism from those who think it an unwarranted projection of human sexual values onto animals or a fallacious appeal to nature.[92] To some extent, both critiques are correct. But they are probably equally applicable to any representation of animal sexuality, including Huxley's and Lawrence's. The facts are inextricable from the values. Such is the danger – and the draw – of ethological thick description.

3.4   Animal Language

Let us return to the nightingale of "Self-Protection." He "is neither hiding himself nor preserving himself nor propagating his species," according to Lawrence.[93] He sings because he was made to sing, because his

---

[90] See Jennifer Terry, "'Unnatural Acts' in Nature: The Scientific Fascination with Queer Animals," *GLQ: A Journal of Lesbian and Gay Studies* 6.2 (2000): 151–93; Catriona Mortimer-Sandilands and Bruce Erickson, eds., *Queer Ecologies: Sex, Nature, Politics, Desire* (Indiana University Press, 2010); and Joan Roughgarden, *Evolution's Rainbow: Diversity, Gender, and Sexuality in Nature and People* (University of California Press, 2009) for a few examples.

[91] Stacy Alaimo, "Eluding Capture: The Science, Culture, and Pleasure of 'Queer' Animals," in *Queer Ecologies: Sex, Nature, Politics, Desire*, ed. Catriona Mortimer-Sandilands and Bruce Erickson (Indiana University Press, 2010): 15–36.

[92] See, for example, Terry's "'Unnatural Acts' in Nature," Greg Garrard, "How Queer is Green?" *Configurations* 18.1–2 (2010): 73–96; and Jovian Parry, "From Beastly Perversions to the Zoological Closet: Animals, Nature, and Homosex," *Journal for Critical Animal Studies* 10.3 (2012): 7–25.

[93] Lawrence, *Complete Poems*, 523, line 7.

song is his reason for being. To defend the nightingale's song as an expression of self, Lawrence rejects any functional role for it. Like art, the bird's song must exist outside the evolutionary economy of advantage and disadvantage if it is to fit within Lawrence's philosophy. For Huxley, though, function and expression are not a zero-sum game. Birdsong can be both an expression of self *and* a biologically useful behavior. Huxley tries to reconcile the two explanations by invoking a separate spheres argument. "To say that song has a certain function," he writes, "is to give an answer to the question of why birds sing. But if you were to ask the ordinary man or women why birds sing, they would probably say, because they feel happy, or excited, or full of life." The layman, Huxley argues, is just as correct as the biologist: "The truth is that whenever any activity of an animal involves consciousness, there are always two answers to our questions about it. One is an immediate answer, in terms of psychology, the other a more remote answer in terms of biological function. And each is in its own sphere a correct answer."[94] Psychology and biology can happily co-exist, he implies, as long as each stays in its own lane.

The quotation above is from *Animal Language*, a 1938 multi-media project created by Huxley, the photographer Ylla, and the sound recordist Ludwig Koch. *Animal Language* combines recordings of different animal noises – a wolf chorus howling, a sea lion bleating, a camel grunting – with photographs of the animals and text, written by Huxley, describing the noises' meanings. The project is significant for several reasons. First, it expands the definition of "language," a term generally reserved solely for humans and often considered the defining difference between humans and other animals. Second, it sheds light on Huxley's vitalism by explaining how he negotiates between the subjective and objective meanings of animal behaviors. And finally, it demonstrates his understanding of animal life as fundamentally social, a view that contradicts a good deal of philosophical thinking on animals but that is consistent with ethological thought today.

Philosophy has long preoccupied itself with the question of what makes humans human, which is to say, what distinguishes us from other animals. Many philosophers have posited language as the gulf that cannot be breached. Descartes, the villain of many a work of animal studies, insisted that while all human beings are capable of speech, "there is no other animal at all, however perfect and pedigreed it may be, that does

---

[94] Julian Huxley and Ludwig Koch, *Animal Language* [1938] (Grosset &Dunlap, 1964), 17–8.

the like."[95] For Descartes, animals' lack of language "attests not merely to the fact that the beasts have less reason than men but that they have none at all."[96] Later philosophers from Rousseau to Herder to Heidegger took a less hardline view than Descartes, but they still made language the defining characteristic of human existence.[97] Most linguists today believe that animals have communication systems and that human language evolved from animal communication, but they maintain that human language is unique in several ways, including the existence of syntactical rules and the ability to recombine signs to create new meanings.[98] Meanwhile poststructuralists, who are anti-Cartesian in many ways, often assume that language is what ushers the human into subjectivity and society; from their point of view it would make no sense to speak of either animal subjectivity or animal society, since neither can exist without language.[99]

Against the Cartesian view, another line of thinking has emphasized not the uniqueness of human language, but its evolution from and continuity with animal communication. Darwin, for example, grants that "Articulate language is ... peculiar to man," but insists that humans share with other animals an inarticulate, gestural language. He analyzes how animals such as dogs, birds, and monkeys communicate emotions through sound.[100] Huxley's *Animal Language*, in similar fashion, declares that nonhuman animals have language but lack speech.[101] That is, animals do not have abstract, arbitrary words for things as humans do, but they can communicate biologically important information, which is for Huxley the defining characteristic of language. Darwin, Huxley, and their followers do not dispute that human language differs from that of animals, but they emphasize the variety, complexity, and usefulness of animal communication rather than its impoverishment relative to human language.

There is today a third point of view on animal language. Some researchers believe that certain animals can learn to use language in the same ways as humans – to recombine signs, to make novel statements,

[95] René Descartes, *Discourse on Method* [1637], 3rd ed., transl. Donald A. Cress (Hackett, 1998), 32.
[96] Ibid.
[97] Oliver, *Animal Lessons*, 61, 79–80, 91–2.
[98] Charles F. Hockett, a linguistic anthropologist, gave perhaps the most influential account of the "design features" of human language, and the distinctions between human language and animal communication, in "The Origin of Speech," *Scientific American* 203 (1960): 88–111.
[99] See, for example, Kelly Oliver's reading of the language barrier in Lacan (*Animal Lessons*, 180–2).
[100] Darwin, *Descent of Man*, 89.
[101] Huxley and Koch, *Animal Language*, 24.

and to communicate with people. The most famous examples of this research include Koko, the gorilla taught to use sign language, Kanzi and Panbanisha, bonobos trained to communicate with a keyboard, and Alex, an African grey parrot adept at speaking with his trainers. The experiments on Koko, Kanzi, Panbanisha, and Alex have not been replicated elsewhere, however, and many other scientists contest the researchers' claims about their test subjects' linguistic abilities.[102] As Noam Chomsky points out, the animal language experiments may also be flawed because they are anthropocentric and biologically inappropriate: "It's an insult to chimpanzee intelligence to consider this their means of communication," he says. "It's rather as if humans were taught to mimic some aspects of the waggle dance of bees and researchers were to say, 'Wow, we've taught humans to communicate.'"[103] In other words, we cannot understand animals' native intelligence by measuring them against a yardstick designed for humans, and, these critics maintain, language is just such a yardstick.

Animal Language assumes a capacious definition of language, and its multi-media form suggests that animal language is best understood not as a set of decontextualized signs, but as part of the rich visual and auditory worlds of animal life. The text includes Huxley's chapters followed by an appendix with a table decoding the meanings of various animal sounds. But the table is incomplete by itself, requiring Koch's accompanying record and Ylla's photographs to give audiences the full experience. The project thus allows us to contextualize human language as merely one part of a wider, multi-sensory communication system, the other elements of which we share with other animals. In this sense, *Animal Language* builds on Darwin's 1872 *Expression of the Emotions in Man and Animals*. Darwin assumed that humans communicate through body language and facial expressions along with speech, and he argued that these bodily expressions evolved from our animal progenitors and are shared with other animals.[104] Thus, while Huxley's text is legible for humans alone, the visual and vocal expressions that Ylla and Koch captured belong to a cross-species communication system.

---

[102] See, for example, Steven Pinker, *The Language Instinct: How the Mind Creates Language* (W. Morrow, 1994), 340–81, and Jane C. Hu, "What Do Talking Apes Really Tell Us?" *Slate* August 20, 2014: www.slate.com/articles/health_and_science/science/2014/08/koko_kanzi_and_ape_language_research_criticism_of_working_conditions_and.html.

[103] Noam Chomsky, "On the Myth of Ape Language" (interview via email by Matt Aames Cucchiaro), *Chomsky.Info* 2007/2008: chomsky.info/2007____.

[104] Charles Darwin, *Expression of the Emotions in Man and Animals* (John Murray, 1872; repr. in *The Complete Work of Charles Darwin Online*, ed. John van Wyhe: www.darwin-online.org.uk), 13.

Animal Language, like Darwin's *Expression of the Emotions*, portrays animal life as expressive and emotional, infused with subjective meaning. In theory, Huxley proposed that the objective function and subjective meaning of animal calls could be separated out into the biological and psychological "spheres" of understanding. In practice, however, he could not help but blur the boundary between the two. The book's appendix includes, as one of three columns in the table accompanying Koch's record, "Probable emotion expressed: Notes." The entries in this column move freely between biological and psychological explanations of different sounds. For example, the red fox's bark, the panda's whinny, and the zebra's whistle are all classified as "sexual calls," their biological function.[105] Yet the red fox's chattering, the corsac fox's grumbling, and the camel's gurgling are all explained in terms of feeling; they express "excitement," "anger," and "pleasure, satisfaction," respectively.[106] One cannot easily parse out their evolutionary function from their subjective meaning. This difficulty indicates a larger inconsistency in Huxley's vitalistic ethology. Sometimes he represents animal emotions as something *added on* to their biological lives, a supplement: mechanism plus consciousness. One might visualize the psychological sphere sitting atop the biological sphere. At other times, however, Huxley seems to adopt a more materialist view in which the emotions are *part of* the mechanism and serve evolutionary functions. From this point of view, it makes no sense to separate the spheres of biology and psychology; there can be only one sphere that reconciles both.

Huxley could not dispense with the psychological analysis of animal calls because he wanted to represent animal life as subjectively full and emotionally fine-tuned. Nor could he dispense with the functional analysis of animal calls, because functional analysis adds yet another crucial layer to his portrait of the animal world: social life. For Huxley, animal language is not just about individual expression – it is also about intersubjective communication. It knits together animal societies. "[F]unctional sounds," he writes, "differ from almost all other functional activities of animals, in that they only exert their effect via the senses of another animal, whether of the same or another species." While Lawrence imagines that the nightingale sings only for himself, Huxley knows that the song has another purpose: "[W]hen the sound produced by an animal has a function, it is to call to its fellows, to frighten its enemies,

---

[105] Huxley and Koch, *Animal Language*, 56, 57, 59.
[106] Ibid., 56, 57.

to attract its mate, to warn its young."[107] Huxley delineates several different types of communicative animal sounds: recognition characters, sexual calls, deflection characters, warning sounds, and true language, i.e. sounds that "impart information of biological value" to other members of the species.[108] Calling all of these sounds *allaesthetic*, "from the Greek roots for *others* and *perception*," he emphasizes their other-oriented character, even as the word *aesthetic* within *allaesthetic* makes space for a more Lawrentian appreciation of their sound.[109]

Many ethologists today share Huxley's view of animal life as intensely social. Perhaps the most famous of these is Frans de Waal, a primatologist at Emory University. De Waal argues in his book *The Ape and the Sushi Master* that culture is not peculiar to humans, but exists in many animal species. His definition of culture centers on social learning: "Culture simply means that knowledge and habits are *acquired* from others – often, but not always, the older generation – which explains why two groups of the same species may behave differently. Because culture implies learning from others, we need to rule out that each individual has acquired a particular trait by itself before we call it cultural."[110] One of de Waal's examples of social learning in animals involves the same kind of sounds that fascinated Huxley:

> [A]s a student I worked in a laboratory in Utrecht where one scientist regularly caught monkeys out of a large group with a net. At first, the monkeys gave warning calls whenever they saw him approach with his dreadful net, but later they also did so when he only walked by. Still later, years after his research had ceased, I noticed that monkeys too young to have known the threat he once posed alarm-called for this man, and for no one else. They must have deduced from the reaction of their elders that he was not to be trusted. I recently heard that the group kept this alarm-call tradition up for decades, still always aimed at the same person![111]

The monkeys' warning call represents at once an expression of fear, an allaesthetic sound, and a social behavior. According to de Waal, it is a manifestation of this group's particular culture; as such, it is very similar to language.

---

[107] Ibid., 16.
[108] Ibid., 23.
[109] Ibid., 16.
[110] Frans de Waal, *The Ape and the Sushi Master: Cultural Reflections of a Primatologist* (Basic Books, 2001), 6.
[111] Ibid., 15.

For Huxley, social behaviors constitute a key part of animal life, but for some of his contemporaries, Lawrence included, they were a source of anxiety. In *Ants* (1930), a popular science book, Huxley describes in vivid detail the world of the ant colony, but he warns against drawing analogies to human society, particularly the "fallacy" that with increasing mechanization and specialization, we are becoming more like the highly specialized and rigidly hierarchical ant. "There is," he declares, "no reason to suppose that man is destined to sterilize nurses or manual workers, to breed armoured or gas-resistant soldiers, communal parents the size of whales, or an intelligentsia all head and no body," as proponents of the human-ant hypothesis feared (or perhaps hoped).[112] Ant society represented for some of his contemporaries a dystopian nightmare of alienated labor; for others, it was herd animals that signified the biggest threat. For example Nietzsche, whose influence on Lawrence is well documented, warned against the herd mentality in humans. Nietzsche admired solitary species such as tigers and eagles for their power, independence, and wildness, but he disdained herd species such as cattle and sheep for being weak and domesticated.[113] "Wherever there are herds, it is the instinct of weakness that has willed the herd," Nietzsche declared.[114] The ideal animal, in his philosophy, is solitary, just as the ideal human animal is independent, refusing to be enslaved to bourgeois civilization.

Following Nietzsche, Lawrence too respected what he saw as the solitary wildness of animals. In *Women in Love*, for example, Ursula is drawn to the very cattle that Nietzsche disparages because she perceives them not as part of a herd, but as lonely individuals: "From the bottom of her heart, from the bottom of her soul, she despised and detested people ... She loved best of all the animals, that were single and unsocial as she herself was. She loved the horses and cows in the field. Each was single and to itself, magical. It was not referred away to some detestable social principle."[115] Ursula's individualistic distaste for society manifests itself here on two levels. It is not just that she prefers animals to people; it is also that she prefers these animals because she identifies with their apparent unsociability. By relating to such a creature, Ursula distances herself

---

[112] Julian Huxley, *Ants* (Jonathan Cape and Harrison Smith, 1930), 112–13.

[113] Alphonso Lingis, "Nietzsche and Animals," in *Animal Philosophy: Essential Readings in Continental Thought*, ed. Matthew Calarco and Peter Atterton (Continuum, 2004): 7–14.

[114] Friedrich Nietzsche, *On the Genealogy of Morality: Revised Student Edition* [1887], ed. Keith Ansell-Pearson, transl. Carol Diethe (Cambridge University Press, 2007), 100–1.

[115] Lawrence, *Women in Love*, 244.

even further from the civilization that she despises.[116] Jeff Wallace asks, in response to this passage, "When Ursula looks at horses and cows, does she not see a principle of asociality which is her own desideratum? *Are* animals magically single?"[117] Wallace attributes this projection to Ursula as a character, while I would attribute it to Lawrence as author, but it seems clear either way that individualism is the lens which refracts this view of cows, not necessarily something that inheres in the cows themselves.

Animal social life did not fit into Lawrence's individualistic primitivism, since animal societies and herds looked too much like the modern human society that he found so objectionable. But animal language nevertheless has a place in Lawrence's poetry, where it reflects encounters between humans and animals. *Birds, Beasts and Flowers* employs frequent apostrophe to speak *to* animals, and in a few cases, the animals speak back. Lawrence's use of animal apostrophe raises the same anxieties about thick description that preoccupied both him and Huxley. Does the poetic speaker have special insight into the inner lives of his animal subjects? Or is he merely projecting his own feelings onto the animals? Can one have any kind of meaningful communication with animals?

Writing of W. H. Auden, a modernist poet who often "talked to" animals and listened to nature, Kelly Sultzbach says that his "later poems strive to work under, over, and across this barrier of language, consciously questioning whether any human can ever speak 'for' Nature."[118] Sultzbach identifies the poem "Natural Linguistics" as a touchstone for Auden's animal dialogues. "Every created thing has ways of pronouncing its ownhood," he declares in this poem, expressing a belief that animals and other natural objects can "speak" in their own ways, if we know how to listen.[119] Later in the poem, he says of animals, "'Dumb' we may call them but surely, our poets are right in assuming / all would prefer that they were rhetorized *at* than *about*."[120] The line implies that poetic

[116] One might contrast this moment in *Women in Love* with Virginia Woolf's bovine and ovine analogies in *Between the Acts* [1941] (Harcourt Brace Jovanovich, 1969). Speaking of people's need for "society apparently, to be with [their] kind," Woolf writes that it is "the very same instinct that cause the sheep and the cows to desire propinquity" (37–8).

[117] Wallace, *D. H. Lawrence, Science and the Posthuman*, 130.

[118] Kelly Sultzbach, *Ecocriticism in the Modernist Imagination*, 146.

[119] W. H. Auden, *Collected Poems*, ed. Edward Mendelson (Vintage, 1991), 848, line 1; quoted in ibid., 187.

[120] Auden, *Collected Poems*, 849, lines 37–8; quoted in Sultzbach, *Ecocriticism in the Modernist Imagination*, 189.

apostrophe is preferable to human discourses which claim knowledge about animals without an attentive "listening" back. I want to argue that Lawrence's poetry works through similar issues as it experiments with speaking about, at, and to animals. Like Auden, Lawrence worries about the presumptuousness of trying to "speak a word *for* Nature" yet longs to capture nature's speech. In poems like "The Mosquito," "Fish," and "She-Goat," Lawrence suggests that much of what we "hear" from animals is projection, but that in certain cases, real communication can take place.

"The Mosquito," an ironic ode to the pesky insect, portrays an antagonistic "conversation" between speaker and mosquito. "How can you put so much devilry / Into that translucent phantom shred / Of a frail corpus?" the speaker demands.[121] Hearing the mosquito's "small, high, hateful bugle," the speaker responds,

> Why do you do it?
> Surely it is bad policy.
>
> They say you can't help it.
>
> If that is so, then I believe a little in Providence protecting the innocent.
> But it sounds so amazingly like a slogan,
> A yell of triumph as you snatch my scalp.[122]

The poem balances between several possible readings. Perhaps the speaker is right, and the mosquito really does bear him ill will. Or perhaps he is over-reading nature, and the "yell of triumph" is no such thing, but merely an involuntary noise from a tiny-brained insect. We might hear echoes of Robert Browning's dramatic monologues in this poem; it is not a stretch to regard the speaker as a slightly unhinged paranoiac railing against an imagined nemesis. Then again, if we draw that conclusion, perhaps we are underestimating the mosquito, letting it win "in this sly game of bluff" it is playing.[123]

At the end of the poem, the speaker squashes the bug and wins the battle. But one detects, beneath the speaker's hatred of his miniature adversary, a bit of grudging respect. "Am I not mosquito enough to out-mosquito you?" he asks.[124] The mosquito's buzz may be "bad policy," a maladaptive habit that helps its enemies locate and kill it. But it might

[121] Lawrence, *Complete Poems*, 332, lines 12–14.
[122] Ibid., 333, lines 43–8.
[123] Ibid., line 34.
[124] Ibid., 334, line 70.

also be the mosquito's version of the nightingale's song, a noisy form of self-expression that conveys no beauty to human ears but that is nevertheless the mosquito's *raison d'être*.[125]

According to Jonathan Culler, a typical function of apostrophe in lyric poetry is to establish the speaker as someone with a special gift: "One who successfully invokes nature is one to whom nature might, in its turn, speak. He makes himself poet, visionary."[126] At times, *Birds, Beasts and Flowers* flirts with this kind of communion. Other times, however, it punctures the visionary fantasy, revealing the mysterious chasm between human and animal. "Fish," for example, begins with the direct address typical of the *Birds, Beasts and Flowers* poems: "Fish, oh Fish."[127] The speaker continues,

> As the waters roll
> Roll you.
> The waters wash,
> You wash in oneness
> And never emerge.
>
> Never know,
> Never grasp.
>
> Your life a sluice of sensation along your sides,
> A flush at the flails of your fins, down the whorl of your tail,
> And water wetly on fire in the grates of your gills;
> Fixed water-eyes.[128]

Speaking to the fish, the speaker attempts to read it and decipher its life. Seeing the fish's body – its fins, tail, gills, eyes – the speaker describes what it is like to inhabit that body. The fish may "never know" the speaker or anyone else, but the speaker claims to know him.

The poem shifts direction gradually, however, and one sign of this shift is that the speaker abandons the "you" of apostrophe in favor of the third-person pronoun "him." Over the course of the poem, the speaker

---

[125] Another poem, "The Blue Jay," lends itself to a similar reading. The speaker (a Lawrence persona, walking with his dog Bibbles), hearing the call of a blue jay, declares, "It's the blue jay laughing at us" (Lawrence, *Complete Poems*, 375, line 17). He resents what he perceives as the bird's mockery, demanding of the blue jay, "Who are you? / Whose boss are you, with all your bully way?" (lines 26–7). As with "The Mosquito," it is difficult to decide if Lawrence really believes blue jays harbor something like malice, or if he intends to portray the speaker as paranoid.

[126] Jonathan Culler, *The Pursuit of Signs: Semiotics, Literature, Deconstruction* (Cornell University Press, 2002), 157.

[127] Lawrence, *Complete Poems*, 334, line 1.

[128] Ibid., 335, lines 9–19.

begins to realize that it is not the fish that lacks knowledge – it is himself.
Upon seeing a pike in a lake, the speaker tries again to make claims about
the fish's life. But upon a second look,

> I left off hailing him.
> I had made a mistake, I didn't know him.
> This grey, monotonous soul in the water,
> This intense individual in shadow,
> Fish-alive.
>
> I didn't know his God.
> I didn't know his God.[129]

Apostrophe here is refigured as presumptuousness. Only when the
speaker "[leaves] off hailing him" can he recognize that he never knew
the fish at all. The speaker, then, is not a visionary, and nature has not
chosen him to whisper secrets in his ear. The moment marks a turn in the
poem, as Carrie Rohman observes; after these lines, the speaker "does not
attempt 'to be a fish' any longer," but instead meditates on the fish's "radical alterity" and the "epistemological limit" that humans face in trying to
know it.[130] Fish live in another world, under another god, and not even
poets can communicate across that chasm.

What is true of the fish, though, is not necessarily true of all the animals in Lawrence's poetic menagerie. "She-Goat," like "Fish," dispenses
with apostrophe, but here it is abandoned in favor not of mysterious
silence but of dialogue. The poem shows a back-and-forth repartee
between the speaker and his goat, an animal much more legible than the
fish. The goat's vocalizations are even portrayed typographically as language, as she calls for the speaker to come to untie her:

> *Merr-err-err! Merr-er-errr! Mer! Mé!*
> *Wait, wait a bit, I'll come when I've lit the fire.*
> *Merrr!*
> *Exactly.*
> *Mé! Mer! Merrrrrrr!!!*
> *Tace, tu, crapa, bestia!*
> *Merr-ererr-ererrrr! Merrrr!*[131]

The goat's calls are represented as merely another foreign language: ital-
icized, using the non-English letter "*é*," interspersed with the speaker's

---

[129] Ibid., 338, lines 108–14.
[130] Rohman, *Stalking the Subject*, 97.
[131] Lawrence, *Complete Poems*, 384, lines 7–13.

English and Italian. (The speaker's Italian line translates, roughly, to "Be quiet, you goat, beast!") The acute accent mark is typically used in Italian to differentiate between homonyms; in the case of the made-up word *"Mé!"* it forecloses the possibility that we could understand the goat as saying the English word "me." The poem, of course, gets to have it both ways – the goat's cry is both "Me!" and not "Me!" to the reader, but either way it is an assertion of her presence. (Later in the poem, the speaker imagines her saying, "That's me!"[132]) Regardless of the linguistic content of these noises, the speaker has no difficulty translating the meaning of the goat's calls – she is tied up in the shed, and she wants to be free.

The relationship between speaker and goat resembles the kind of inter-species communication that Donna Haraway and Vicki Hearne associate with training. Writing about her companionship with her dog Cayenne, Haraway says, "We are training each other in acts of communication we barely understand."[133] Training acknowledges the subjectivity and agency of all parties; it relies not on full and transparent knowledge of one another, nor on the visionary insights that poetic apostrophe connotes, but on "greeting rituals" and mutual responsiveness.[134] For Hearne, training forms a kind of language that allows human and animal to "travel together."[135] It does not necessarily create a paradise of love and equality. In Lawrence's poem, the speaker retains power over the leashed goat, and the two seem more annoyed with each other than overcome with fondness. Nevertheless, through living together speaker and goat have trained each other, cobbling together a form of communication that is ad hoc and provisional but nevertheless effective.

It is one thing to imagine that wild animals are solitary, noble, fully realized individuals, unsullied by civilization. But for Lawrence, this fantasy could not be sustained when it came to household animals, who so obviously exist in a web of social relationships. "She-Goat" represents the intrusion of the domestic, the ordinary, and the sociable into *Birds, Beasts and Flowers*. And, it turns out, the intrusion is not so bad, even from a Lawrentian point of view. The goat is domesticated but never servile – she pays no attention to the speaker when he orders her to "*[c]ome down, crapa, out of that almond tree!*"[136] She has a mind

[132] Ibid., 386, line 48.
[133] Haraway, *When Species Meet*, 16.
[134] Ibid., 19–27.
[135] Vicki Hearne, *Adam's Task: Calling Animals by Name* (Skyhorse, 2007), 42.
[136] Lawrence, *Complete Poems*, 385, line 35.

of her own, and "leaps the rocks" with "sheer will."[137] If she were more obedient and less willful, she would annoy the speaker less often, but it is precisely her disobedience and willfulness that demand his grudging respect. She is like St. Mawr, the horse in Lawrence's 1925 novella of the same name who has a "recalcitrant agency" that, in Philip J. Armstrong's words, "refuses ... subservience" and thus elicits Lawrence's admiration.[138] "She-Goat" is perhaps the only Lawrence poem to reconcile the expressive and functional meanings of animal behavior. The goat's bleats are at once a functional call to the speaker and an irrepressible expression of self.

3.5   Animal Spirits

In "Self-Protection," after praising the nightingale for its beautiful song and the tiger for its magnificent stripes, Lawrence expresses admiration for a smaller, meeker animal: the unassuming mouse. "Even mice play quite beautifully at shadows," he writes, "And some of them are brilliantly piebald."[139] Compared to the other animals of "Self-Protection," the mouse might seem, well, mousy. But for Lawrence, it is just as full of vivacious energy, which it channels into play. Playfulness, like vibrant coloration and exuberant song, expresses the animal spirits that, for Lawrence, exceed biological usefulness and can never be reduced to selective advantage. If all art is quite useless, so is all play, and for Lawrence, gloriously so.

Play was equally important to Huxley as a kind of animal behavior that is useless but that animals carry out for its own sake. Huxley believed that play was unique to the "higher animals" – i.e. mammals and birds – and that it could be divided into two categories. "From the point of view of its evolution and its biological meaning, play seems to have a double origin," he explains. "There is the play which is biologically useful as a preparation for adult life" – think of wolf cubs wrestling each other as practice for hunting – "[a]nd there is the play which results from a mere surplus of energy being directed into pleasurable or exciting outlets; this, if we want to distinguish it, we can call sport."[140] Huxley's notion of sportive play is perhaps the clearest example of his vitalism. Animals that

[137] Ibid., 386, lines 50, 52.
[138] Armstrong, *What Animals Mean in the Fiction of Modernity*, 146.
[139] Lawrence, *Complete Poems*, 523, lines 20–1.
[140] H. G. Wells, Julian Huxley, and G. P. Wells, *The Science of Life*, (Doubleday, Doran, 1931), vol. 4, 1254–5.

play for the joy of play are not mere machines, made only of genes and proteins or drives, releases, and motor responses. They are subjects with feelings, pursuing pleasure just as we do.

Animal play, particularly in birds, seems to have been an enduring interest of Huxley's. His 1916 paper "Bird-Watching and Biological Science" warned would-be ornithologists, "It is always well to remember that some actions of birds" – including play and, in some cases, singing – "seem to be gone through simply for the sake of releasing energy in a pleasurable way, simply because the bird enjoys doing them."[141] He also wrote a 1924 article, "Birds' Play and Pleasure," which describes birds' "Olympic games of the air."[142] And in *The Science of Life* (1929–30), he and co-authors H. G. Wells and G. P. Wells devoted a seven-page section to "Play" within a chapter on vertebrate behavior. Around the same time, his book *Bird-Watching and Bird Behaviour* (1930), which collects in essay form six BBC radio lectures, gave special attention to the play antics of birds. Huxley's ethological interest in animal play is not as well known as his interest in courtship, but it nevertheless formed a crucial part of his thinking on animal subjectivity.

Huxley believed that most mammals play while juveniles as training for activities such as hunting, whereas most birds play merely to expend energy and enjoy themselves.[143] How could he tell that birds play for pleasure? According to Huxley, it is obvious; one simply needs to exercise a little empathy. Describing a group of birds cavorting through the air in acrobatic fashion, Huxley declares, "[T]he reason for the performance is not far to seek. It is sheer pleasure in motion and its control – play, or sport, if you will, but in any case the same pleasure which we ourselves find in diving, or tobogganing, or skiing, or motoring. Many kinds of birds thus play tricks in the air for the mere pleasure of playing them."[144] Birds, in Huxley's view, are emotionally similar to humans and have a sense of fun and excitement akin to ours. Somersaulting through the air seems like fun to Huxley, and he can identify no other purpose for it, so he concludes inductively that it is fun for the birds too.

Describing animal play also gives Huxley the opportunity to empathetically catch their spirit of fun and channel it into his own prose. So,

[141] Julian Huxley, "Bird-Watching and Biological Science: Some Observations on the Study of Courtship in Birds," *The Auk* 33.2 (1916): 256–70, quote on 262.
[142] Julian Huxley, "Birds' Play and Pleasure," *The New Statesman*, January 19, 1924, 417–419, quote on 418.
[143] Wells, Huxley, and Wells, *The Science of Life*, vol. 4, 1254–5.
[144] Julian Huxley, *Bird-Watching and Bird Behaviour* (Chatto and Windus, 1930), 20.

for example, when detailing the kinds of bird play he has witnessed, he reports, "I have seen our own English heron, for all its size and apparent stolidity, go through the most extraordinary series of somersaults from four to five hundred feet up."[145] The line is a mischievous wink to readers, inviting them to imagine not just stolid English herons but stolid English gentlemen tumbling through the air in a very un-English manner. The playful prose even sneaks into the *Science of Life* textbook, whose discussion of animal play begins with the didactic language of scientific definition but quickly turns to a more imaginative register. "What is the biological function of play?" Huxley asks. "Let us consider a few examples to clear our minds about this question. We are standing in the bows of a steamer in the Mediterranean. Some distance away we see a series of leaping forms, one behind the other, each curving over in a semicircle to dive below the surface and re-emerge a few seconds after. They are a file of dolphins."[146] By the third sentence, Huxley is no longer in the realm of scientific fact; he is in the world of fiction. What follows is a detailed narrative of dolphins playing with a ship, "twisting up," "circl[ing] right round the ship," and "gambol[ing] around the bows." In the conclusion to this passage, Huxley writes, "Those who prefer everything to be sensible and simple have suggested that porpoises really frequent the bows of ships to rub barnacles and other encumbrances off their backs; but the unanimous verdict of those who have watched them is that this is not so – the porpoises are not being reasonable, they are being playful."[147] We might expect Huxley himself to be one of "those who prefer everything to be sensible," and one who would reject the intuitions of dolphin-watchers as insufficiently scientific. But what he says of the porpoises might justly be said of the writer too – he is not being reasonable here, he is being playful.

Animal play continues to fascinate and puzzle ethologists today, who have catalogued play behavior in many species but seem no closer than the scientists of Huxley's day were to arriving at a firm biological understanding of it. Marc Bekoff and Colin Allen explain, "Attempts to define it functionally face the problem that it is not obvious that play serves any particular function either at the time at which it is performed or later in life. Indeed several authors have been tempted into defining

[145] Ibid.
[146] Wells, Huxley, and Wells, *The Science of Life*, 1252.
[147] Ibid.

play as functionless behavior."[148] Bekoff and Allen settle for a provisional definition of play as motor activities that *appear* purposeless, reserving the possibility that a purpose will be found with further study. Yet they follow Huxley in preserving the notion of uselessness in their definition. Subjective experiences such as pleasure in play cannot be measured or even proven to occur, but zoologists who study play behaviors continue to invoke these terms – as long as they are safely contained within scare quotes or punctuated by question marks. As Maxeen Biben puts in her study of play-fighting in squirrel monkeys, "But why not invoke fun?"[149] The query captures in its very semantics the tenuous yet persistent position that pleasure, shorn of usefulness, continues to have in ethological studies of play.

For Lawrence, animals' play reflects what he calls joie de vivre, a drive that he is careful to distinguish from other animal impulses that are biologically useful. In "Fish," for example, the speaker, meditating on what feelings the fish might experience, proposes, "Joie de vivre, and fear, and food, / All without love."[150] Joie de vivre is separate from sexual desire, appetite for food, and fear, feelings which help animals to survive and propagate and thus have evolutionary utility. It does not even belong to the same language – the speaker's turn to French, his exclamation "Quelle joie de vivre / Dans l'eau!" point to its otherness.[151] Joie de vivre is not limited to the fish "dans l'eau." Lawrence also identifies it in the little dog "Bibbles," whose playful spirit "turn[s] the day suddenly into a black tornado of *joie de vivre*."[152] And his early short story "Second-Best" (1914) recognizes it in a mole, who is "like a very ghost of joie de vivre" in its playfulness, "delighted to ecstasy by the sunlight and the hot, strange things that caressed its belly and its nose."[153]

[148] Marc Bekoff and Colin Allen, "Intentional Communication and Social Play: How and Why Animals Negotiate and Agree to Play," in *Animal Play: Evolutionary, Comparative, and Ecological Perspectives*, ed. Marc Bekoff and John A. Byers (Cambridge University Press, 1997): 97–114, quote on 99.
[149] Maxeen Biben, "Squirrel Monkey Play Fighting: Making the Case for a Cognitive Training Function for Play," in *Animal Play: Evolutionary, Comparative, and Ecological Perspectives*, ed. Marc Bekoff and John A. Byers (Cambridge University Press, 1997): 161–82, quote on 165.
[150] Lawrence, *Complete Poems*, 336, lines 59–60.
[151] Ibid., lines 61–2.
[152] Ibid., 397, line 59.
[153] D. H. Lawrence, *The Prussian Officer and Other Stories* [1914], ed. John Worthen (Penguin, 1995), 115. It bears mentioning that the mole in "Second Best" is killed, its joie de vivre stamped out because it is a pest. Its death symbolically mirrors the death of joie de vivre in the protagonist, Frances, as she settles for a "second best" suitor.

A later poem, "Little Fish" (1929), reiterates the role of joie de vivre in fish life. Only five lines long, the poem is itself a little "Fish." It mixes a playful, child-like style with a vitalist understanding of animal life and animal play:

> The tiny fish enjoy themselves
> in the sea.
> Quick little splinters of life,
> their little lives are fun to them
> in the sea.[154]

To call the fish "splinters of life" is to imply that they are made of a special kind of matter imbued with life – textbook vitalism. Meanwhile, the style of "Little Fish" mimics its subjects' playfulness. It is itself a little poem, full of repetition like a nursery rhyme, minor in import, yet within its own small scope lively and fun.

Huxley, it is worth noting, would not have agreed with Lawrence that fish can have fun. In *The Science of Life*, after describing the playful dolphins, he declares, "No fish would ever behave like this. Fish will leap out of the water, but only to avoid their enemies; they will keep poised in the current of a stream, but only because that is the business of their lives."[155] It is not clear even today which of the two is right. Zoologists have been hesitant to ascribe play behaviors to fish, but a few, including the psychologist Gordon M. Burghardt, have argued that fish, along with other unlikely creatures, including turtles and frogs, do indeed play.[156] Lawrence's perception of playfulness in the fish's darting and leaping, then, may be merely a poet's projection, but it may also be a real psychological possibility.

Other playful animals pepper Lawrence's poetry, where they signify the primitive, vitalistic essence of animal life. "Humming-Bird," for example, a poem from *Birds, Beasts and Flowers*, envisions prehistoric hummingbirds expressing their vital spark through play. "While life was a heave of Matter, half inanimate," intones the speaker, "[t]his little bit chipped off in brilliance" and became the hummingbird.[157] Fragments of vital matter, the hummingbirds play by "racing down the avenues" and "whizzing through the slow, vast, succulent stems."[158] In a later poem published in

[154] Lawrence, *Complete Poems*, 466, lines 1–5.
[155] Wells, Huxley, and Wells, *The Science of Life*, 1252.
[156] See Chapter 13, "The Origins of Vertebrate Play: Fish That Leap, Juggle, and Tease," in Gordon M. Burghardt, *The Genesis of Animal Play: Testing the Limits* (MIT Press, 2005), 309–58.
[157] Lawrence, *Complete Poems*, 372, lines 6–7.
[158] Ibid., lines 4, 8.

Pansies, "When I Went to the Circus," Lawrence reads animals' playfulness as a reproach to humans who have forgotten that ancient impulse. The horses, elephants, monkeys, dogs, and human acrobats of the circus engage in a kind of embodied play that their audience cannot appreciate. "[A]ll the creatures seemed to enjoy the game," the speaker claims, but the audience is envious and resentful.[159] The moral?

> When modern people see the carnal body dauntless and flickering gay
> playing among the elements neatly, beyond competition
> and displaying no personality,
> modern people are depressed.[160]

The joie de vivre of animal play, according to Lawrence, is our "birthright," if only we remembered how to claim it.[161]

3.6 Thick Description

For readers today, it is hard to believe that any circus animals Lawrence might have seen were really enjoying themselves. Circuses have become notorious for animal abuse, and we know now that large wild animals like elephants and tigers suffer psychologically in that sort of captive environment. It is easy to accuse Lawrence of projection: he perceives the circus animals as having fun simply because it fits his preconceived notions about primitive animal spirits versus modern society. Another observer, a Kafka or a Rilke, would likely have seen something very different: animals imprisoned, exiled from their native lands, condemned to repeat meaningless ritual movements before an audience. (Kafka's story "A Report to an Academy," for example, describes the capture and imprisonment of an ape by European hunters, while Rilke's poem "The Panther" describes the titular creature pacing anxiously behind bars. Both texts emphasize the misery of captive animals.) Play, like all animal behaviors, is easy to misunderstand. And at the circus or elsewhere, when people misrecognize animals' feelings – and some misrecognition seems inevitable – the stakes are high.

Thick description of animal behavior, then, is not just a scientific and aesthetic problem – it is also an ethical one. Our dealings with animals hinge on our understanding of them. We read their emotional states from their behaviors and respond accordingly, but we can never be sure

---

[159] Ibid., 445, line 34.
[160] Ibid., lines 42–5.
[161] Ibid., 446, line 55.

our interpretations are right. Neither Lawrence nor Huxley has much to say directly about animal ethics, but their understanding of animals – as feeling, expressive subjects not unlike human beings – leads necessarily to the conclusion that animals demand ethical consideration. This consideration depends upon our reading – or misreading – of animals, and thus cannot be separated from the epistemological debates of zoology and the literary questions surrounding animal representations. Thick description is a murky morass of epistemological, literary, and ethical entanglements, one that Aldous Huxley and the classical ethologists preferred to avoid, but that Julian Huxley and D. H. Lawrence dared to wade into.

Other modernists waded in too. The next chapter focuses on a group of writers who saw animal subjectivity through a slightly different lens. While Huxley and Lawrence emphasized animals' emotions, these writers focused instead on their sensory experiences. They imagined animals not as primitive artists, but as primitive scientists and philosophers. And they aimed at nothing less than the exploration of animal worlds.

CHAPTER 4

Bloomsbury's Comparative Psychology: Bertrand Russell, Julian Huxley, J. B. S. Haldane, Virginia Woolf

What is it like to be a snail, a dog, or a bee?[1] What is it like to see the world through their eyes, smell it through their noses, or sense it through their feelers? For many scientists and writers in the modernist period, such questions defined the study of animal subjectivity. To understand animals as subjects, they believed, one had to enter their *perspectives*. In Germany, the Expressionist painter Franz Marc asked, "How does a horse see the world?" A few years later, the biologist Jakob von Uexküll asked what constituted the *Umwelt*, or world, of a tick.[2] In Prague, Kafka was writing stories like "Investigations of a Dog" and "A Report to an Academy" voiced by animal narrators.[3] In Russia, Viktor Shklovsky was reading Tolstoy's "Kholstomer," a story focalized through a horse, and using it to develop his theory of defamiliarization.[4] In Japan, readers devoured Natsume Soseki's *I Am a Cat*, a satire of middle-class life presented through feline eyes. And in England, intellectuals including Bertrand Russell, Julian Huxley, J. B. S. Haldane, and Virginia Woolf were exploring animal perspectives to reconsider the nature of knowledge and uncover strange, novel views of the world.

Russell, Huxley, Haldane, and Woolf's views on animal perspectives drew on the legacy of comparative psychology, a discipline that emerged in the late Victorian period and flourished until the rise of behaviorism

---

[1] I allude here to Thomas Nagel's well-known essay "What Is It Like to Be a Bat?"

[2] See Franz Marc, "How Does a Horse See the World?" [1920], transl. Ernest Mundt and Peter Selz, in *Theories of Modern Art: A Source Book by Artists and Critics*, ed. Herschel Browning Chipp (University of California Press, 1968), 178–9, and Jakob von Uexküll, *A Foray into the Worlds of Animals and Humans*, [1934] transl. Joseph D. O'Neil (University of Minnesota Press, 2010), 44–52.

[3] Kafka's other animal stories include "Josephine the Singer, or the Mouse Folk," "The Burrow," and, of course, *The Metamorphosis*.

[4] See Victor Shklovsky's "Art as Technique" [1917], in *Russian Formalist Criticism: Four Essays*, transl. Lee T. Lemon and Marion J. Reis (University of Nebraska Press, 1965), 3–24, which introduces the term *ostranenie*, or defamiliarization, and deploys "Kholstomer" as an example of the technique.

in the 1920s.[5] Comparative psychologists aimed to understand human and animal minds from the inside. Margaret Washburn, author of the textbook *The Animal Mind*, described comparative psychology's purview as "knowledge of how the world looks from the point of view of our brother animals."[6] Part of the school that Judith Ryan calls "empiricist psychology," comparative psychologists saw animals, including humans, as diffuse bundles of sense-impressions rather than well-defined selves oriented around an ego.[7] Russell, Huxley, Haldane, and Woolf's notions of animal minds also draw on this empiricist tradition; the question of what animal subjectivity is like, for them, is principally a question of what sensations animals feel.

Russell captured the spirit of this approach to animal subjectivity when he wrote, in *Portraits from Memory and Other Essays* (1956), "Animals, including human beings, view the world from a center consisting of the here and now. Our senses, like a candle in the night, spread a gradually diminishing illumination upon objects as they become more distant."[8] Russell's words imply, first, that humans are not qualitatively different from other species – the parenthetical aside "including human beings" subordinates the category of human beings to the more inclusive and important category of "animals." This assumption rests on the Darwinian postulate that there is continuity between human and animal "mental powers."[9] Second, Russell zeroes in on the animal perspective – the unique and ever-changing standpoint from which it perceives the world around it. And third, Russell portrays the *senses* as the medium of experience and, implicitly, knowledge, for all species. The analogy of candlelight illuminating the world around the subject recalls the trope of knowledge as enlightenment. Russell thus indicates that humans and other species experience and create knowledge through vision and other sensory perceptions, a belief that places him within the empiricist tradition.

---

[5] In this chapter, "Huxley" will refer to Julian Huxley, and Aldous Huxley will be referred to by his full name.

[6] Margaret Washburn, *The Animal Mind: A Text-Book of Comparative Psychology*, 3rd ed. (Macmillan, 1926), 22.

[7] Judith Ryan, *The Vanishing Subject*, 12. Ryan's arguments about empiricist psychology, its revision of the concept of the self, and its influence on literary modernism correspond closely with my own; but she does not delve into comparative psychology or representations of animal minds, whereas I think comparative psychology's notion of animal subjectivity was a crucial means for disseminating ideas about the subject of sensation into modernist culture at large.

[8] Bertrand Russell, *Portraits from Memory and Other Essays* (Simon & Schuster, 1956), 178.

[9] See Darwin's *Descent of Man*, especially chapters 2 and 3, titled "Comparison of the Mental Powers of Man and the Lower Animals," which argue that human and animal mental faculties differ only in degree, not in kind.

For both comparative psychology and its intellectual heirs, animal perspectives led to an unraveling and reweaving of empirical knowledge. Animal perspectives recast knowledge as a collection of partial, subjective observations distilled through animal senses, not a phenomenon unique to the human mind. Biology's unraveling of empiricism began in the nineteenth century. Physiologists showed that the senses, far from being transparent vehicles of information, were instead fallible and limited biological systems; psychologists, meanwhile, revealed the probability of unconscious beliefs and biases.[10] The fantasy of a purely rational scientist who could transcend his own animality had, as Carrie Rohman shows, been exposed and dismantled in early modernist works like H. G. Wells's *Island of Doctor Moreau*.[11] Science could no longer be absolute or objective once scientists were understood as human animals with animal senses and psyches. Thus, modern scientists like Huxley and Haldane came to believe that multiplying perspectives was the best path to knowledge; no single perspective would do.

This chapter maps the travels of animal perspectives across science, philosophy, and literature in modernist Britain. Comparative psychology evolved in the late nineteenth and early twentieth centuries embroiled in debates over whether animals' subjective experiences could be studied in a scientific way – while skeptics and behaviorists answered, "no," most comparative psychologists said "yes." Russell studied comparative psychology in the teens as he developed his theory of mind, and his redefinition of subjectivity reflects an empiricist intellectual lineage shared with the comparative psychologists. Huxley and Haldane, meanwhile, took up comparative psychology in their essays "Philosophic Ants" and "Possible Worlds," using the field's questions about animal perspectives as a thought experiment to reshape the epistemological foundations of science itself.

These scientific and philosophical forays into animal perspectives form the context in which Woolf wrote her fictional representations of animal subjects, primarily in "The Mark on the Wall" (1917), "Kew Gardens" (1919), and *Flush* (1933). Woolf was probably not directly acquainted with the scientific literature on animal psychology, but she

---

[10] Peter Garratt discusses the trajectory of British empiricism in the nineteenth century as questions about the subjectivity of the perceiving self came to the fore. He argues that the skepticism about epistemology we usually associate with modernism actually has its roots in the Victorian period. See Peter Garratt, *Victorian Empiricism: Self, Knowledge, and Reality in Ruskin, Bain, Lewes, Spencer, and George Eliot* (Fairleigh Dickinson University Press, 2010).

[11] Rohman, *Stalking the Subject*, 69–72.

was acquainted with Huxley, Haldane, and Russell, and thus with the ideas about knowledge and subjectivity that became attached to animal perspectives in modernist scientific thought. Russell, Huxley, and Haldane were peripheral members of the Bloomsbury circle that centered on Woolf and her sister, Vanessa Bell. All were visitors to Garsington Manor, the home of Lady Ottoline Morrell and a popular destination for the London intelligentsia. Woolf, Russell, and Haldane would also have met at the Cambridge Heretics Society, a group founded in 1909 for intellectual debate and the promotion of unorthodox views.[12]

For Woolf, animal perspectives offered a way to challenge fusty, patriarchal orthodoxies about knowledge. They also provided a method for aesthetic experimentation, defamiliarizing the London haunts Woolf and her friends knew so well. Most importantly, animal perspectives helped Woolf explore the limits, and the necessity, of empathic epistemology. Pursuing further the paths laid down by Huxley, Haldane, Russell, and the comparative psychologists, Woolf's fiction meditates on the challenges and possibilities that arise when the empiricist self aims to move beyond direct experience and apprehend the revelatory strangeness of animal worlds.

4.1   Comparative Psychology and the Problem of Animal Experience

Comparative psychology was, in the period between 1890 and 1930, a modernist discipline, aligned with modernist literary themes such as a plurality of perspectives, an exploration of consciousness, and a desire to denaturalize our own point of view and see the world through different eyes. As Lorraine Daston argues, comparative psychology's preoccupation with animal *perspectives* is a historically specific phenomenon. Before the

---

[12] See Ann Banfield, *The Phantom Table: Woolf, Fry, Russell and the Epistemology of Modernism* (Cambridge University Press, 2000) for an account of Woolf and Russell's acquaintance. Woolf was also a casual acquaintance of Huxley's (though she was better friends with Aldous); she mentions him in a 1935 diary entry but says she did not recognize him at first; see Virginia Woolf, *The Diary of Virginia Woolf*, vol. 4, ed. Anne Olivier Bell and Andrew McNeillie (Harcourt Brace Jovanovich, 1982), 357. It seems likely that they would have met in the teens at Garsington Manor as well – Huxley was a frequent visitor; see Huxley, *Memories*, vol. 1, 114. Woolf's acquaintance with Haldane is more difficult to document. Holly Henry claims, in *Virginia Woolf and the Discourse of Science*, that Woolf read and knew Haldane (3, 68). The only specific meeting between Woolf and Haldane that I have been able to uncover is described in the appendix to *The Essays of Virginia Woolf*, vol. 3, which states that when Woolf went to Cambridge in 1924 to deliver her "Character in Fiction" lecture to the Heretics Society, she had dinner with several people "including the eminent Heretic J. B. S. Haldane" (501).

late nineteenth century, people were certainly interested in animal minds, but they did not conceptualize knowledge about these other minds in terms of putting oneself in the animal's place or inhabiting its point of view. Contrasting the late Victorian study of animal minds with the medieval study of angels, Daston points out that while medieval theologians wanted to understand angels' structures of thinking, they would never have put the question in terms of what it is like to be an angel. Only with the nineteenth-century rise of objectivity and subjectivity, Daston claims, did the question of what it is subjectively like to be an animal come to dominate the study of animal cognition.[13]

Early animal psychologists had fairly consistent ideas about what animal consciousness was like. It was, they believed, embodied rather than cerebral, passive rather than active, ruled by sensation rather than thought. The American comparative psychologist Edward Thorndike affords a representative example of how the typical turn-of-the-century scientist understood animal experience. Thorndike was not especially sentimental or sympathetic when it came to animals. He eschewed all but the most rigidly experimental methods for studying animal minds, and some of his experiments in a Columbia University laboratory were criticized for being cruel and unfeeling.[14] Yet when it came to describing what it felt like to be an animal, Thorndike could not help waxing poetic. In *Animal Intelligence* (1911) he wrote that when watching animals, one "gets, or fancies he gets, a fairly definite idea of what the intellectual life of a cat or dog feels like." It is a kind of consciousness, he claims, that "contains little thought about anything," one in which "we feel the sense-impulses in their first intention, so to speak, when we feel our own body, and the impulses we give to it." Thorndike compared animal consciousness to the kind of experience humans might have when swimming:

> One feels the water, the sky, the birds above, but with no thoughts *about* them or memories of how they looked at other times, or aesthetic judgments about their beauty; one feels no *ideas* about what movements he will make, but feels himself to make them, feels his body throughout.

[13] Lorraine Daston, "Intelligences: Angelic, Animal, Human," in *Thinking with Animals: New Perspectives on Anthropomorphism*, ed. Lorraine Daston and Gregg Mitman (Columbia University Press, 2005): 37–58.

[14] Robert Boakes, *From Darwin to Behaviourism: Psychology and the Minds of Animals* (Cambridge University Press, 1983), 72. Thorndike was accused of keeping his animals in a state close to starvation and of confining them in small, unnatural boxes. Boakes suggests that the criticism was unfounded, and that "the condition had been far less drastic" than Thorndike's critics assumed (72).

> Self-consciousness dies away. The meanings, and values, and connections
> of things die away. One feels sense-impressions, has impulses, feels the
> movements he makes; that is all.[15]

Thorndike's lyrical evocation of animal consciousness makes it seem
appealing in the way that meditation and yoga seem appealing: as a
retreat from the stresses of intellectual work, social demands, or ideology. Repeating the word "feel" six times in this short passage, Thorndike
establishes his main claim about animal consciousness: it is dominated by
feeling, not thinking. It represents a more direct and embodied relationship with the environment. It is, for Thorndike, a purer state of being.

Many other scientists and writers shared Thorndike's understanding of
animal consciousness, and it formed an important alternative strand of
modernist primitivism. The animal life of pure sensation that Thorndike
describes is not one of primal violence, as Freud or Hemingway envisioned. Nor is it one of unrestrained sexual passion, as Lawrence thought.
Instead, comparative psychology's primitivism fixates on the mundane,
passive experiences of animals and humans – the way water feels against
skin, the way sunlight looks, the colors in a field of vision. Filtered
through the prism of empiricism rather than Freudianism, comparative
psychology's primitivism romanticizes not deep-seated, dark instincts, but
sensations at the porous border between self and environment.

Though comparative psychologists had distinct ideas about what animals' subjective experiences were like, substantiating these ideas proved
difficult. Margaret Floy Washburn's textbook *The Animal Mind*, first published in 1908, defends the scientific legitimacy of comparative psychology, but also expresses the epistemological unease that characterized the
field. "We have wonderfully advanced, within the last twenty-five years,
in knowledge as to how the world looks from the point of view of our
brother animals," she claims in the 1926 third edition, citing hundreds
of scientific studies that purport to answer questions about animals' cognitive abilities, learning processes, and sensory perceptions.[16] But while
she is sanguine about her discipline's accomplishments, she does not
gloss over its epistemological fuzziness. To begin with, the assumption
that animals have minds – or even that other humans have minds – is
an inference on which most of psychology (save behaviorism) rests, and
yet one that cannot be proven. "The science of human psychology," she
writes, "has to reckon with this unbridgeable gap between minds as its

[15] Edward Lee Thorndike, *Animal Intelligence: Experimental Studies* (Macmillan, 1911), 123.
[16] Washburn, *The Animal Mind*, 3rd ed., 22.

chief difficulty."[17] The gap between the human psychologist and the animal, however, is even larger. As Washburn says, "If my neighbor's mind is a mystery to me, how great is the mystery which looks out of the eyes of a dog, and how insoluble the problem presented by the mind of an invertebrate animal, an ant or a spider!"[18]

The mystery deepens when Washburn considers that other species have different sense organs than humans and thus experience sensations we know nothing of. "[W]e cannot imagine a color or a sound or a smell that we have never experienced," she says; "how much less the sensations of a sense radically different from any that we possess!"[19] Dogs live in a world of smells we never perceive; birds and other animals see colors invisible to humans; whales communicate using sounds beyond humans' range of hearing. As the philosopher Thomas Nagel famously argued, it is virtually impossible to imagine how a bat experiences echolocation, since humans have no sense quite like it.[20] What Washburn's words suggest is that, after comparative psychology, we cannot assume our human view of the world is true and complete. We must recognize that many animals have sensory experiences, and even something like knowledge, which we lack.

Washburn alludes to the empiricist foundations of comparative psychology by quoting John Locke. Locke says that no mind can "invent or frame one new simple idea," and Washburn cites this claim as evidence that we cannot imagine some of the colors, sounds, or smells that other animals experience.[21] Locke's empiricist philosophy proposes that we have no innate knowledge; the mind is a tabula rasa, to be imprinted with knowledge derived from sensory experiences. Comparative psychologists mostly shared this assumption, and it is one of the major points of division between comparative psychology and classical ethology. Ethologists like Konrad Lorenz and Niko Tinbergen were more interested in studying animals' inborn, instinctive behaviors, while comparative psychologists focused instead on animals' sensations and learned behaviors.

Conwy Lloyd Morgan, one of the earliest and most influential comparative psychologists, promoted this empiricist foundation for the field in books like *Animal Life and Intelligence* (1891) and *Introduction to Comparative Psychology* (1894). A student of Darwin's protégé George

[17] Washburn, *The Animal Mind*, 1st ed. (Macmillan, 1908), 1.
[18] Ibid., 2.
[19] Ibid., 3.
[20] Nagel, "What Is It Like to Be a Bat?" 438.
[21] Washburn, *The Animal Mind*, 1st ed., 3.

Romanes, Morgan combined a Lockean stress on the primacy of sensation with a Darwinian insistence on the continuity between human and animal minds. "The sense-experience," Morgan writes, "forms the foundation of our psychical life; and it can hardly be questioned that it forms the foundation of the psychical life of animals."[22] What *is* questionable is whether animals' sense-experiences can be known in any scientific sense. Writing about bees, Morgan observes, "It is not improbable that the ocelli serve mainly the purpose of directing the insect to a glimmer of light, the opening of the nest, for example; while the method of vision in the many-facetted eyes, the so-called mosaic vision, is quite different from anything of which we have or can have experience."[23] He goes on to ask, "[M]ust not one infer that the nature of the sense-experience of this insect is a secret she keeps to herself, even if she be philosopher enough to fancy she has guessed it?"[24] His prose at once enacts comparative psychological knowledge – the function of the bee's ocelli – and renounces the very possibility of it.

Morgan's playful suggestion that the bee might herself be a philosopher points to comparative psychology's epistemological relativism. If knowledge emerges from sensory experience, and animals have different sensory experiences from humans, then human knowledge must be relative, merely one "philosophy" among many. H. G. Wells picked up on this relativism in a mostly positive review of *An Introduction to Comparative Psychology*. Noting that Morgan did not believe animals other than humans could reason or form abstract concepts, Wells responds that dogs, having "a power of olfactory discrimination infinitely beyond our own, may have on that basis a something not strictly 'rational' perhaps, but higher than mere association and analogous to and parallel with the rational." Wells goes on to tease the author: "It may even be that Professor Lloyd Morgan's dog, experimenting on Professor Lloyd Morgan with a dead rat or bone to develop some point bearing upon olfactory relationships, would arrive at a very low estimate indeed of the powers of the human mind."[25] Wells is poking fun at Morgan for a certain lack of imagination in evaluating the mental abilities of animals, but in fact Morgan was more imaginative than Wells gives him credit for: he

[22] C. Lloyd Morgan, *An Introduction to Comparative Psychology* [1894], ed. Daniel N. Robison (University Publications of America, 1977), 157.
[23] Ibid., 158.
[24] Ibid., 159.
[25] H. G. Wells, "The Mind in Animals," *The Saturday Review*, 22 December 1894, 683–4, quote on 684.

anticipated Wells's comedic figure of the dog as scientist by imagining the bee as a potential philosopher.

Comparative psychology's relativism is perhaps best expressed in its language of "worlds." The notion of animal worlds is commonly associated with the German biologist Jakob von Uexküll, whose 1934 book *A Foray into the Worlds of Animals and Humans* aimed to understand the *Umwelten*, translated as "worlds" or "environments," of different creatures. Uexküll argued that an animal's world consists of "perception signs" attached to objects in the environment that are significant to that animal. The tick, for instance, lives in an *Umwelt* composed of three perception signs: the smell of a mammal, the feeling of skin, and the temperature of the mammal whose blood it feeds on. Other animals have more complicated *Umwelten*, but they operate in essentially the same way.[26] Uexküll, however, was not the first to suggest that different animals inhabit different subjective worlds. Morgan too used the rhetoric of worlds to understand animal minds. "[W]e must remember," he cautions readers, "that it is not merely that the same world is differently mirrored in different minds, but that they are two different worlds. If there is any truth in what I have urged in the last chapter, we *construct* the world that we see." Comparing the minds of dogs and humans, Morgan continues, "The question, then, is not – How does the world mirror itself in the mind of the dog? but rather – How far does the symbolic world of the dog resemble the symbolic world of man?"[27] Forty years before Uexküll, Morgan pointed out that it would be wrong to assume we as humans have objective knowledge of the singular world. Instead, both humans and dogs construct worlds; both worlds are mediated by the subject's biology; and neither is more or less real than the other.

Morgan devoted most of his career to comparative psychology, but late in life he began to express more serious doubts about scientific method as a tool for understanding animals. In 1912 he wrote to Henry Eliot Howard, "I often think that a sort of unanalyzed sympathetic artistic sense sets a man nearer to the secret of the animal mind than scientific thought which is at home in the midst of a more intellectual mode of psychological development."[28] Intuition, he suggested, might get us just as close to understanding animal minds as scientific practice does. We might even say that Morgan came to lose faith in the possibility of a

---

[26] Uexküll, *A Foray into the Worlds of Animals and Humans*, 50–1.
[27] C. Lloyd Morgan, *Animal Life and Intelligence* (E. Arnold, 1891), 336.
[28] Quoted in Burkhardt, *Patterns of Behavior*, 94–5. The quote is originally from a letter addressed to Howard, dated 29 May 1912, in the Howard Papers at Oxford University.

scientifically reliable answer to the problem of other minds, and instead placed his faith in the empathic possibilities of art. In the meantime, as psychologist Alan Costall has argued, Morgan's work inadvertently contributed to the rise of behaviorism. Morgan's *Introduction to Comparative Psychology* contained the following proscription, known now as Morgan's Canon: "In no case is an animal activity to be interpreted in terms of higher psychological processes if it can be fairly interpreted in terms of processes which stand lower in the scale of psychological evolution and development." Morgan certainly did not mean to foreclose all appeals to animal consciousness or intelligence in explaining animal behaviors, but, Costall argues, that is exactly how most of his followers interpreted it.[29]

Thus the "fall" of comparative psychology in the 1920s and 1930s. In its place emerged John B. Watson's school of behaviorism, which ruled introspection an inadmissible method for psychology, and Niko Tinbergen's ethology, which similarly excluded any study of the subjective meanings of animal behaviors. Watson and Tinbergen did not deny that animals might have consciousness, but they did declare animal consciousness outside the scope of science; as Watson wrote, "One can assume either the presence or absence of consciousness anywhere in the phylogenetic scale without affecting the problems of behavior by one jot or tittle; and without influencing in any way the mode of experimental attack upon them."[30] Turn-of-the-century comparative psychology welcomed uncertainty, subjectivity, and imaginative forays into animal worlds as a part of science. But by the 1930s, a new division of labor had emerged: experimentally verifiable animal behaviors belonged to science, imagined animal perspectives to art.

4.2   Russell and the Subject as Sense-Data

Between science and art we might locate Bertrand Russell, a philosopher and Bloomsbury compatriot who shared the comparative psychologists' empiricist background. Russell is best known today for his *Principia Mathematica* (1910–13), coauthored with Alfred North Whitehead, and for works like *The ABC of Relativity* (1925), which popularized modern physics. He was also a political activist who went to prison during World War I for his pacifist activities. And he was a regular visitor to

---

[29] Alan Costall, "Lloyd Morgan and the Rise and Fall of 'Animal Psychology,'" *Society and Animals* 6.1 (1998): 13–29.

[30] John B. Watson, "Psychology as the Behaviorist Views It," *The Psychological Review* 20.2 (1913): 158–77, quote on 161.

Garsington Manor during the teens, where he befriended the Woolfs, D. H. Lawrence, Aldous Huxley, and other writers. First and foremost, though, Russell was a philosopher, and during the period 1912–21 he developed a philosophy founded on sensations and "sense-data." As Ann Banfield demonstrates in *The Phantom Table*, Russell's philosophy was an important influence on Woolf; I would add that comparative psychology was an important influence on Russell, and that his work helped to disseminate comparative psychological ideas about subjectivity. Russell's early work disentangled the concept of "perspective" from the human subject, while *The Analysis of Mind* (1921) extended concepts borrowed from animal psychology to humans. Russell's ventures into philosophy and psychology show that he rejected common-sense notions of mind and envisioned instead a zoomorphic human subject, modeled after the animal subjects of comparative psychology.

Russell's early philosophy reconceptualizes the physical world through the language of the senses. He outlines, in *Our Knowledge of the External World* (1914) and "The Relation of Sense-Data to Physics" (1914), an account of physical matter *as* sense-data. We are used to thinking of an object, such as a table, as a solid, unchanging thing that merely appears different depending upon where we are standing. A person standing at the head of a table receives different sensory impressions than a person standing at its side, but we do not think of this as any indication that the table itself is different. Russell, however, argues that the "table" *is* in fact a series of related sense-data, and not a single, consistent object. "All the aspects of a thing are real," he writes, "whereas the thing is a merely logical construction."[31] Russell's language echoes Morgan, who claimed that "we *construct* the world that we see" and that different creatures' constructed worlds are equally real. Russell is making an even more counterintuitive claim; however, he regards sense-data "as not mental, and as being, in fact, part of the actual subject-matter of physics."[32] It is sense-data, rather than matter (or mind), that is the essence of the world.

The world according to Russell is thus a system of perspectives. By "perspective," however, he does not mean a psychological perspective belonging to a conscious subject, but instead a spatial, geometric perspective. In *The Analysis of Mind*, he clarifies that a perspective can, but need not, be occupied by a human or a living thing. Photographic plates, he suggests, afford the best example of a nonmental entity with

[31] Bertrand Russell, *Our Knowledge of the External World* [1914] (W.W. Norton, 1929), 94.
[32] Bertrand Russell, *Mysticism and Logic* [1910] (W.W. Norton, 1929), 149.

a perspective; they receive and record sense-data with no semblance of a mind.[33] When perspectives *are* inhabited by subjects, Russell considers these subjects more similar to the photographic plate than to any traditional concept of self. The subject, for him, is not a preexisting entity that *has* sensations; instead, experiences of sense-data *constitute* the subject.[34] As Banfield argues, one of the central goals of Russell's philosophical project is to "par[e] down the I."[35] Russell's philosophy reenvisions the subject as the perspective, a concept that levels out human, animal, and mechanical points of view. Subjects of the liberal humanist or psychoanalytic sorts are nowhere in Russell's work, but subjectivity is everywhere.

Russell distinguishes semantically between perspectives that are inhabited by a human or animal subject and those that are not, using the term "private worlds" to describe the former.[36] Like Morgan before him and Haldane and Uexküll after, Russell sees in the plurality of "worlds" a more apt designation than the singular "world" to describe the things around us. "Worlds" and "perspectives" emphasize that there is no single perfect, objective world or perspective in his philosophy. These words also minimize the contribution of the conscious self in favor of the subject's *position*. Worlds function as spaces that the subject may inhabit and outlooks that the subject may take, but exist prior to and independent of the subject itself.

Thus far it seems that Russell has little, if anything, to say about "mind" or psychology. And it is true that he thought philosophy should not assume the existence of consciousness a priori, but should approach the concept with skepticism. Yet he is not quite the advocate of impersonality or reductionist materialism that he might seem from the discussion above. In fact, Russell took a "psychological turn" around 1918 in preparation for writing *The Analysis of Mind*, and his foray into psychology depended on the interventions of the comparative psychologists. Works like *Our Knowledge of the External World* tear down humanist understandings of mind by reducing it to a holding-place for sense-data; *The Analysis of Mind*, written after Russell read up on comparative psychology, builds a new understanding of the mind that is sparer and more zoomorphic than the old one.

Russell began studying psychology in prison, where he read the works of many comparative psychologists include Thorndike,

---

[33] Bertrand Russell, *The Analysis of Mind* [1921] (George Allen & Unwin, 1949), 129–31.
[34] Ibid., 13.
[35] Banfield, *The Phantom Table*, 162.
[36] Russell, *Our Knowledge of the External World*, 93.

Washburn, Morgan, and Watson.[37] Watson plays a major role in *The Analysis of Mind*, and what Richard F. Kitchener calls a "flirtation with behaviorism" is a central act in Russell's psychological turn.[38] Watson called for psychology to be an objective science. This meant rejecting introspective methods of investigation and making empirically observable behaviors, rather than mental states, the object of study. He ran his psychological experiments on rats without caring about the rats' conscious processes; the psychology of humans, he argued, should similarly "dispense with consciousness."[39] Mental states, in his schema, could be reduced to "faint throat, chest, and laryngeal movements." Thinking was, he insisted, a physiological activity not qualitatively different from playing tennis.[40]

Behaviorism attracted Russell because he too doubted the existence of consciousness, at least as it is normally conceived. His doubt reflects the influence not just of Watson, but also of Franz Brentano and William James, two of the "empiricist psychologists" that, Judith Ryan argues, contributed to the turn-of-the-century redefinition of the subject as "a fluid, unbounded self essentially composed of sense impressions, a self that was not distinct from its surroundings."[41] Consciousness is not empirically observable, and Russell though that any philosophy or science worth its salt should not assume its existence a priori. Furthermore, "paring down the I" is a keystone of Russell's philosophy, and behaviorism represents one logical extension of this train of thought. Behaviorism pares down the "I" until there is no "I" left at all.

Yet Russell stops short of the behaviorists, reaching an account of mind that is closer to that of comparative psychologists like Morgan than to behaviorist psychologists like Watson. In his attempt to distil the concept of mind to its essence, Russell reaches two irreducible parts: sensations and images, a word he uses to mean remembered sensations. The latter is an exclusively mental phenomenon, corresponding to

---

[37] Russell's list of "Philosophical books read in prison" (1918) includes Washburn's *The Animal Mind*, along with many works on human psychology; *The Analysis of Mind* cites Thorndike, Morgan, and Watson. See "Appendix III: Philosophical Books Read in Prison," in *The Collected Papers of Bertrand Russell*, vol. 8, ed. John G. Slater (George Allen & Unwin, 1986): 315–28.

[38] Richard F. Kitchener, "Bertrand Russell's Flirtation with Behaviorism," *Behavior and Philosophy* 32.2 (2004): 273–91.

[39] Watson, "Psychology as the Behaviorist Views It," 176.

[40] John B. Watson, "*The Analysis of Mind*, Bertrand Russell," *The Dial* 72 (1922): 98; quoted in Kitchener, "Bertrand Russell's Flirtation with Behaviorism," 281–2.

[41] Ryan, *The Vanishing Self*, 12. For Brentano and James's influence on Russell, see Russell, *The Analysis of Mind*, 9–26.

nothing in the observable world, and thus inadmissible to the behaviorists.[42] Images are accessible only through introspection. So are private sensations, such as feelings in our own bodies that cannot be observed externally but are nevertheless real.[43] Thus, introspection cannot be entirely eliminated from the practice of psychology. In short, Russell diverges from the behaviorists because he believes psychology must account for an internal mental life. This mental life is, at its heart, nothing more than sensations and their echoes, but for Russell it is real and it is not fully explicable through external observation alone.

Russell's notion of mental life sounds a lot like the comparative psychologists' notion of what it is like to be an animal. And like most comparative psychologists, Russell believed that humans' and animals' mental lives are not qualitatively different. He encourages his readers "to remember that from the protozoa to man there is nowhere a very wide gap either in structure or in behaviour. From this fact it is a highly probable inference that there is also nowhere a very wide mental gap."[44] Assuming mental continuity among all species, Russell contends that "there is probably more to be learnt about human psychology from animals than about animal psychology from human beings."[45] The statement flips the script of anthropomorphism; rather than anthropomorphizing animals, Russell proposes zoomorphizing humans. What many psychologists would agree is true of other species – that their experience is composed of sensations (present and past) and not subordinated to a coherent ego – Russell argues is true of humans as well.

In applying animal psychology to humans, Russell creates a vision of the human that is more in accord with modernist versions of subjectivity, particularly Woolf's.[46] Recasting mind in terms of perspectives, Russell's works elevate sensations and images themselves at the expense of the

---

[42] Russell, *The Analysis of Mind*, 144–52.

[43] Ibid., 117.

[44] Ibid., 41.

[45] Ibid., 43.

[46] In this claim I am in agreement with Banfield, who identifies parallels between the Russellian and Woolfian subjects (though Banfield does not address the role of animal psychology's ideas about subjectivity in contributing to these parallels). Timothy Mackin, in "Private Worlds, Public Minds: Woolf, Russell, and Photographic Vision," *Journal of Modern Literature* 33.3 (2010): 112–30, has made a counterargument that Woolf disagrees with Russell's ideas about private worlds and mental life, saying, "Woolf clearly does have her suspicions of the 'I,' but that doesn't mean she is willing to abandon the personal" (121). I think Mackin is right about Woolf, but wrong about Russell. Despite Russell's desire to get rid of concepts like "consciousness" that are not empirically verifiable, he never quite eradicates the personal – it remains a key part of his theory of mind in the form of private sensations and images.

experiencing subject. We learn, from studying animals, that we are like them. Despite humans' belief in our own complicated selfhood, Russell argues that we are actually, like the animals, mere bundles of sensations and images, open to and constituted by the sense-data of the world.

4.3   Huxley, Haldane, and the Philosophical Animals

Enter Julian Huxley and J. B. S. Haldane, close friends, fellow biologists, popular science writers and, like Russell, inheritors of comparative psychology. Both had a reputation for "scientism" – the belief that science represents the most reliable way of knowing the world and that scientific progress is the key to human progress. The reputation is not undeserved, and yet Huxley and Haldane also brought their scientific skepticism to bear on science itself, expressing wariness about its promises of knowledge and objectivity. In Huxley's "Philosophic Ants" (1922) and Haldane's "Possible Worlds" (1927), the authors reflected on "biological relativity" and how it colors and limits scientific knowledge. And crucially, both used the trope of the animal philosopher or animal scientist in their essays, a trope we have already seen in Morgan's philosophic bee and H. G. Wells's scientific dog. The figure of the philosophical animal helped Huxley and Haldane put human knowledge in perspective.

Huxley's "Philosophic Ants: A Biologic Fantasy" begins with a fable of intelligent ants. Ants are ectothermic creatures whose rates of activity depend on temperature. These intelligent ants thus notice not that some days seem warmer than others, but that some days seem to last longer than others. Attempting to make sense of their oddly-rhythmed world, the intelligent ants progress from religious to scientific explanations. This bit of fiction, clearly an allegory for the Scientific Revolution and the persecution of early scientific thinkers like Galileo, also paves the way for Huxley's reflections on "biological relativity." Biological relativity represents Huxley's attempt to import the concept of relativity, then in vogue in English intellectual circles, from physics to the life sciences. Physics tells us that two observers, traveling at different speeds, will make different observations about the motion of a third object, and both will be right. Huxley's notion of biological relativity says that two observers (say, an ant and a human), equipped with different biological traits, will make different observations about the external world, and both will be right.

The upshot of Huxley's ant fable is to relativize humans' empirical knowledge of the world. "We are," he says, "but parochial creatures endowed only with sense-organs giving information about the agencies normally found in our own little environment."[47] This insight is similar to Morgan's recognition that the dog and the human both live in "symbolic worlds." The project that Huxley begins in "Philosophic Ants," and Haldane finishes in "Possible Worlds," is to extend that claim from the realm of psychology into the realm of the philosophy of science. Huxley and Haldane recognized the relativity of human knowledge, but they also looked for ways to reconcile this relativism with their faith that human knowledge could still be expanded and made more reliable through scientific practice.

"Possible Worlds," which cites "Philosophic Ants" and is clearly inspired by it, aims to reexamine our assumptions about the nature of reality by "considering whether a plausible world or a coherent experience might not exist in which they are not fulfilled."[48] Haldane challenges common sense through a series of thought experiments in which he constructs hypothetical "possible worlds," many belonging to hyperintelligent animals. "How does the world appear to a being with different senses or instincts from our own?" he asks, "and if such beings postulated a reality behind these appearances, what would they regard as real?"[49] The essay goes on to explore how a dog, barnacle, and bee, endowed with different senses and instincts, might perceive and make sense of the world.

Perhaps the most memorable character in "Possible Worlds" is the philosophical barnacle, Haldane's rejoinder to Huxley's philosophic ants. The barnacle is rooted to a surface, where it can move its arms and stalks to "explore a sharply limited volume of space."[50] It has a crude sense of sight and of direction, but no more:

> 'The world,' it says, 'is what we can sweep with our arms. Things come into it, and my visions are of some use to me in telling me of things that will come into being in it, but they are notoriously deceptive. I know that when a vision becomes very large it is time for me to shut my shell, though sometimes even a very large vision does not portend any real event ... Visions are visions and realities are realities, and no good will come of mixing them up.'[51]

Like Huxley, Haldane turns to the conventions of fable, whimsically endowing the barnacle with language and philosophy. Beneath this anthropomorphism, however, lies a realistic foundation of barnacle

[47] Huxley, *Essays of a Biologist*, 161.
[48] Haldane, *Possible Worlds*, 261.
[49] Ibid., 264–5.
[50] Ibid., 276.
[51] Ibid., 277.

sense-experience. The barnacle constructs its world from sensations past and present. Its mind, like a Lockean tabula rasa, is inscribed with the patterns of experience. The barnacle's speech teaches us that there is nothing inevitable about associating seeing with believing. Had we evolved to have poor eyesight and excellent senses of hearing or smell, we would structure our notion of reality differently.

Haldane was not a pure empiricist, though; he recognized that animal minds are not truly tabulae rasae, but come preetched with instincts. Here it is worth mentioning that Haldane was a geneticist and a key figure in the modern evolutionary synthesis, which combined natural selection with Mendelian genetics. As a geneticist, Haldane attributed mental phenomena partly to inherited traits such as instincts, not solely to environmental factors such as sense-experience. Take, for example, an animal with highly developed instincts, like the bee. How would a thinking bee explain the nature of reality? Haldane says that a bee's instincts would lead it to consider duties the principal component of reality and external objects only a secondary component. "I do not see why we should deny the bee the reality of her duty world," he declares. "Duties are, I suspect, as real as material things, which is not perhaps saying much."[52]

The point of these thought experiments is to demonstrate that our knowledge depends on our human senses and instincts, and that our perspective is just one among many. Our knowledge of the world is constrained by our biology. "My own suspicion," wrote Haldane, "is that the universe is not only queerer than we suppose, but queerer than we *can* suppose."[53] We can make progress in debunking common sense and imagining other perspectives, but eventually we will hit a wall. Haldane seemed to take pleasure in these limitations, asserting, "I do not feel that any of us know enough about the possible kinds of being and thought, to make it worth while taking any of our metaphysical systems very much more seriously than those at which a thinking barnacle might arrive."[54]

Yet Haldane also remained optimistic about the future of science because there is still much to be learned from taking other perspectives into account. Though "our present ignorance of animal psychology" means that his hypothetical creatures are probably far from their real-world counterparts, the qualifier "present" suggests that Haldane believed scientists would better comprehend animal minds in the future. Indeed,

[52] Ibid., 273.
[53] Ibid., 286.
[54] Ibid., 280.

an understanding of animal perspectives plays a crucial role in the development of science itself for Haldane. "Our only hope of understanding the universe," he declared, "is to look at it from as many different points of view as possible."[55]

This faith that it is possible to look at the universe from other points of view connects Haldane and Huxley to Russell. Though all three wrote out of the empiricist tradition, they also believed in a form of empathic epistemology that allows us to know things beyond our own direct experience. Empathic epistemology is what allows us to emerge from our own private worlds and build collective kinds of knowledge, like philosophy and science. Russell, Huxley, and Haldane all rejected solipsism; as Russell said, "I do not think this theory [solipsism] can be refuted, but I also do not think that anybody can sincerely believe it."[56] Likewise, the stance that animal minds are fully opaque to us cannot be refuted, but few who spend any amount of time observing animals can sincerely believe it.

"Philosophic Ants" and "Possible Worlds" are not themselves works of comparative psychology, but instead theoretical exercises in constructing knowledge from different subject positions. Yet comparative psychology's influence on both essays is evident. It led Huxley and Haldane to employ the fiction of the philosophical animal, to recognize that knowledge is subjective, and to embrace introspection and speculation within scientific thinking. The scientist's perspective, as we learned from Morgan, is already subjective, conditioned by his or her human frames of reference and human senses. But Huxley and Haldane suggest that we can still garner knowledge from other points of view. We remain, like the barnacle, rooted in our own perspectives, but we can stretch outside of them.

4.4   Woolf and the Aesthetics of Animal Experience

Virginia Woolf wrote frequently about animals: butterflies, moths, birds, cats, and dogs populate her work and reveal a naturalist's fascination with other creatures. Woolf's engagement with natural history has drawn attention from other critics.[57] Most notably, Gillian Beer has explored

[55] Ibid., 285–6.
[56] Bertrand Russell, *My Philosophical Development* [1959] (Routledge, 1995), 78.
[57] For studies of *Lepidoptera* in Woolf, see Rachel Sarsfield, "From the Chrysalis to the Display Case: The Butterfly's 'Voyage Out' in Virginia Woolf," in *Insect Poetics*, ed. Eric C. Brown (University of Minnesota Press, 2006): 87–111; Harvena Richter, "Hunting the Moth: Virginia Woolf and the Creative Imagination," in *Virginia Woolf: Revaluation and Continuity*, ed. Ralph Freedman (University of California Press, 1980): 13–28; and Christine Froula, "Out of the Chrysalis: Female

how Darwinian ideas about time and prehistory infused Woolf's writing.[58] Bonnie Kime Scott, meanwhile, suggests that Woolf's fiction revisits her childhood forays into natural history, especially insect-collecting.[59] And Christina Alt argues that Woolf's animals and plants reflect awareness of both Victorian natural history and modern biology. Alt shows that Woolf admired the ethology of W. H. Hudson, the proto-ecological entomology of Eleanor Ormerod, and the laboratory biology of Marie Stopes.[60] Not only did Woolf appreciate the new approaches to the study of nature, she also used them to help articulate her literary theory, which rejects pinning down and taxonomic classification in favor of observing life in its fleeting, ever-changing movement. For Woolf, Alt concludes, "writing is not a process of capturing, classifying, and arranging words for display, but rather one of observing and recording the behaviour of words," as if they were themselves animals.[61]

Ecocritics have also begun to reclaim Woolf as an environmentally sensitive writer, and her animals can be understood as part of her ecological consciousness. Most notably, Louise Westling and Kelly Sultzbach have explored parallels between Woolf's writing and the ecophenomenology of Maurice Merleau-Ponty. Merleau-Ponty, whose 1957–8 "Nature" lectures drew on embryology, Jakob von Uexküll's *Umwelten*, and Konrad Lorenz's ethological work on animal instincts, "[built] a case for the profound interrelationship of creatures with their environments," Westling writes.[62] For Merleau-Ponty as for Woolf, "our sensations are the active expression of relationship, a continuing *communion* with the living world."[63] Sultzbach, meanwhile, explores how Woolf's evocations of the sensory world prefigure ecophenomenology by flattening out the divide between subject and environment in order to emphasize

---

Initiation and Female Authority in Virginia Woolf's *The Voyage Out*," in *Virginia Woolf: A Collection of Critical Essays*, ed. Margaret Homan (Prentice-Hall, 1993): 136–61. The 2010 International Conference on Virginia Woolf focused on Woolf's engagements with nature; see Kristin Czarnecki and Carrie Rohman, eds., *Virginia Woolf and the Natural World: Selected Papers from the Twentieth Annual International Conference on Virginia Woolf* (Clemson University Digital Press, 2011). Animal studies criticism of Woolf will be discussed later in this chapter.

[58] Gillian Beer, "Virginia Woolf and Prehistory," in *Arguing with the Past: Essays in Narrative from Woolf to Sidney*, by Gillian Beer (Routledge, 1999): 159–82.

[59] Bonnie Kime Scott, *In the Hollow of the Wave: Virginia Woolf and Modernist Uses of Nature* (University of Virginia Press, 2012), 42–70.

[60] Alt, *Virginia Woolf and the Study of Nature*, 152–4, 135–47, 114–27.

[61] Ibid., 190.

[62] Louise Westling, "Merleau-Ponty's Human-Animality Intertwining and the Animal Question," *Configurations* 18.1–2 (2010): 161–80, quote on 167.

[63] Louise Westling, "Virginia Woolf and the Flesh of the World," *New Literary History* 30 (1999): 855–75, quote on 864.

their shared materiality and "interrelated existence."[64] Woolf's animal subjects, including the human ones, are open to their environments through their senses, and her experiments in prose aim to evoke these phenomenological worlds.

Woolf's animal subjects-in-worlds represent not only a precocious form of ecophenomenology, but also her own literary version of comparative psychology. She was acquainted with Russell, Huxley, and Haldane, and stories like "The Mark on the Wall," "Kew Gardens," and *Flush* demonstrate that she shared their interest in animal perspectives and the epistemological questions they raise. These works also show that for Woolf, writing animal subjects was an opportunity to develop some of her signature modernist techniques – a mutable point of view, defamiliarizing imagery, and delayed decoding. Woolf's thinking animals enact a zoomorphic form of subjectivity as Russell's subjects do, and they interrogate human knowledge just as the philosophical ants, barnacles, and bees of Huxley and Haldane's essays do. Her animal representations also foreground something that lies latent in Russell, Huxley, and Haldane's work: that nonhuman perspectives can be a source of aesthetic novelty and pleasure.

"The Mark on the Wall" (1917) frames animal subjectivity as an attractive alternative to complicated, inward-facing human subjectivity. The story relates the thoughts of an unnamed narrator as she observes a mark on the wall in her living room and wonders what it might be. Though her thoughts begin with and periodically return to the mark, they also spin out dizzyingly into other topics – lost possessions, Shakespeare, self-reflection, Sundays past, the South Downs, the nature of knowledge, trees, to name a few. The narrator's stream of consciousness flows rapidly and unpredictably. Only when another character speaks and identifies the mark on the wall as a snail do the narrator's speculation and the story end.

One might be tempted to read "The Mark on the Wall" as a celebration of modernism's new techniques for representing consciousness. But the narrator is troubled by the rapid upheaval in her stream of consciousness. "The inaccuracy of thought!" she despairs at one point; at another she muses, "I want to think quietly, calmly, spaciously, never to be interrupted, never to have to rise from my chair, to slip easily from one thing

[64] Sultzbach, *Ecocriticism in the Modernist Imagination*, 84.

to another, without any sense of hostility, or obstacle."[65] But thought does not accommodate this desire, manifesting itself instead in stormier ways: "Everything's moving, falling, slipping, vanishing ..."[66] Douglas Mao has argued that Woolf's work reflects a modernist backlash against human subjectivity. Modernity, he suggests, "could be construed as an affair of consciousness gone awry, a phenomenon of subjectivity grown rapacious and fantastically powerful."[67] Modernists like Woolf sought, instead, "immunity to thinking and knowing, the noble repose that comes of being out of reach of human persuasion."[68] "The Mark on the Wall" betrays this kind of doubt about human consciousness, portraying it as "inaccurate," confusing, and tempestuous. Woolf's narrator seeks the "noble repose" that lies outside of human consciousness.

The story encodes a potential solution to this fatigue by imagining animal forms of consciousness, using imagery that recalls the primitivism of comparative psychology. The narrator wishes for "a world which one could slice with one's thoughts as a fish slices the water with his fin, grazing the stems of the water-lilies, hanging suspended over nests of white sea eggs ... How peaceful it is down here, rooted in the centre of the world and gazing up through the grey waters, with their sudden gleams of light and their reflections."[69] The passage begins with a simile describing the narrator's wish for the process of thinking to be sharper, clearer, and under her control, but the paragraph is quickly derailed by the simile's second half, in which she imagines what it is like to be a fish. Echoing Thorndike's description of animal consciousness as resembling the sensations of swimming, the narrator finds pleasure in the moment when her thought is diverted to the fish's underwater world and its calm passivity. This fantasy suggests that it is most desirable not to exercise control over the stream of consciousness and "slice" the world with it, but instead to have an experience akin to the fish's. For its experience, composed of appealing impressions like the feel of the water-lilies or the look of light refracted through the water, is peaceful and passive, without intellectual struggle.

[65] Virginia Woolf, *The Complete Shorter Fiction of Virginia Woolf*, ed. Susan Dick (Harcourt Brace Jovanovich, 1985), 84–5.

[66] Ibid., 89.

[67] Mao, *Solid Objects*, 8.

[68] Ibid., 9. Mao goes on to argue that modernists turned to the object world for relief from human subjectivity and ideology.

[69] Woolf, *Complete Shorter Fiction*, 87–8; Woolf's ellipsis.

The daydream comes to an end, however, with the aside, "if it were not for Whitaker's Almanack – if it were not for the Table of Precedence!"[70] "Whitaker's Almanack" and the "Table of Precedence" allude to an earlier part of the narrator's internal monologue in which she contemplates "the masculine point of view which governs our lives, which sets the standard, which establishes Whitaker's Table of Precedence" (a table that laid out the order of rank for the English aristocracy), and which in modern times may yet "be laughed into the dustbin … leaving us all with an intoxicating sense of illegitimate freedom."[71] The almanac and table are metonymies for a restrictive and patriarchal ideological apparatus; they also represent the frustrating vagaries of human thought, asserting themselves and interrupting the reverie despite the narrator's wishes. Yet Woolf offers us a glimpse of possibility for an alternative way of being. Animal subjectivity, in the form of the fish, offers a different kind of experience.

Science and philosophy, like Whitaker's Almanack, are tied up with the patriarchal ideology that Woolf opposes, and the narrator expresses distrust of these sorts of knowledge at several points in the story. "The ignorance of humanity!" she thinks to herself.[72] "Nothing is proved, nothing is known," she declares; "And if I were to get up at this very moment and ascertain that the mark on the wall is really – what shall I say? – the head of a gigantic old nail … what should I gain? Knowledge? Matter for further speculation?"[73] To examine the mark more closely would produce some kind of empirical verification of its nature, but the narrator doubts that this would create knowledge on any but the most superficial level. Woolf criticizes the certitude of "learned men," putting their epistemology on a level with the superstitions of "witches and hermits."[74] In expressing skepticism about the truth-value of what passes for knowledge, Woolf brings to the surface an undercurrent hidden in Russell, Huxley, and Haldane's texts (those "learned men"!). While they insist that the multiplicity of perspectives allows us to reject solipsism and garner knowledge from beyond our private worlds, the fear that this provisional kind of almost-knowledge isn't good enough seems to lurk behind their claims. Only Woolf, however, actually gives voice to this fear.

[70] Ibid., 88.
[71] Ibid., 86.
[72] Ibid., 84.
[73] Ibid., 87.
[74] Ibid.

Yet Woolf shares Russell, Huxley, and Haldane's interest in opening up the horizons of knowledge and not simply discounting the very possibility of it. In the following passage, the narrator imagines inhabiting a strange point of view and attempting to construct knowledge from this vantage point:

> But after life. The slow pulling down of thick green stalks so that the cup of the flower, as it turns over, deluges one with purple and red light. Why, after all, should one not be born there as one is born here, helpless, speechless, unable to focus one's eyesight, groping at the roots of grass, at the toes of the Giants? As for saying which are trees, and which are men and women, or whether there are such things, that one won't be in a condition to do for fifty years or so. There will be nothing but spaces of light and dark, intersected by thick stalks, and rather higher up perhaps, rose-shaped blots of an indistinct colour – dim pinks and blues – which will, as time goes on, become more definite, become – I don't know what ...[75]

The passage begins by meditating on what happens "after life," perhaps from the perspective of the corpse as it is buried and plants grow over it. But at some point, the perspective changes, shifting from the dead to a subject "born there," "at the roots of grass." Holly Henry points out that this moment resonates with Haldane's "Possible Worlds" because both texts focus on "multiple and alien perspectives," especially those that operate on scales much smaller or larger than human perception. She suggests that the perspective here is that of an insect.[76] I think that it could represent an insect, or perhaps a tree, since a tree would grow taller over fifty years and things "higher up" might gradually "become more definite" for it, and since the narrator imagines tree consciousness elsewhere in the story. Whatever the subject inhabiting this private world, it is one that creates knowledge from its sensations of spaces, colors, and blots; it makes inferences about whether trees and people are real entities or not. Its nonhuman epistemology converges uncannily with the philosophical ants and barnacles of Huxley and Haldane's essays. The subject's knowledge is contingent and provisional, never reaching the level of certainty that "learned men" believe they have attained. Indeed, the narrator ends this train of thought with an acknowledgement of *not* knowing, implying that there can be no recuperation of absolute knowledge. Yet the passage suggests that seeking to know one's world empirically, while always an incomplete and flawed project, is also a way of engaging with

---

[75] Ibid., 84; Woolf's ellipses.
[76] Henry, *Virginia Woolf and the Discourse of Science*, 90.

that world on an aesthetic level. It allows one to look outward, appreciating the "rose-shaped blots" and "pinks and blues" in one's environment.

"The Mark on the Wall" explores the perspectives of a fish, a tree, and, of course, humans, but not of the snail on the wall itself. When another character remarks to the narrator, "All the same, I don't see why we should have a snail on our wall," the narrator thinks, "Ah, the mark on the wall! It was a snail," and the story ends.[77] To name the mark a snail is to fix it and thus to foreclose all the other possibilities that led to the narrator's imaginings in the first place – or so the story's logic goes. As Christina Alt suggests, the story "can be read as a deferral of classification, and conclusive categorization is presented as inimical to the creative process."[78] But in the later story "Kew Gardens" (1919), a story that Woolf envisioned as "dancing in unity" with "The Mark on the Wall," the creature that was an opaque object, a stopper in the narrator's stream of consciousness, becomes instead a fleshed-out subject.[79]

"Kew Gardens" can be read as a sequel to "The Mark on the Wall" not only because both share the snail image, but also because both stories center on the multiplicity of perspectives. While "The Mark on the Wall" spotlights a single character's protean consciousness, "Kew Gardens" embraces multiple characters as focalizers, including an animal. The story revolves around several pairs of people walking by a flowerbed, where a snail embarks on smaller-scale perambulations. The third-person narrator's vantage point at the flowerbed remains constant, but the characters move in and out of focus, their thoughts, conversations, and actions occupying a few paragraphs each. The snail, like the human characters, has thoughts and takes deliberate actions, and Woolf represents its simple experience as a richness of sensation.

Perspective shifts in "Kew Gardens" on the level of style as well as plot. The narrator's voice ranges from a third-person objective narration, in which characters are described as they would appear to an outsider, to a third-person limited narration that registers a character's thoughts, to interior monologue, and finally to the free indirect discourse for which Woolf is so well known. This mutability in the narrator's position reflects the story's thematic focus on the diversity of perspectives. Woolf's flowerbed, like Russell's table, is constituted by the different subjective views of it. And, like Huxley and Haldane, Woolf recognizes that fiction is

---

[77] Woolf, *Complete Shorter Fiction*, 89.
[78] Alt, *Virginia Woolf and the Study of Nature*, 171.
[79] Virginia Woolf, *A Writer's Diary: Being Extracts from the Diary of Virginia Woolf*, ed. Leonard Woolf (Harcourt, 2003), 22.

perhaps the best tool for capturing this array of perspectives. It is the prerogative of Woolf's third-person fictional narrator to weave in and out of different characters' private worlds.

The snail, like the flowerbed, serves as a focal point for the story. Its perspective represents an aesthetic experiment in defamiliarization as well as an exploration of animal cognition. Woolf introduces us to the snail through a passing remark in the first paragraph: "The light fell either upon the smooth grey back of a pebble, or the shell of a snail with its brown circular veins."[80] The narration here remains objective and external. Objective language introduces the snail's next appearance as well:

> In the oval flower-bed the snail, whose shell had been stained red, blue and yellow for the space of two minutes or so, now appeared to be moving very slightly in its shell, and next began to labour over the crumbs of loose earth which broke away and rolled down as it passed over them. It appeared to have a definite goal in front of it, differing in this respect from the singular high stepping angular green insect who attempted to cross in front of it, and waited for a second with its antennae trembling as if in deliberation, and then stepped off as rapidly and strangely in the opposite direction.[81]

The narrator occupies some position outside the snail and grasshopper, a vantage point from which the snail "appears" to be moving and thinking, the grasshopper's "deliberation" qualified by the phrase "as if."

At this point, however, the passage turns to a more subjective perspective as the narrator enters the mind of the snail:

> Brown cliffs with deep green lakes in the hollows, flat, blade-like trees that waved from root to tip, round boulders of grey stone, vast crumpled surfaces of a thin crackling texture – all these objects lay across the snail's progress between one stalk and another to his goal. Before he had decided whether to circumvent the arched tent of a dead leaf or to breast it there came past the bed the feet of other human beings.[82]

With the phrase "[b]rown cliffs," the narrative re-orients readers to a snail's-eye view of the garden. Woolf presents in this sentence an impressionistic micro-landscape that invites readers to see tiny pebbles and leaves and blades of grass in a new way. When we imagine ourselves looking through the eyes of a snail, the minutiae of a flowerbed become objects of wonder. Of course, we are not fully inside the snail's private

---

[80] Woolf, *Complete Shorter Fiction*, 90.
[81] Ibid., 91.
[82] Ibid., 91–2.

world here – the narration remains third person and maintains human mediation of the snail's perspective. The metaphors of cliffs, deep lakes, trees, and boulders rely on a human scale. We can only understand what seems vast to the snail by comparing it to what seems vast to us. Woolf does not ask readers to abandon their human frame of reference entirely, and indeed, it would be impossible to do so because, in Morgan's words, "we cannot think of [animal minds] in any other terms than those of human consciousness."[83] But she does fashion for us an encounter with a strange perspective, showing us glimpses of another world that partly overlaps with our own.

Woolf's snail is more than just a new lens for aesthetic contemplation, however. He is also a subject who registers his sensations in conscious thought, as becomes clear the next time the narration returns to him:

> The snail had now considered every possible method of reaching his goal without going round the dead leaf or climbing over it. Let alone the effort needed for climbing a leaf, he was doubtful whether the thin texture which vibrated with such an alarming crackle when touched even by the tips of his horns would bear his weight; and this determined him finally to creep beneath it, for there was a point where the leaf curved high enough from the ground to admit him. He had just inserted his head in the opening and was taking stock of the high brown roof and was getting used to the cool brown light when two other people came past outside on the turf.[84]

As in the accounts of the comparative psychologists, in this passage the snail's thoughts are tied directly to the sensory world – the crackle and thinness of the dead leaf, the coolness and light of its underside. The snail is no unconscious automaton; he is aware of these stimuli and what they mean. As Alt observes, he has "the ability to evaluate conditions, feel doubt, and make decisions."[85] He exhibits logical reasoning when he "determines" to crawl under the leaf rather than over it. This moment of anthropomorphic ratiocination might trigger skepticism in some readers, but I think it would meet the approval of at least one scientist who studied comparative psychology – Darwin. The snail's assessment of the leaf echoes Darwin's claim, in his 1881 *Formation of Vegetable Mould Through the Action of Worms*, that earthworms assess the size and shape of leaves as they drag them into their underground tunnels. "We can hardly escape from the conclusion that worms show some degree of intelligence in their

[83] Morgan, *Animal Life and Intelligence*, 335.
[84] Woolf, *Complete Shorter Fiction*, 93–4.
[85] Alt, *Virginia Woolf and the Study of Nature*, 148.

manner of plugging up their burrow," he declared.[86] In addition, Kelly Sultzbach suggests that the snail's intentional behavior in this moment might reflect the influence of Frederick Gamble's *The Animal World* (1911), which argued that animals have not only awareness but also a "power of choice."[87] Woolf's rational snail, then, is consonant with some contemporaneous scientific representations of invertebrate minds.

Like "The Mark on the Wall," "Kew Gardens" presents animal experience as a welcome alternative to human subjectivity. The human characters are haunted by their memories, "the spirits of the dead," or the inadequacy of conversation, but the snail experiences no such discomfort. His private world represents an attractive respite from the human world. However, one of the human characters in "Kew Gardens" does experience a strange and refreshing state of consciousness that resembles animal experience. An elderly woman, passing the flowers, sees them "as a sleeper waking from a heavy sleep sees a brass candlestick reflecting the light in an unfamiliar way."[88] This defamiliarizing vision allows her to transcend (or, perhaps, descend beneath, as the snail descends beneath the leaf) the inanity of the conversation she is having: "[she] ceased even to pretend to listen to what the other woman was saying. She stood there letting the words fall over her, swaying the top part of her body slowly backwards and forwards, looking at the flowers."[89] Sultzbach writes that in this moment the woman "becomes a kind of flower" as she experiences "an unconscious lull in her attachment with the human world, allowing her to hear the pattern of words, and to express the physicality of the flowers as she sways her stalk-like body with the breeze."[90] It is a passive, nonlinguistic, yet meaningful moment and, I would add, it approximates the kind of primitivist experience that Woolf and the comparative psychologists associated with animals. People, Woolf implies, can feel this way too, and readers, projecting themselves into the perspectives of animal subjects, can temporarily access this kind of animal experience.

---

[86] Charles Darwin, *The Formation of Vegetable Mould Through the Action of Worms* (John Murray, 1881; repr. in *The Complete Work of Charles Darwin Online*, ed. John van Wyhe: www.darwin-online.org.uk), 91. Eileen Crist has explored Darwin's representations of worm cognition and their implications for scientific studies of animals. See Eileen Crist, "The Inner Life of Earthworms: Darwin's Argument and Its Implications," in *The Cognitive Animal: Empirical and Theoretical Perspectives on Animal Cognition*, ed. Marc Bekoff, Colin Allen, and Gordon M. Burghardt (MIT Press, 2002): 3–8.

[87] Frederick Willaim Gamble, *The Animal World* (Williams and Norgate, 1911), 143; quoted in Sultzbach, *Ecocriticism in the Modernist Imagination*, 99.

[88] Woolf, *Complete Shorter Fiction*, 93.

[89] Ibid.

[90] Sultzbach, *Ecocriticism in the Modernist Imagination*, 100.

In 1933, more than a decade after Woolf began to explore animal perspectives in "The Mark on the Wall" and "Kew Gardens," she revisited the
subject at greater length. Her book *Flush* presents a biography of Elizabeth
Barrett Browning's dog, indirectly narrating the poet's courtship with and
marriage to Robert Browning. *Flush* is many things to many critics: an
experiment with the forms of biography and *Bildungsroman*, a feminist
text, a challenge to fascism, an interrogation of anthropomorphism, and a
mapping of interspecies connections.[91] As several critics have noted, *Flush*
also contains parallels with zoological studies past and present. Jeanne
Dubino, for example, identifies in the book an exploration of Darwinian
coevolution between humans and dogs.[92] David Herman and Kendalyn
Kendall-Morwick, meanwhile, claim that the representation of Flush's
world is similar to Uexküll's representations of animal *Umwelten*.[93] And
Craig Smith suggests that Woolf's methods prefigure those of cognitive
ethologists like Donald Griffin (who helped found the field in the 1970s)
by engaging in a form of "critical anthropomorphism."[94]

---

[91] David Herman's "Modernist Life Writing and Nonhuman Lives: Ecologies of Experience in
Virginia Woolf's *Flush*," *Modern Fiction Studies* 59.3 (2013): 547–68 argues that *Flush* is a "metabi-
ographical text" that adapts the conventions of life writing to better represent connections across
gender, class, and species. Karalyn Kendall-Morwick's "Mongrel Fiction: Canine Bildung and the
Feminist Critique of Anthropocentrism in Woolf's *Flush*," *Modern Fiction Studies* 60.3 (2014):
506–26 interprets the text as an alternative form of *Bildungsroman* that offers a more networked,
multiplicitous account of character formation than the classical male *Bildungsroman* does. Kari
Weil, in *Thinking Animals*, reads *Flush* as a feminist rebuttal to Freud's *Civilization and its
Discontents* that reclaims animal instincts and "begins to envision an alternative civilization to that
of the fathers" (87–96, quote on 93). Anna Snaith's "Of Fanciers, Footnotes, and Fascism: Virginia
Woolf's *Flush*," *Modern Fiction Studies* 48.3 (2002): 614–36 analyzes the text's politics surrounding
hierarchy and finds that it reflects Woolf's opposition to the rise of fascism. Dan Wylie's "The
Anthropomorphic Ethic: Fiction and the Animal Mind in Virginia Woolf's *Flush* and Barbara
Gowdy's *The White Bone*," *Interdisciplinary Studies in Literature and Environment* 9.2 (2002): 115–
31 argues that Woolf's style of anthropomorphism is an ethical attempt to build interspecies community. Jutta Ittner's "Part Spaniel, Part Canine Puzzle: Anthropomorphism in Woolf's *Flush* and
Auster's *Timbuktu*," *Mosaic* 39.4 (2006): 181–96 sees Woolf's text as taking part in a traditional
form of anthropomorphism that subordinates animals to humans (as opposed to Auster's text,
which represents a "new anthropomorphism" that is non-hierarchical). And Derek Ryan's "From
Spaniel Club to An*i*malous Society: Virginia Woolf's *Flush*," in *Contradictory Woolf: Selected Papers
from the Twenty-First Annual International Conference on Virginia Woolf*, ed. Derek Ryan and Stella
Bolaki (Clemson University Digital Press, 2012): 158–65 turns to Donna Haraway's notion of
companion species to argue that *Flush* "journey[s] away from hierarchical, essentialist categorisa-
tions ... towards a more open, entangled zone of human and animal" (158).

[92] Jeanne Dubino, "The Bispecies Environment, Coevolution, and *Flush*," in *Contradictory Woolf:
Selected Papers from the Twenty-First Annual International Conference on Virginia Woolf*, ed. Derek
Ryan and Stella Bolaki (Clemson University Digital Press, 2012): 150–7.

[93] Herman, "Modernist Life Writing and Nonhuman Lives," 559–60; Kendall-Morwick, "Mongrel
Fiction," 517–19.

[94] Craig Smith, "Across the Widest Gulf: Nonhuman Subjectivity in Virginia Woolf's *Flush*,"
Twentieth Century Literature 48.3 (2002): 348–61.

To this vein of criticism linking *Flush* and zoology, I would add that Woolf's understanding of animal subjectivity draws on the comparative psychology tradition. Flush is a philosophical animal constructing knowledge from his vantage point as a dog, placing Woolf in company with Morgan, Huxley, and Haldane as she explores the epistemological possibilities of imagining animal perspectives. But *Flush* also casts an ironic light on the primitivism that characterized comparative psychology and Woolf's own earlier representations of animal experience. Woolf's nephew and biographer Quentin Bell observed that "*Flush* is not so much a book by a dog lover as a book by someone who would love to be a dog."[95] But if Woolf wanted to be a dog, it is not because she saw Flush's dog subjectivity as a peaceful retreat from human consciousness. Rather, it is because Flush's perspective helps to satisfy an intellectual curiosity about other worlds, not unlike the curiosity that motivates Huxley and Haldane's essays.

Morgan argued that sense-experience "forms the foundation of the psychical life of animals," and Flush is no exception. Indeed, *Flush*'s representations of the dog's sensory life have elicited attention from many critics, including Kelly Sultzbach, Dan Wylie, David Herman, and Karalyn Kendall-Morwick.[96] Woolf's olfactory and tactile imagery is particularly vivid when she describes Flush's puppyhood rambles through the countryside:

> The cool globes of dew or rain broke in showers of iridescent spray about his nose; the earth, here hard, here soft, here hot, here cold, stung, teased and tickled the soft pads of his feet. Then what a variety of smells interwoven in subtlest combination thrilled his nostrils; strong smells of earth, sweet smells of flower; nameless smells of leaf and bramble; sour smells as they crossed the road; pungent smells as they entered bean-fields.[97]

As Wylie points out, Woolf is engaging in a "process of translation" here, trying to render dog experience in human terms.[98] The passage includes enough visual cues – dew, flowers, bean-fields – to keep human readers oriented, but its most powerful appeals are to the senses of touch and smell, the dominant senses that help Flush navigate his morning walk. By imagining the feelings of dew beneath our feet and

[95] Quentin Bell, *Virginia Woolf: A Biography* (Harcourt, 1972), 410.
[96] Sultzbach, *Ecocriticism in the Modernist Imagination*, 109–12; Wylie, "The Anthropomorphic Ethic," 117–19; Herman, "Modernist Life Writing and Nonhuman Lives," 557; Kendall-Morwick, "Mongrel Fiction," 517–19.
[97] Virginia Woolf, *Flush* [1933], ed. Elizabeth Steele (Blackwell, 1999), 6.
[98] Wylie, "The Anthropomorphic Ethic," 118.

spray in our face, and the smells of dirt and flowers, readers can almost imagine what it is like to be a dog.

Flush's experience is mostly, but not fully, constituted by sensations like these. Like Haldane's philosophical bee, he is also a creature of instinct, and Woolf describes what the activation of these instincts feels like to Flush. When he notices the smell of game – "hare" or "fox" – it triggers inherited instincts which Woolf encodes as a kind of race-memory: "Off he flashed like a fish drawn in a rush through water further and further. He forgot his mistress; he forgot all human kind. He heard dark men cry 'Span! Span!' He heard whips crack. He raced; he rushed. At last he stopped bewildered; the incantation faded."[99] Woolf suggests that Flush has inherited the memories of his ancient spaniel ancestors, a Lamarckian image of inheritance that few biologists in the 1930s would have given credence to. But she is aiming to represent the experience of an instinctive behavior, one that compels Flush to chase as if he were a "fish drawn ... through water." Flush does not understand why he responds to the scent of game this way; his instincts overpower his reason.

When describing Flush's sensory life, Woolf frequently uses the technique of delayed decoding. A term invented by Ian Watt to describe one of Joseph Conrad's impressionist techniques, delayed decoding is a device in which an author or narrator relates the sense-impressions of an event before, or without, explaining the event's meaning.[100] The result is a defamiliarization of the scene and temporary disorientation of the reader. For example, in one episode Flush visits "mysterious arcades filmed with clouds and webs of tinted gauze. A million airs from China, from Arabia, wafted their frail incense into the remotest fibres of his senses. Swiftly over the counters flashed yards of gleaming silk; more darkly, more slowly rolled the ponderous bombazine. Scissors snipped, coins sparkled. Paper was folded; strings tied."[101] From the passage's imagery – the smell of incense, the sound of scissors, the gleam of money – readers infer that Elizabeth Barrett has taken Flush shopping. But the delayed decoding foregrounds not the event itself, but Flush's experience of it. Flush does not understand shopping in human terms, as an errand or a transaction. Instead, he surrenders himself to the sights, sounds, and smells of the shop.

---

[99] Woolf, *Flush*, 6.
[100] Watt, *Conrad in the Nineteenth Century*, 175–6.
[101] Woolf, *Flush*, 15–17.

Flush's sense-experience leads him to create nonhuman forms of knowledge. Like the philosophical ant, bee, and barnacle, Flush has a dog-philosophy all his own: "[I]t was in the world of smell that Flush mostly lived. Love was chiefly smell; form and colour were smell; music and architecture, law, politics and science were smell. To him religion itself was smell."[102] An empiricist dog, Flush develops abstract ideas from sensory perceptions. It is hard to believe that Woolf did not have in mind here Haldane's description of the intellectual dog in "Possible Worlds." Haldane writes that dogs have strong emotional responses to smells, and that "[i]f dogs had a religion they would certainly flood their holy buildings with that 'doggy' smell which is the material basis of their herd instincts."[103] He suspects that their emotional responses to smells would make dogs of a more religious than scientific temperament, but declares that if dogs did develop a science, they would "classify things according to their smells" rather than their sizes or appearances.[104] When Woolf writes that science, religion, law, and many other categories of understanding, for Flush, *are* smell, she approaches the same conclusions that Haldane does, with similar implications. If Flush's religion emerges from sensory perceptions, so must human religion, rather than being handed down from on high. And religious experience, then, is significant *as* experience, rather than as unveiling of truth.

Flush's olfactory philosophy, science, and religion also resonate with that of another modernist dog philosopher: the narrator of Kafka's "Investigations of a Dog." This story revolves around a scientifically minded canine who conducts "researches" into important matters of dog metaphysics, including the all-consuming question of where food comes from.[105] "Investigations" probably did not influence *Flush* – Kafka's story was written in 1922 but not published until 1931 and not translated into English until 1933.[106] Nevertheless, the stories' commonalities reveal how widespread the trope of the philosophical animal was in the 1920s and 1930s, and how closely bound to literary experimentation.

[102] Ibid., 67.
[103] Haldane, *Possible Worlds*, 267.
[104] Ibid.
[105] Franz Kafka, "Investigations of a Dog" [1931], transl. Willa and Edwin Muir, in *The Complete Stories*, by Franz Kafka (Schocken Books, 1971): 310–46.
[106] Richard T. Gray, Ruth V. Gross, Rolf J. Goebel, and Clayton Koelb, *A Franz Kafka Encyclopedia* (Greenwood Press, 2005), 94. The first English translation was by Willa and Edwin Muir, as part of *The Great Wall of China* (1933). Woolf reports being "finished" with *Flush* on January 15th, 1933 (*A Writer's Diary*, 187) and does not mention ever reading Kafka, so influence seems unlikely.

The juxtaposition also illuminates what is unique about *Flush*. Its representations of animal consciousness are less enigmatically allegorical – which is to say less Kafkaesque – than those of "Investigations of a Dog." They are closer to the "realistic animal stories" that Allan Burns has described as "literary extensions of natural history" than to the fantastic and fabulistic world of Kafka's animal tales.[107] *Flush*'s descriptions of animal consciousness, like those of comparative psychology, are grounded in the mundane everyday life of dogs.

Woolf builds Flush's intellectual life on a foundation of sensations strung together through associations, a paradigm that comparative psychologists used to explain how animals learn. Morgan, drawing on the associationist psychology of J. S. Mill and Alexander Bain, claimed that association of ideas in animals "is the means – the sole means – by which experience is made available for the guidance of action."[108] In other words, he thought that it was through association of ideas, and not through abstract logic or reason, that animals learned. Woolf's account of Flush's learning process echoes Morgan's associationist claims. When Elizabeth Barrett takes Flush for walks in Regent's Park, he tries to run free as he used to in the countryside, but is hindered by his leash. Soon, Flush learns the law of the park: "Setting one thing beside another, he had arrived at a conclusion. Where there are flower-beds there are asphalt paths; where there are flower-beds and asphalt paths, there are men in shiny top-hats; where there are flower-beds and asphalt paths and men in shiny top-hats, dogs must be led on chains."[109] Woolf uses the term "conclusion" to name Flush's newfound knowledge, but it is a conclusion reached not by logical thinking, but instead by "setting one thing beside another," or associating things.

Flush's representation of animal subjectivity often echoes comparative psychological ideas, but it diverges from comparative psychology in one important way. Woolf satirizes the primitivism of psychologists like Thorndike and of her own earlier writing about animal subjectivity in "The Mark on the Wall" and "Kew Gardens." Flush's life may be rich in sensations, but it does not always resemble the passive pleasures of floating in water, free of human cares:

> [T]hough it would be pleasant for the biographer to infer that Flush's life in late middle age was an orgy of pleasure transcending all description; to maintain that while the baby day by day picked up a new word and thus

[107] Allan Burns, "Extensions of Vision: The Representation of Nonhuman Points of View," *Papers on Language and Literature* 38.4 (2002): 339–50, quote on 350.
[108] Morgan, *Introduction to Comparative Psychology*, 90.
[109] Woolf, *Flush*, 17–18.

removed sensation a little further beyond reach, Flush was fated to remain for ever in a Paradise where essences exist in their utmost purity, and the naked soul of things presses on the naked nerve – it would not be true. Flush lived in no such Paradise. The spirit, ranging from star to star, the bird whose furthest flight over polar snows or tropical forests never brings it within sight of human houses and their curling wood-smoke, may, for anything we know, enjoy such immunity, such integrity of bliss. But Flush had lain upon human knees and heard men's voices. His flesh was veined with human passions; he knew all grades of jealousy, anger and despair.[110]

Here Woolf offers one of the clearest articulations of this form of primitivism, but it is one laced with irony, and one that the biographer-narrator comes to reject. Flush's life is not all pleasure and purity and sensations unmediated by ideology – "the naked soul of things press[ing] on the naked nerve." Karalyn Kendall-Morwick identifies in this passage a satire of "the anti-humanist aesthetics of [D. H.] Lawrence" and other modernists because it refuses to idealize Flush's animal being.[111] It is no prelapsarian paradise to be a dog. Perhaps it is because dogs live with humans that they are barred from this primitivist Utopia, the biographer-narrator suggests; perhaps the bird that never encounters humans does live a life of peaceful purity. But for all the animals of our acquaintance, the primitivist fantasy is just that – a fantasy.

Woolf also gently lampoons the sexual primitivism of fellow modernists like Lawrence and Paul Gauguin when she describes Flush's sex life. When the Brownings marry and move to Italy, Flush begins a new life as a free-range dog, and he mates indiscriminately with the other dogs he comes across, satisfying the urge whenever it strikes him with no signs of inhibition. Woolf's narrator says, "Flush knew what men can never know – love pure, love simple, love entire; love that brings no train of care in its wake; that has no shame; no remorse; that is here, that is gone, as the bee on the flower is here and gone."[112] In its euphemistic language, the description is likely mocking the Victorian biographer-narrator through whom Woolf voices the entire book. This figure can say no more than that Flush "embraced" other dogs, that he "followed the horn wherever the horn blew and the wind wafted it."[113] Yet Victorian prudery is clearly not Woolf's only target. The idealization of animal sexuality, the anaphora ("love pure, love simple, love entire," etc.), the piling on

[110] Ibid., 68.
[111] Kendall-Morwick, "Mongrel Fiction," 513.
[112] Woolf, *Flush*, 60.
[113] Ibid., 61.

of subordinate clauses – all this suggests a more contemporary object of parody: Lawrence. Consider these lines from "Tortoise Shout," a Lawrence poem about tortoise sex: "Sex, which breaks us into voice, sets us calling across the deeps, calling, calling for the complement, / Singing, and calling, and singing again, being answered, having found."[114] *Flush*'s description of dog sex is stylistically similar, but where Lawrence's tone is earnest, Woolf's is wry.

Primitivism, *Flush* implies, is less a theory of how animals really live than a fantasy of how people would like to live. Like other modes of representing animals, from sentimental anthropomorphism to rigid mechanomorphism (to borrow a phrase from Eileen Crist), primitivism projects human values onto animals. As Bertrand Russell once joked,

> It seem[s] that animals always behave in a manner showing the rightness of the philosophy entertained by the man who observes them ... In the seventeenth century, animals were ferocious, but under the influence of Rousseau they began to exemplify the cult of the Noble Savage ... Throughout the reign of Queen Victoria all apes were virtuous monogamists, but during the dissolute 'twenties their morals underwent a disastrous deterioration.[115]

We can ask, of any representation of animal subjectivity, how far it is true to the animal itself, and how far it is a projection of human ideology. Woolf and Russell both use playful humor to foreground this question, reminding us that if animal experience looks like an alluring respite from human anxieties, it may be because people want to see it that way. "It would be pleasant," to borrow the words of *Flush*'s narrator, but "it would not be true."

This push and pull – is the dog's perspective a manifestation of empathic epistemology or a screen on which to project human desires? – is at the heart of *Flush*. The question comes to the fore most obviously in the novel's representation of Barrett Browning's relationship with Flush. Though the two form a close bond, "there were vast gaps in their understanding. Sometimes they would lie and stare at each other in blank bewilderment."[116] It is not only Barrett Browning who sometimes fails to penetrate the mystery of Flush's mind; the narrator does as well. As Jutta Ittner and Dan Wylie have pointed out, the third-person, apparently omniscient narrator of *Flush* is not always omniscient when it comes

---

[114] Lawrence, *Complete Poems*, 366, lines 81–2.
[115] Russell, *My Philosophical Development*, 95–6.
[116] Woolf, *Flush*, 21.

to Flush's mind. The narration is at times empathically canine, at other times ironically detached.[117] Adopting the voice of the biographer, Woolf is in a position to represent the normally inaccessible consciousness of the dog, offering insight into those aspects of Flush's subjective life that even his closest companions could not understand. Yet the biographer-narrator confronts the limitations of human constructs in understanding and describing the full extent of Flush's experience. "Not even Mr. Swinburne could have said what the smell of Wimpole Street meant to Flush on a hot afternoon in June," Woolf writes; even the most sensuous of poets cannot find words for the sensations a dog feels.[118] The story reaches, in Wylie's words, "a necessary failure of the imagination to *be* Flush."[119]

Flush is thus a failure in the same sense that comparative psychology was a failure. As Washburn marveled, "how great is the mystery which looks out of the eyes of a dog," an irresolvable mystery. Or, as Morgan lamented, "the pity of it is that we cannot think of [animal minds] in any other terms than those of human consciousness. The only world of constructs that we know is the world constructed by man."[120] But it is not just that the project of knowing an animal mind will necessarily end in failure; it is also that such a failed project is necessary. It is necessary epistemologically, as Russell, Huxley, and Haldane showed, to put human knowledge in its proper place, not on a pedestal but within a wider system of perspectives. And it is necessary ethically as an act of empathy that leads us to respect animal others. Not only to respect them, but also to think of better ways to improve their lots, whether they are house dogs like Flush or wild animals like "the bird whose furthest flight over polar snows or tropical forests never brings it within sight of human houses." To recognize animals as subjects, as Woolf and her intellectual forerunners do, is to enter some kind of ethical relationship with them; to imagine animals' perspectives is to ask what constitutes, *for them*, pain or pleasure, a poor life or a rich one.

4.5   The Afterlife of Comparative Psychology

The aspects of comparative psychology that made it most relevant to philosophy and literature – its subjectivism, uncertainty, and closeness to fiction – also made it unscientific in the eyes of opponents. As historians

[117] Ittner, "'Part Spaniel, Part Canine Puzzle,'" 185–6; Wylie, "The Anthropomorphic Ethic," 121–2.
[118] Woolf, *Flush*, 67.
[119] Wylie, "The Anthropomorphic Ethic," 118.
[120] Morgan, *Animal Life and Intelligence*, 335.

like Robert Boakes have shown, psychology had to root out anecdotes, introspection, and other soft methods in favor of experimentation, quantitative data, and objectivity in order to become a professional science.[121] But even though midcentury science ruled questions about animals' subjective experiences inadmissible, people never lost interest in animal subjectivity. Comparative psychology's legacy lives on in two contemporary fields of intellectual inquiry: animal studies and cognitive ethology.

Animal studies continues to build on the interest in animal perspectives that Russell, Huxley, Haldane, and Woolf shared. In "The Animal That Therefore I Am," Jacques Derrida's exploration of the challenges animals pose to Western philosophy pivots on an animal's point of view – that of his cat. This cat, he writes, "can allow itself to be looked at, no doubt, but also – something that philosophy perhaps forgets, perhaps being this calculated forgetting itself – it can look at me. It has its point of view regarding me."[122] It is this recognition of the cat as a someone who looks back at him that spurs Derrida to rethink animals' role in philosophy. Leading animal studies scholar Cary Wolfe, meanwhile, makes animal perspectives part of his posthumanist philosophy. He argues that thinking about animals' sensory lives allows us to reconfigure vision itself, understanding seeing as not a humanist process of knowledge and mastery, but merely another function of the animal sensorium.[123] And a recent issue of *Modern Fiction Studies* titled "Animal Worlds in Modern Fiction" testifies to the growing importance of animal perspectives within literary studies.[124] The questions that launched comparative psychology into the intellectual world of modernism continue to trail animal studies today.

Some scientists, meanwhile, have also returned to the question of what we can know about animals' subjective experiences. In recent years, a new brand of subjectivism has come back into fashion: cognitive ethology. A field pioneered by Donald R. Griffin in the 1970s, cognitive ethology studies the relationship between animal behavior and consciousness. Marc Bekoff, for example, combines scientific method with fiction and empathic epistemology, writing that in his research, "I become coyote, I become penguin. I try to step into animals' sensory and locomotor worlds to discover what it might be like to be a given individual, how they sense their surroundings, and how they behave and move about in

---

[121] Boakes, *From Darwin to Behaviourism.*
[122] Derrida, "The Animal That Therefore I Am," 380.
[123] Wolfe, *What is Posthumanism?*, 127–42.
[124] The issue is *Modern Fiction Studies* 60.3 (Fall 2014), edited by David Herman.

certain situations."[125] Cognitive ethologists imagine animal perspectives just as the major figures in this chapter did, and they are equipped with more robust scientific evidence for their claims about animal cognition than was available in the 1920s. They even continue to use the trope of the philosophical animal, a trope that seems to become more and more literal as time goes on. For example, some cognitive ethologists debate whether nonhuman animals have a "theory of mind," or an ability to attribute mental states to others.[126] Not all scientists agree that cognitive ethology's methods are sufficiently rigorous, but the field's growth reflects a return of the kind of subjectivism that comparative psychologists and thinkers across disciplines embraced at the turn of the twentieth century. It is a willingness to make space for speculation, empathy, and even fiction within scientific thinking. When it comes to understanding animal minds today, the modernist imagination shared by Woolf, Russell, Huxley, Haldane, Washburn, Morgan, and many others is still with us.

[125] Marc Bekoff, *Minding Animals: Awareness, Emotions, and Heart* (Oxford University Press, 2002), 11.

[126] See, for example, David Premack and Guy Woodruff, "Does the Chimpanzee Have a Theory of Mind?" *Behavioral and Brain Sciences* 1.4 (1978): 515–26; Joseph Call and Michael Tomasello, "Does the Chimpanzee Have a Theory of Mind? 30 Years Later," *Trends in Cognitive Sciences* 12.5 (2008): 187–92; and Alain Morin, "What Are Animals Conscious Of?" in *Experiencing Animal Minds: An Anthology of Animal-Human Encounters*, ed. Julie A. Smith and Robert W. Mitchell (Columbia University Press, 2012): 246–60.

Conclusion

What of the modernist imagination remains in contemporary representations of animal subjectivity? As the previous pages suggest, H. G. Wells perceived animals as agents of resistance, challenging anthropocentric visions of human sovereignty over the planet. Aldous Huxley saw animals as mysterious subjects whose very presence makes an ethical demand upon us to respect the other we cannot fully know. For D. H. Lawrence, animals were best conceptualized as natural expressionist artists, channeling their vitality and emotions into song or coloration or play. And to Virginia Woolf, animals' perceptual worlds were sources of aesthetic novelty and beauty. Each of these ideas continues to reverberate in contemporary popular science discourse, where the modernists' scientific and aesthetic fascination with animal life coincides with a growing recognition of its fragility. The following four case studies suggest that the modernist visions remain captivating today, even as the broader animal discourse has shifted to recognize that we are living in the age of the sixth mass extinction and animal life is more vulnerable than ever.

Tardigrade

The tardigrade, or water bear, a tiny but tough aquatic animal about half a millimeter in size, was perhaps the breakout star of the 2014 television series *Cosmos: A Spacetime Odyssey*. The tardigrade may be small and weirdly cute, with its round, pinkish, bear-shaped body and eight wriggling legs, but, as host Neil deGrasse Tyson points out, it is surprisingly robust. Tardigrades, he says, can live on icy mountains, in volcanoes, and in the depths of the ocean; they can even survive exposure in outer space. They tolerate a wide range of environmental conditions. Their resilience has made the phylum an extraordinary evolutionary success. As Tyson observes, tardigrades have been around for about 500 million years old – they have survived all five mass extinction events in the earth's history.

They are living fossils from the Cambrian explosion. "A visitor from another world," he concludes, "could be forgiven for thinking of earth as the planet of the tardigrades."[1]

Tardigrades' extreme versatility has made them a popular subject of scientific research in recent years. Biologists have successfully recovered living tardigrades from an Antarctic moss sample that had been frozen for thirty years; exposed them to toxic chemicals and the vacuum of outer space, both of which they survived; and rehydrated living tardigrades from moss and lichen samples that had been kept dry for years.[2] Most recently, researchers have sequenced tardigrade genomes in an effort to discover what genetic adaptations make them so "extremotolerant," or resilient in extreme environments. They found proteins unique to tardigrades which suppress damage and offer the creatures protection from punishing conditions.[3]

Since *Cosmos* aired, the tardigrades have become staples of popular science and technology discourse as an emblem of environmental resilience.[4] "Tardigrades roamed the earth and seas far before humans did – and will most likely outlast us," declares Maeve McDermott, a blogger for *National Geographic*. "Will the tardigrades be nature's last organisms standing? Only time will tell."[5] It's not hard to imagine a future in

---

[1] Neil deGrasse Tyson, "Some of the Things that Molecules Do," *Cosmos: A Spacetime Odyssey*, Fox, March 16, 2014.

[2] Megumu Tsujimoto, Satoshi Imura, and Hiroshi Kanda, "Recovery and Reproduction of an Antarctic Tardigrade Retrieved from a Moss Sample Frozen for Over 30 Years," *Cryobiology* 72.1 (2016): 78–81; N. Møbjerg, A. Jørgensen, D. Persson, M. Bjørn, H. Ramløov, and R. M. Kristensen, "Survival in Extreme Environments – On the Current Knowledge of Adaptations in Tardigrades," *Acta Physiologica* 202 (2011): 409–20; Lorena Rebecchi, Tiziana Altiero, Roberto Guidetti, Michele Cesari, Roberto Bertolani, Manuela Negroni, and Angela M. Rizzo, "Tardigrade Resistance to Space Effects: First Results of Experiments on the LIFE-TARSE Mission on FOTON-M3," *Astrobiology* 9.6 (2007): 581–91; Roberto Guidetti and K. Ingemar Jönsson, "Long-Term Anhydrobiotic Survival in Semi-Terrestrial Micrometazoans," *Journal of Zoology* 257 (2002): 181–7.

[3] Takuma Hashimoto, Daiki D. Horikawa, et al., "Extremotolerant Tardigrade Genome and Improved Radiotolerance of Human Cultures Cells by Tardigrade-Unique Protein," *Nature Communications* 7.12808 (2016): 1–14.

[4] See, for example, Rachel Becker, "Tardigrades Can Live 30 Years in a Freezer and Survive in Space, and Now We Know Why," *The Verge* September 20, 2016: www.theverge.com/2016/9/20/12990274/tardigrade-extreme-water-bears-genome-sequence; George Dvorsky, "Scientists Finally Figured Out Why Tardigrades are So Indestructible," *Gizmodo* September 20, 2016: http://www.gizmodo.com/genes-hold-the-key-to-the-water-bears-indestructibility-1786814698; Matt Simon, "Absurd Creature of the Week: The Incredible Critter That's Tough Enough to Survive in Space," *Wired* March 21, 2014: www.wired.com/2014/03/absurd-creature-week-water-bear/; and Laura Geggel, "Super Species: Animals with Extreme Powers Invade Museum," *LiveScience* April 1, 2015: www.livescience.com/50333-life-at-the-limits.html.

[5] Maeve McDermott, "5 Reasons Why the Tardigrade is Nature's Toughest Animal," *National Geographic TV Blogs* March 19, 2014: www.tvblogs.nationalgeographic.com/2014/03/19/5-reasons-why-the-tardigrade-is-natures-toughest-animal/.

which there are few signs of life in the poisoned water, the acid oceans, or on the overheated earth – H. G. Wells foresaw something rather similar at the end of *The Time Machine* – but tardigrades will probably still be around. The notion that these tiny animals, rather than human beings, might be the inheritors of the earth would have delighted Wells, who envisaged the land as an empire of ants and the sea as an empire of cephalopods. If the species' history is any indication, the water bears will still roam the earth and seas long after our own species has been reduced to fossils in the geological strata of the Anthropocene.

Octopus

In the spring of 2016, an octopus named Inky made headlines by escaping from his tank at the National Aquarium of New Zealand and slithering down a drainpipe that emptied into Hawke's Bay. Reporter Dan Bilefsky of the *New York Times* called it "an audacious night-time escape," describing Inky as a "nimble contortionist" to rival Houdini.[6] Inky's story captivated the public, largely because it fits into the narrative pattern of a clever rascal who captures our hearts by eluding capture. Like Irene Adler, who earned Sherlock Holmes's respect in Arthur Conan Doyle's story by outsmarting the famous detective, Inky became an exhibit attesting to the intelligence of his kind. Rob Yarrell, the aquarium's national manager, said that Inky was always "a curious boy" and "a bit of a surprise octopus" – and, we might infer, he is all the more lovable for his unpredictability and intelligence.[7]

Octopuses have attracted a great deal of scientific and popular attention because they challenge many of biology's traditional assumptions about animal minds. They are invertebrates, and they are distant from humans phylogenetically – our last common ancestor likely lived 500 to 700 million years ago.[8] Until recently, few scientists attributed much, if any, intelligence to invertebrates, reserving it for "higher" animals – i.e. those more closely related to humans. Over the last few years,

[6] Dan Bilefsky, "Inky the Octopus Escapes from a New Zealand Aquarium," *The New York Times* April 13, 2016: www.nytimes.com/2016/04/14/world/asia/inky-octopus-new-zealand-aquarium .html.
[7] Eleanor Ainge Roy, "The Great Escape: Inky the Octopus Legs It to Freedom from Aquarium," *The Guardian* April 12, 2016: www.theguardian.com/world/2016/apr/13/the-great-escape -inky-the-octopus-legs-it-to-freedom-from-new-zealand-aquarium.
[8] Sy Montgomery, "Deep Intellect," *Orion Magazine* October 2011: www.orionmagazine.org/article/ deep-intellect/.

however, a more complicated picture has emerged. Octopuses, it appears, *are* highly intelligent creatures, but their intelligence evolved separately from humans'. They have large brains relative to other invertebrates, and they can learn to run mazes and maybe even to use tools.[9] And Inky is not the only octopus to resist human efforts at control. In an essay for the environmental magazine *Orion*, Sy Montgomery write that "[o]ctopuses in captivity actually escape their watery enclosures with alarming frequency. While on the move, they have been discovered on carpets, along bookshelves, in a teapot, and inside the aquarium tanks of other fish – upon whom they have usually been dining." To keep captive octopuses busy and happy, Montgomery reports, aquarists give them toys and puzzles; a Cincinnati aquarium has even developed an *Octopus Enrichment Handbook*.

One of the most common metaphors that popular science writers use to describe octopuses is to say that they are aliens. "No sci-fi alien is so startlingly strange" as an octopus, Montgomery declares. The philosopher Peter Godfrey-Smith says that "[m]eeting an octopus is like meeting an intelligent alien."[10] When, in 2015, researchers sequenced the genome of the California two-spot octopus, the University of Chicago neurobiologist Clifton Ragsdale jokingly summarized their findings by saying, "It's the first sequenced genome from something like an alien."[11] Octopuses can taste with their suckers, change color and texture to camouflage themselves, and perhaps even "think" with their arms, where three-fifths of their neurons are located.[12] Whatever kind of subject an octopus is, it is undoubtedly startling different from a human subject. To even begin to imagine its experience is a mind-bending proposition.

Unlike the laboratory animals that Aldous Huxley described in *Antic Hay*, destined for experimentation and death in captivity, Inky managed to get away. Octopuses more generally, though, remind us that Huxley's ethos of observation and thin description still has a part to play in contemporary animal studies. There is still so much we don't understand about these creatures; to attempt to explain their experience is almost certainly an act of projection more than of empathy. The octopus encounter, as Montgomery and others describe it, is an encounter with an other who

[9] Ibid.
[10] Peter Godfrey-Smith, "Philosophy and the Octopus," *WAMC: Academic Minute* March 30, 2011: www.wamc.org/post/dr-peter-godfrey-smith-harvard-university-philosophy-and-octopus.
[11] Alison Abbott, "Octopus Genome Holds Clues to Uncanny Intelligence," *Nature* August 12, 2015: www.nature.com/news/octopus-genome-holds-clues-to-uncanny-intelligence-1.18177.
[12] Montgomery, "Deep Intellect."

looks back at us, perhaps even touches us, and yet remains in large part unknowable, "alien." To borrow a turn of phrase from Derrida, the octopus looks at us; ethics perhaps begins there.[13]

Whale

Whales have been beloved symbols of the conservation movement for over forty years. These charismatic megafauna are now also considered key exemplars of animal culture, typically defined as the acquisition of novel behaviors through social learning between and within generations.[14] Whales communicate with each other via vocalizations popularly known as whale songs. The songs are predominantly used by males as a form of sexual display. Whale songs are one of the earliest documented cases of cultural transmission in animals; the animals learn their song patterns from listening to each other. Recent research by Ellen C. Garland and others indicates that in humpback whales, songs are not only passed down from parents to offspring, but also horizontally, from members of one whale population to another, creating a constantly evolving shared refrain.[15]

In his poem "Whales Weep Not!" D. H. Lawrence contrasts warm-blooded, lustful whales with the cold ocean in which they live:

> They say the sea is cold, but the sea contains
> the hottest blood of all, and the wildest, the most urgent.
>
> All the whales in the wider deeps, hot are they, as they urge on and on, and dive
> beneath the icebergs.
> The right whales, the sperm-whales, the hammer-heads, the killers
> there they blow, there they blow, hot wild white breath out of the sea![16]

Lawrence saw whales as another part of the pattern of primitive, untroubled animal sexuality. But he could not have known in 1930 that whales also fit into his vision of animal artists, creatures whose

[13] Derrida says, "The animal looks at us, and we are naked before it. Thinking perhaps begins there" ("The Animal That Therefore I Am," 397).

[14] For a discussion of animal cultures, see de Waal, *The Ape and the Sushi Master.*

[15] Ellen C. Garland, Jason Gedamke, Melinda L. Rekdahl, Michael J. Noad, Claire Garrigue, and Nick Gales, "Humpback Whale Song on the Southern Ocean Feeding Grounds: Implications for Cultural Transmission," *PLOS One* 8.11 (2013): e79422; and Ellen C. Garland, Anne W. Goldizen, Melinda L. Rekdahl, Rochelle Constantine, Claire Garrigue, Nan Daeschler Hauser, M. Michael Polle, Jooke Robbins, and Michael J. Noad, "Dynamic Horizontal Cultural Transmission of Humpback Whale Song at the Ocean Basin Scale," *Current Biology* 21.8 (2011): 687–91.

[16] Lawrence, *Complete Poems*, 694, lines 1–5.

expressions of exuberant emotion in song form a prototype for human art-making. Whale choruses were not discovered until 1967, when biologists Roger Searle Payne and Scott McVay began studying humpback whale songs. They went on to record and release the album *Songs of the Humpback Whale* in 1970, which became a hit and contributed to the rise of the "Save the Whales" movement. The songs were considered evidence of the intelligence and cultural complexity of cetacean species.[17]

One whale, known as 52 Blue, has found a special place in the culture of popular science. In a piece for the digital magazine *The Atavist*, essayist Leslie Jamison explains that in 1992, a naval air station in Washington state detected a strange noise in the ocean, at a frequency of 52 hertz.[18] At first, technicians were unsure what the source of the noise was, but then an officer realized that the sound was a blue whale. Typically, blue whales sing at 15–20 hertz, so 52 Blue's call was abnormally high-pitched – so high-pitched, in fact, that other whales never responded to his calls, presumably unable to recognize them. After a 2004 scientific paper by William A. Watkins in *Deep Sea Research*, 52 Blue became fabled among followers who thought of him as "the loneliest whale in the world."

Jamison's essay, which toggles back and forth between the researchers who studied 52 Blue (and found his viral legend baffling) and the devotees who came to identify with the solitary whale many years later, is characterized by the same tension that infuses D. H. Lawrence's poetry: the idea that anthropomorphizing animals is at once intellectually intolerable and artistically fruitful. The people who (over)identify with the blue whale find in him a kind of creative vitality that inspires them to make art of their own: a tattoo for one, songs for another, paintings for a third. Ultimately Jamison, like Lawrence, attempts to carve a path that would let her have it both ways, searching for an immediacy outside anthropomorphic symbolism without abandoning the meaningfulness that humans have built up around the whale. "What if we grant the whale his whale-ness, grant him furlough from our metaphoric employ, but still grant the contours of his second self – the one we've made – and admit what he's done for us?" she suggests. "*That's really something*. If we let the whale cleave in two – into his actual form and the apparition of

what we needed him to become – then we let these twins swim apart. We
free each figure from the other's shadow. We watch them cut two paths
across the sea."

Mantis Shrimp

In a 2012 episode of the popular science program *Radiolab*, the speakers
take on color perception, a subject which has fascinated scientists and
artists from Newton to Goethe. To illustrate differences among species
in color vision, they turn to the mantis shrimp, a small, brightly-colored,
pugilistic creature inhabiting coral reefs which may have a wider range
of color perception than any other animal. While human eyes have
three color receptors, allowing us to perceive red, green, and blue light
wavelengths, and some birds and fish have a fourth photoreceptor for
ultraviolet light, the mantis shrimp has sixteen types of photoreceptors
in its eyes. The result? "A pugnacious, Muhammad Ali seagoing animal
with incredibly great visual sense," as a Radiolab host describes it.[19] Or, as
Matthew Inman, author of the webcomic *The Oatmeal* puts it, "where we
see a rainbow, the mantis shrimp sees a THERMONUCLEAR BOMB
of light and beauty."[20]

The mantis shrimp's range of color vision, unparalleled in the animal
kingdom, has drawn the attention of not only podcast fans but also scientists curious about what all of those photoreceptors are for. *Radiolab*
and *The Oatmeal* imagined that the mantis shrimp sees a vast, complex
rainbow of colors we cannot even imagine. But researchers Hanne H.
Thoen, Martin J. Howe, Tsyr-Huei Chiou, and Justin Marshall found
that mantis shrimp are actually not very good at discriminating between
colors – in fact, they are much worse at it than humans are. These results
might seem disappointing, but they may suggest something far more
intriguing – that mantis shrimp "use a previously unknown color vision
system based on temporal signaling combined with scanning eye movements, enabling a type of color *recognition* rather than *discrimination*"
(my italics).[21] Researchers can make inferences about this process of color

---

[19] Jay Abumrad and Robert Krulwich, "Colors," *Radiolab*, podcast audio, May 21, 2012, www.radio-
lab.org/story/211119-colors/.
[20] Matthew Inman, "Why the Mantis Shrimp is My New Favorite Animal," *The Oatmeal*: www.theo-
atmeal.com/comics/mantis_shrimp.
[21] Hanne H. Thoen, Martin J. Howe, Tsyr-Huei Chiou, and Justin Marshall, "A Different Form of
Color Vision in Mantis Shrimp," *Science* 343.6169 (2014): 411–13, quote on 411.

recognition, but we cannot picture it – it is an "entirely unique form of vision," they say, adapted for the shrimp's life as a marine predator.[22]

If Virginia Woolf, Julian Huxley, J. B. S. Haldane, or Jakob von Uexküll had known about the mantis shrimp and its brilliant, violent world among the coral, it would have confirmed their sense that our own perceptual sphere is just one among many. No doubt those writers and scientists who daydreamed about how a dog, snail, ant, barnacle, or tick sees the world would have found in the mantis shrimp rich material for speculation. The creature itself, with its iridescent blues, greens, and reds, is a marvel to look at, but to look at the world through its eyes is to imagine the most vibrant coral reef ever caught on film, and then to know that is probably not the half of it.

Animal Stories in the Age of Extinction

What the modernists perceived only in occasional glimmers was that, just as they were opening up animal worlds to the imagination, global capitalism was beginning to raze actual animal worlds with unprecedented efficiency. They knew that something called "nature" was threatened by something called modernization. But they could not foresee the acres of Canadian boreal forest cut down to mine the tar sands beneath, the shorebirds covered in spilled oil in the Gulf of Mexico, the caves littered with dead bats in New York, the kilometers of bleached coral reef off the Australian coast: the relentless winnowing down of animal worlds, deliberately at first and then, as with the corals, despite our efforts to save them.

In the age of the sixth mass extinction, it would be naïve to overstate the efficacy of animal stories, literary or scientific, for creating a more ethical way of living with other kinds of beings. We have lots of stories, and ever fewer species. At the same time, it would be naïve to think that any ethical or political action can happen without the sense of meaning and value that narrative brings. George Levine argues, in *Darwin Loves You*, that Darwin's writing offers a secular vision of a "re-enchanted world," one which "seeks a feeling for the organism, values the extraordinary differences that mark the range of organic life, and depends on imagination (anthropomorphic perhaps, but not anthropocentric), honoring difference, recognizing penguins for penguins."[23] Re-enchantment, Levine writes, runs the risk of "laps[ing] into a mere aestheticism," but

[22] Ibid.
[23] Levine, *Darwin Loves You*, 274.

at its best it may "energize the ethical," forming "a small first step toward a more humane and a more joyful, a more open, a more knowledgeable and attentive relation not only to the natural world but to the communities we inhabit."[24] An example of that "more knowledgeable and attentive relation" can be found in the work of the philosopher Thom van Dooren. His book *Flight Ways* tells stories of endangered birds "at the edge of extinction." Van Dooren is motivated by a faith that talking about animals matters, not just as a way of accurately reflecting the world, but as a way of changing it. "Story" is, for him, a verb, a way of contributing "to the emergence of 'what is.'" "Stories are part of the world," he writes, "and so they participate in its becoming."[25]

Somewhere between Darwin's Victorian re-enchantment and van Dooren's Anthropocene animal stories lie the animal subjects of modernist literature and science. They are not animal rights propaganda or environmentalist manifestos; there are no guarantees that they will "work." There is just the possibility that they might, in some small way, help story a more attentive, more loving relationship with the world that houses all our animal worlds.

[24] Ibid., 254.
[25] Thom van Dooren, *Flight Ways: Life and Loss at the Edge of Extinction* (Columbia University Press, 2014), 10.

Bibliography

Abbott, Alison. "Octopus Genome Holds Clues to Uncanny Intelligence," *Nature* August 12, 2015: www.nature.com/news/octopus-genome-holds-clues-to-uncanny-intelligence-1.18177.

Abumrad, Jay and Robert Krulwich. "Colors," *Radiolab*, podcast audio, May 21, 2012: www.radiolab.org/story/211119-colors/.

Agamben, Giorgio. *The Open: Man and Animal*, transl. Kevin Attell (Stanford University Press, 2004).

Alaimo, Stacy. *Bodily Natures: Science, Environment, and the Material Self* (Indiana University Press, 2010).

   "Eluding Capture: The Science, Culture, and Pleasure of 'Queer' Animals," in *Queer Ecologies: Sex, Nature, Politics, Desire*, ed. Catriona Mortimer-Sandilands and Bruce Erickson (Indiana University Press, 2010): 51–72.

Allen, David Elliston. *The Naturalist in Britain: A Social History* (Allen Lane, 1976).

Alt, Christina. "Extinction, Extermination, and the Ecological Optimism of H.G. Wells," in *Green Planets: Ecology and Science Fiction*, ed. Gerry Canavan (Wesleyan University Press, 2014): 25–39.

   Virginia Woolf and the Study of Nature (Cambridge University Press, 2010).

Anderson, Thomas J. "Aepyornis as Moa: Giant Birds and Global Connections in Nineteenth-Century Science," *British Journal for the History of Science* 46.4 (2013): 675–93.

Anker, Peder. *Imperial Ecology: Environmental Order in the British Empire, 1895–1945* (Harvard University Press, 2001).

Arata, Stephen D. "The Occidental Tourist: Dracula and the Anxiety of Reverse Colonization," *Victorian Studies* 33.4 (1990): 621–45.

Armstrong, Philip J. *What Animals Mean in the Fiction of Modernity* (Routledge, 2008).

Arrowsmith, Rupert Richard. *Modernism and the Museum: Asian, African, and Pacific Art and the London Avant-Garde* (Oxford University Press, 2011).

Auden, W. H. *The Dyer's Hand and Other Essays* (Random House, 1962).

Baker, Robert S. "Science and Modernity in Aldous Huxley's Interwar Essays and Novels," in *Aldous Huxley: Between East and West*, ed. C. C. Barfoot (Rodopi, 2001): 35–58.

Bakhtin, Mikhail. *Rabelais and His World* [1965], transl. Helene Iswolsky (Indiana University Press, 1984).

Banfield, Ann. *The Phantom Table: Woolf, Fry, Russell and the Epistemology of Modernism* (Cambridge University Press, 2000).

Bartley, Mary M. "Courtship and Continued Progress: Julian Huxley's Studies on Bird Behavior," *Journal of the History of Biology* 28 (1995): 91–108.

Batchelor, John. "Conrad and Wells at the End of the Century," *The Critical Review* 38 (1998): 69–82.

Becker, Rachel. "Tardigrades Can Live 30 Years in a Freezer and Survive in Space, and Now We Know Why," *The Verge* September 20, 2016: www.theverge.com/2016/9/20/12990274/tardigrade-extreme-water-bears-genome-sequence.

Beer, Gillian. *Darwin's Plots: Evolutionary Narrative in Darwin, George Eliot and Nineteenth-Century Fiction* [1983] (Ark Paperbacks, 1985).

   "Darwin and the Uses of Extinction," *Victorian Studies* 51.2 (2009): 321–31.

   "Translation or Transformation? The Relations of Literature and Science," in *Open Fields: Science in Cultural Encounter*, by Gillian Beer (Clarendon Press, 1996): 173–95.

   "Virginia Woolf and Prehistory," in *Arguing with the Past: Essays in Narrative from Woolf to Sidney*, by Gillian Beer (Routledge, 1999): 159–82.

Bekoff, Marc. *Minding Animals: Awareness, Emotions, and Heart* (Oxford University Press, 2002).

Bekoff, Marc and Colin Allen. "Intentional Communication and Social Play: How and Why Animals Negotiate and Agree to Play," in *Animal Play: Evolutionary, Comparative, and Cognitive Perspectives*, ed. Marc Bekoff and John A. Byers (Cambridge University Press, 1998): 97–114.

Bell, Quentin. *Virginia Woolf: A Biography* (Harcourt, 1972).

Bennett, Jane. *Vibrant Matter: A Political Ecology of Things* (Duke University Press, 2010).

Bergonzi, Bernard. *The Early H.G. Wells: A Study of the Scientific Romances* (Manchester University Press, 1961).

Bernard, Claude. *Introduction to the Study of Experimental Medicine* [1865], transl. Henry Copley Greene (Dover, 1957).

Biben, Maxeen. "Squirrel Monkey Play Fighting: Making the Case for a Cognitive Training Function for Play," in *Animal Play: Evolutionary, Comparative, and Cognitive Perspectives*, ed. Marc Bekoff and John A. Byers (Cambridge University Press, 1998): 161–82.

Bilefsky, Dan. "Inky the Octopus Escapes from a New Zealand Aquarium," *The New York Times* April 13, 2016: www.nytimes.com/2016/04/14/world/asia/inky-octopus-new-zealand-aquarium.html.

Boakes, Robert. *From Darwin to Behaviourism: Psychology and the Minds of Animals* (Cambridge University Press, 1984).

Bowering, Peter. *Aldous Huxley: A Study of the Major Novels* (Oxford University Press, 1969).

Bowler, Peter J. *Reconciling Science and Religion: The Debate in Early Twentieth-Century Britain* (University of Chicago Press, 2001).

Science for All: The Popularization of Science in Early Twentieth-Century Britain (University of Chicago Press, 2009).

Bown, Nicola. "'Entangled Banks': Robert Browning, Richard Dadd and the Darwinian Grotesque," in *Victorian Culture and the Idea of the Grotesque*, ed. Colin Trodd, Paul Barlow, and David Amigoni (Ashgate, 1999): 119–42.

British Instructional Films. *The Cuckoo's Secret* (British Film Institute National Archive, 1922).

Romance in a Pond (British Film Institute National Archive, 1932).

Browne, Janet. *Charles Darwin: The Power of Place* (Princeton University Press, 2003).

Buettinger, Craig. "Antivivisection and the Charge of Zoophil-Psychosis in the Early Twentieth Century," *The Historian* 55.2 (1993): 277–88.

"Women and Antivivisection in Late Nineteenth-Century America," *Journal of Social History* 30.4 (1997): 857–72.

Burghardt, Gordon M. *The Genesis of Animal Play: Testing the Limits* (MIT Press, 2005).

Burkhardt, Richard W. "Huxley and the Rise of Ethology," in *Julian Huxley: Biologist and Statesman of Science*, ed. C. Kenneth Waters and Albert Van Helden (Rice University Press, 1992): 127–49.

Patterns of Behavior: Konrad Lorenz, Niko Tinbergen, and the Founding of Ethology (University of Chicago Press, 2005).

"The Founders of Ethology and the Problem of Animal Subjective Experience," in *Animal Consciousness and Animal Ethics: Perspectives from the Netherlands*, ed. Marcel Dol (Van Gorcum, 1997): 1–15.

Burns, Allan. "Extensions of Vision: The Representation of Nonhuman Points of View," *Papers on Language and Literature* 38.4 (2002): 339–50.

Cain, Joe. "Julian Huxley, General Biology and the London Zoo, 1935–42," *Notes and Records of the Royal Society* 64 (2010): 359–78.

Call, Joseph and Michael Tomasello. "Does the Chimpanzee Have a Theory of Mind? 30 Years Later," *Trends in Cognitive Sciences* 12.5 (2008): 187–92.

Cantor, Paul A. and Peter Hufnagel. "The Empire of the Future: Imperialism and Modernism in H.G. Wells," *Studies in the Novel* 38.1 (2006): 36–56.

Chan, Winnie. *The Economy of the Short Story in British Periodicals of the 1890s* (Routledge, 2007).

Chaudhuri, Amit. *D.H. Lawrence and 'Difference'* (Clarendon Press, 2003).

Chiba, Yoko. "Japonisme: East–West Renaissance in the Late 19th Century," *Mosaic* 31.2 (1998): 1–20.

Chomsky, Noam. "On the Myth of Ape Language" (interview via email by Matt Aames Cucchiaro), *Chomsky.Info* 2007/8: chomsky.info/2007.

Clark, Ronald. *J.B.S.: The Life and Work of J.B.S. Haldane* [1968] (Bloomsbury, 2011).

Clayton, Jay. "Genome Time: Post-Darwinism Then and Now," *Critical Quarterly* 55.1 (2013): 57–74.

"The Modern Synthesis: Genetics and Dystopia in the Huxley Circle," *Modernism/Modernity* 23.4 (2016): 875–96.

Conrad, Joseph. *Heart of Darkness* [1899], ed. Ross C. Murfin (Bedford/St. Martin's, 2011).

Lord Jim [1899–1900] (Doubleday, 1920).

The Selected Letters of Joseph Conrad, ed. Laurence Davies (Cambridge University Press, 2015).

Costall, Alan. "Lloyd Morgan and the Rise and Fall of 'Animal Psychology,'" *Society and Animals* 6.1 (1998): 13–29.

Cowles, Henry M. "A Victorian Extinction: Alfred Newton and the Evolution of Animal Protection," *British Journal for the History of Science* 46.4 (2013): 695–714.

Crist, Eileen. *Images of Animals: Anthropomorphism and Animal Mind* (Temple University Press, 1999).

"The Inner Life of Earthworms: Darwin's Argument and Its Implications," in *The Cognitive Animal: Empirical and Theoretical Perspectives on Animal Cognition*, ed. Marc Bekoff, Colin Allen, and Gordon M. Burghardt (MIT Press, 2002): 3–8.

Culler, Jonathan. *The Pursuit of Signs: Semiotics, Literature, Deconstruction* (Cornell University Press, 2002).

Cyon, Elie de. "The Anti-Vivisectionist Agitation" [1883], in *Animal Welfare and Anti-Vivisection 1870–1910*, vol. 3, ed. Susan Hamilton (Routledge, 2004): 223–35.

Czarnecki, Kristin and Carrie Rohman, eds. *Virginia Woolf and the Natural World: Selected Papers from the Twentieth Annual International Conference on Virginia Woolf* (Clemson University Digital Press, 2011).

Darwin, Charles. *The Descent of Man and Selection in Relation to Sex*, vol. 1 (John Murray, 1871; repr. in *The Complete Work of Charles Darwin Online*, ed. John van Wyhe: www.darwin-online.org.uk).

Expression of the Emotions in Man and Animals (John Murray, 1872; repr. in *The Complete Work of Charles Darwin Online*, ed. John van Wyhe: www .darwin-online.org.uk).

The Formation of Vegetable Mould Through the Action of Worms (John Murray, 1881; repr. in *The Complete Work of Charles Darwin Online*, ed. John van Wyhe: www.darwin-online.org.uk).

On the Origin of Species by Means of Natural Selection [1859], ed. J. W. Burrow (Penguin Books, 1985).

Daston, Lorraine. "Intelligences: Angelic, Animal, Human," in *Thinking with Animals: New Perspectives on Anthropomorphism*, ed. Lorraine Daston and Gregg Mitman (Columbia University Press, 2005): 37–58.

Daston, Lorraine and Gregg Mitman. "Introduction: The How and Why of Thinking with Animals," in *Thinking with Animals: New Perspectives on Anthropomorphism*, ed. Lorraine Daston and Gregg Mitman (Columbia University Press, 2005): 1–14.

Deleuze, Gilles and Félix Guattari. *A Thousand Plateaus: Capitalism and Schizophrenia*, transl. Brian Massumi (University of Minnesota Press, 1987).

Denisoff, Dennis. "Decadence and Aestheticism," in *The Cambridge Companion to the Fin de Siècle*, ed. Gail Marshall (Cambridge University Press, 2007): 31–52.

Derrida, Jacques and David Wills. "The Animal That Therefore I Am (More to Follow)," *Critical Inquiry* 28.2 (2002): 369–418.

Descartes, René. *Discourse on Method* [1637], 3rd ed., transl. Donald A. Cress (Hackett, 1998).

Desmond, Adrian. *Huxley: From Devil's Disciple to Evolution's High Priest* (Perseus, 1999).

de Waal, Frans. "Anthropomorphism and Anthropodenial: Consistency in Our Thinking About Humans and Animals," *Philosophical Topics* 27.1 (1999): 255–80.

The Ape and the Sushi Master: Cultural Reflections of a Primatologist (Basic Books, 2001).

Diski, Jenny. *What I Don't Know About Animals* (Yale University Press, 2011).

Dryden, Linda. *Joseph Conrad and H.G. Wells: The Fin-de-Siècle Literary Scene* (Palgrave Macmillan, 2015).

Dubino, Jeanne. "The Bispecies Environment, Coevolution, and Flush," in *Contradictory Woolf: Selected Papers from the Twenty-First Annual International Conference on Virginia Woolf*, ed. Derek Ryan and Stella Bolaki (Clemson University Digital Press, 2012): 150–7.

Durant, John R. "The Tension at the Heart of Huxley's Evolutionary Ethology," in *Julian Huxley: Biologist and Statesman of Science*, ed. C. Kenneth Waters and Albert Van Helden (Rice University Press, 1992): 150–60.

Dutton, Denis. "Aesthetics and Evolutionary Psychology," in *The Oxford Handbook of Aesthetics*, ed. Jerrold Levinson (Oxford University Press, 2005): 693–705.

Dvorsky, George. "Scientists Finally Figured Out Why Tardigrades are So Indestructible," *Gizmodo* September 20, 2016: http://gizmodo.com/genes-hold-the-key-to-the-water-bears-indestructibility-1786814698.

Ebbatson, Roger. *Lawrence and the Nature Tradition: A Theme in English Fiction, 1859–1914* (Harvester Press, 1980).

The Evolutionary Self: Hardy, Forster, Lawrence (Harvester Press, 1982).

Ebury, Katherine. *Modernism and Cosmology: Absurd Lights* (Palgrave Macmillan, 2014).

Egerton, Frank N. *Roots of Ecology: Antiquity to Haeckel* (University of California Press, 2012).

Ellis, David. *D.H. Lawrence: Dying Game, 1922–1930* (Cambridge University Press, 1998).

Elton, Charles S. *Animal Ecology* (Macmillan, 1927).

The Ecology of Animals [1933] (Methuen, 1960).

The Ecology of Invasions by Animals and Plants [1958] (University of Chicago Press, 2000).

Esposito, Maurizio. *Romantic Biology, 1890–1945* (Routledge, 2016).

Ferber, Michael. *Romanticism: A Very Short Introduction* (Oxford University Press, 2010).

Fernihough, Anne. *D.H. Lawrence: Aesthetics and Ideology* (Oxford University Press, 1993).

Firchow, Peter. *Aldous Huxley: Satirist and Novelist* (University of Minnesota Press, 1972).

Fisher, R. A. *The Genetical Theory of Natural Selection: A Complete Variorum Edition* [1930], ed. Henry Bennett (Oxford University Press, 1999).

Forman, Ross G. "When Britons Brave Brazil: British Imperialism and the Adventure Tale in Latin America, 1850–1918," *Victorian Studies* 42.3 (1999): 455–87.

Freud, Sigmund. *Civilization and Its Discontents* [1930], transl. James Strachey (W.W. Norton, 1961).

Totem and Taboo [1913], transl. James Strachey (W.W. Norton, 1950).

Froula, Christine. "Out of the Chrysalis: Female Initiation and Female Authority in Virginia Woolf's The Voyage Out," in *Virginia Woolf: A Collection of Critical Essays*, ed. Margaret Homan (Prentice-Hall, 1993): 136–61.

Gang, Joshua. "Mindless Modernism," *NOVEL* 46.1 (2013): 116–32.

Garland, Ellen C., Anne W. Goldizen, Melinda L. Rekdahl, et al. "Dynamic Horizontal Cultural Transmission of Humpback Whale Song at the Ocean Basin Scale," *Current Biology* 21.8 (2011): 687–91.

Garland, Ellen C., Jason Gedamke, Melinda L. Rekdahl, et al. "Humpback Whale Song on the Southern Ocean Feeding Grounds: Implications for Cultural Transmission," *PLOS One* 8.11 (2013): e79422.

Garrard, Greg. "How Queer is Green?" *Configurations* 18.1–2 (2010): 73–96.

Garratt, Peter. *Victorian Empiricism: Self, Knowledge, and Reality in Ruskin, Bain, Lewes, Spencer, and George Eliot* (Fairleigh Dickinson University Press, 2010).

Gaycken, Oliver. *Devices of Curiosity: Early Cinema and Popular Science* (Oxford University Press, 2015).

Geggel, Laura. "Super Species: Animals with Extreme Powers Invade Museum," *LiveScience* April 1, 2015: www.livescience.com/50333-life-at-the-limits.html.

Genette, Gérard. *Narrative Discourse: An Essay in Method*, transl. Jane E. Lewin (Cornell University Press, 1983).

Gilbert, Sandra. *Acts of Attention: The Poems of D.H. Lawrence* (Cornell University Press, 1972).

Godfrey-Smith, Peter. "Philosophy and the Octopus," *WAMC: Academic Minute* March 30, 2011: http://wamc.org/post/dr-peter-godfrey-smith-harvard-university-philosophy-and-octopus.

Goodall, Jane. "Learning from the Chimpanzees: A Message Humans Can Understand," *Science* 282.5397 (1998): 2184–5.

Granofsky, Ronald. *D.H. Lawrence and Survival: Darwinism in the Fiction of the Transitional Period* (McGill-Queen's University Press, 2003).

Gray, Richard T., Ruth V. Gross, Rolf J. Goebel, and Clayton Koelb. *A Franz Kafka Encyclopedia* (Greenwood Press, 2005).

Guerrini, Anita. *Experimenting with Humans and Animals: From Galen to Animal Rights* (Johns Hopkins University Press, 2003).

Guidetti, Roberto and K. Ingemar Jönsson. "Long-Term Anhydrobiotic Survival in Semi-Terrestrial Micrometazoans," *Journal of Zoology* 257 (2002): 181–7.

Hagen, Joel B. *An Entangled Bank: The Origins of Ecosystem Ecology* (Rutgers University Press, 1992).

Haldane, J. B. S. *Possible Worlds* [1927] (Transaction, 2009).

Hamilton, Susan. "Introduction," in *Animal Welfare and Anti-Vivisection 1870–1910: Nineteenth-Century Woman's Mission*, ed. Susan Hamilton (Routledge, 2004): xiv–xlvii.

Hammond, J. R. *H.G. Wells and the Short Story* (St. Martin's Press, 1992).

Haraway, Donna. *When Species Meet* (University of Minnesota Press, 2008).

Harris, Mason. "Vivisection, the Culture of Science, and Intellectual Uncertainty in The Island of Doctor Moreau," *Gothic Studies* 4.2 (2002): 99–115.

Hashimoto, Takuma, Daiki D. Horikawa, Yuki Saito, et al. "Extremotolerant Tardigrade Genome and Improved Radiotolerance of Human Cultures Cells by Tardigrade-Unique Protein," *Nature Communications* 7.12808 (2016): 1–14.

Hearne, Vicki. *Adam's Task: Calling Animals by Name* (Skyhorse, 2007).

Henry, Holly. *Virginia Woolf and the Discourse of Science: The Aesthetics of Astronomy* (Cambridge University Press, 2003).

Herman, David. "Modernist Life Writing and Nonhuman Lives: Ecologies of Experience in Virginia Woolf's *Flush*," *Modern Fiction Studies* 59.3 (2013): 547–68.

Herwig, Malte. "The Unwitting Muse: Jakob von Uexküll's Theory of Umwelt and Twentieth-Century Literature," *Semiotica* 134:1 (2001): 553–92.

Heywood, Christopher. "Birds, Beasts and Flowers: The Evolutionary Context and Lawrence's African Literary Source," *The D.H. Lawrence Review* 15 (1982): 87–105.

"The History of the Aquarium," *ZSL London Zoo*: www.zsl.org/zsl-london-zoo/exhibits/the-history-of-the-aquarium.

Hockett, Charles F. "The Origin of Speech," *Scientific American* 203 (1960): 88–111.

Holmes, John. "Literature and Science vs. History of Science," *Journal of Literature and Science* 5.2 (2012): 67–71.

Howard, Eliot. *Territory in Bird Life* (John Murray, 1920).

The Nature of a Bird's World (Cambridge University Press, 1925).

Hu, Jane C. "What Do Talking Apes Really Tell Us?" *Slate* August 20, 2014: www.slate.com/articles/health_and_science/science/2014/08/koko_kanzi_and_ape_language_research_criticism_of_working_conditions_and.html.

Hurley, Kelly. *The Gothic Body: Sexuality, Materialism, and Degeneration at the Fin de Siècle* (Cambridge University Press, 1996).

Huxley, Aldous. *Antic Hay* (George H. Doran, 1923).
  Brave New World [1932] (TriadGrafton, 1977).
  Eyeless in Gaza [1936] (Harper Perennial, 1964).
  "Introduction," in *The Letters of D.H. Lawrence*, ed. Aldous Huxley (Heinemann, 1956): ix–xxxiv.
  Literature and Science [1963] (Ox Bow, 1991).
  Point Counter Point [1928] (Dalkey Archive Press, 2009).
  Those Barren Leaves [1925] (Dalkey Archive Press, 1998).
Huxley, Julian. "A 'Disharmony' in the Reproductive Habits of the Wild Duck," *Biologisches Zentralblatt* 32 (1912): 621–3.
  "A Journey in Relativity," *North American Review* 218.1 (1923): 67–75.
  Ants (Jonathan Cape and Harrison Smith, 1930).
  "Bird-Watching and Biological Science: Some Observations on the Study of Courtship in Birds," *The Auk* 33.2 (1916): 25670.
  Bird-Watching and Bird Behaviour (Chatto & Windus, 1930).
  "Birds' Play and Pleasure," *The New Statesman*, January 19, 1924: 417–19.
  The Captive Shrew and Other Poems of a Biologist (Basil Blackwell, 1932).
  "The Courtship-Habits of the Great Crested Grebe," *Proceedings of the Zoological Society of London* 35 (1914): 491–562.
  "Editor's Introduction," in *Animal Ecology* [1927], ed. Charles Elton (Macmillan, 1936): ix–xvii.
  Essays of a Biologist [1923] (Penguin, 1939).
  Essays in Popular Science [1926] (Chatto and Windus, 1933).
  "Man vs. Tsetse Fly," *The Listener* May, 31 1933: 863–5.
  Memories, vol. 1 (George Allen and Unwin, 1970).
  "Protective Colouring," *The Field*, February, 8 1936: 187.
Huxley, Julian and Ludwig Koch. *Animal Language* [1938] (Grosset & Dunlap, 1964).
Huxley, Thomas H. *Evolution and Ethics and Science and Morals* [1886–94] (Prometheus Books, 2004).
Huxley, Thomas H. "On the Hypothesis that Animals are Automata, and Its History" [1874], in *The Huxley File*, ed. Charles Blinderman and David Joyce: http://alepho.clarku.edu/huxley/
Inman, Matthew. "Why the Mantis Shrimp is My New Favorite Animal," *The Oatmeal*: http://theoatmeal.com/comics/mantis_shrimp.
Inniss, Kenneth. *D.H. Lawrence's Bestiary: A Study of His Animal Trope and Symbol* (Mouton, 1971).
Isenberg, Andrew C. *The Destruction of the Bison: An Environmental History, 1750–1920* (Cambridge University Press, 2000).
Ittner, Jutta. "Part Spaniel, Part Canine Puzzle: Anthropomorphism in Woolf's Flush and Auster's Timbuktu," *Mosaic* 39.4 (2006): 181–96.
James, Simon J. *Maps of Utopia: H.G. Wells, Modernity and the End of Culture* (Oxford University Press, 2012).
James, William. *The Principles of Psychology*, vol. 1 (Henry Holt, 1890).
Jamison, Leslie. "52 Blue," *The Atavist* 40 (2014): https://magazine.atavist.com/52-blue.

Jay, Martin. "Modernism and the Specter of Psychologism," *Modernism/Modernity* 3.2 (1996): 93–111.

Kafka, Franz. "A Report to an Academy" [1917], transl. Willa and Edwin Muir, in *The Complete Stories*, by Franz Kafka (Schocken Books, 1971): 281–91.

"Investigations of a Dog" [1931], transl. Willa and Edwin Muir, in *The Complete Stories*, ed. Franz Kafka (Schocken Books, 1971): 310–46.

Kant, Immanuel. *The Critique of Judgment [1790]*, transl. Werner S. Pluhar (Hackett, 1987).

Keats, John. *The Complete Poetical Works and Letters of John Keats* (Houghton, Mifflin and Company, 1899).

Keen, Suzanne. *Victorian Renovations of the Novel: Narrative Annexes and the Boundaries of Representation* (Cambridge University Press, 2005).

Kendall-Morwick, Karalyn. "Mongrel Fiction: Canine Bildung and the Feminist Critique of Anthropocentrism in Woolf's Flush," *Modern Fiction Studies* 60.3 (2014): 506–26.

Kinkead-Weekes, Mark. *D.H. Lawrence: Triumph to Exile, 1912–1922* (Cambridge University Press, 1996).

Kiskadden, Peggy. Interview with David K. Dunaway, in *Aldous Huxley Recollected: An Oral History*, by David K. Dunaway (AltaMira, 1999): 32–4.

Kitchener, Richard F. "Bertrand Russell's Flirtation with Behaviorism," *Behavior and Philosophy* 32.2 (2004): 273–91.

Knight, Leah. "Historicising Early Modern Literature and Science: Recent Topics, Trends, and Problems," *Journal of Literature and Science* 5.2 (2012): 56–60.

Kolbert, Elizabeth. *The Sixth Extinction: An Unnatural History* (Henry Holt, 2014).

Lansbury, Coral. *The Old Brown Dog: Women, Workers, and Vivisection in Edwardian England* (University of Wisconsin Press, 1985).

Latour, Bruno. *Reassembling the Social: An Introduction to Actor-Network Theory* (Oxford University Press, 2005).

Lawrence, D. H. *Mornings in Mexico* [1927], ed. Virginia Crosswhite Hyde (Cambridge University Press, 2009).

The Complete Poems of D.H. Lawrence, ed. Vivian de Sola Pinto and Warren Roberts (Penguin, 1993).

The Letters of D.H. Lawrence, Volume II: June 1913–October 1916, ed. George J. Zytaruk and James T. Boulton (Cambridge University Press, 1981).

The Prussian Officer and Other Stories [1914], ed. John Worthen (Penguin, 1995).

Lawrence, D. H. *The Rainbow* [1915], ed. Mark Kinkead-Weekes (Cambridge University Press, 1989).

Women in Love [1920] (Thomas Seltzer, 1922).

Levine, George. *Darwin Loves You: Natural Selection and the Re-Enchantment of the World* (Princeton University Press, 2006).

Darwin the Writer (Oxford University Press, 2011).

Lingis, Alphonso. "Nietzsche and Animals," in *Animal Philosophy: Essential Readings in Continental Thought*, ed. Matthew Calarco and Peter Atterton (Continuum, 2004): 7–14.

Lippit, Akira Mizuta. *Electric Animal: Toward a Rhetoric of Wildlife* (University of Minnesota Press, 2000).

Love, Heather. "Close Reading and Thin Description," *Public Culture* 25.3 (2013): 401–34.

Mackin, Timothy. "Private Worlds, Public Minds: Woolf, Russell, and Photographic Vision," *Journal of Modern Literature* 33.3 (2010): 112–30.

Mao, Douglas. *Solid Objects: Modernism and the Test of Production* (Princeton University Press, 1998).

Marc, Franz. "How Does a Horse See the World?" [1920], transl. Ernest Mundt and Peter Selz, in *Theories of Modern Art: A Source Book by Artists and Critics*, ed. Herschel Browning Chipp (University of California Press, 1968): 178–9.

Marovitz, Sanford E. "Aldous Huxley's Intellectual Zoo," *Philological Quarterly* 48.4 (1969): 495–507.

May, Keith M. *Aldous Huxley* (Elek, 1972).

May, Michael. "Recordings that Made Waves: The Songs that Saved the Whales," *National Public Radio* December 26, 2014: www.npr .org/2014/12/26/373303726/recordings-that-made-waves-the-songs-that-saved-the-whales.

McCarthy, Jeffrey Mathes. *Green Modernism: Nature and the English Novel, 1900 to 1930* (Palgrave, 2016).

McDermott, Maeve. "5 Reasons Why the Tardigrade is Nature's Toughest Animal," *National Geographic TV Blogs* March 19, 2014: http://tvblogs .nationalgeographic.com/2014/03/19/5-reasons-why-the-tardigrade-is-natures-toughest-animal/.

McHugh, Susan. *Animal Stories: Narrating Across Species Lines* (University of Minnesota Press, 2011).

Meckier, Jerome. "Quarles Among the Monkeys: Huxley's Zoological Novels," *Modern Language Review* 68 (1973): 268–82.

Miller, Geoffrey. *The Mating Mind: How Sexual Choice Shaped the Evolution of Human Nature* (Anchor, 2001).

Mitchell, Sally. *Frances Power Cobbe: Victorian Feminist, Journalist, Reformer* (University of Virginia Press, 2004).

Montgomery, Sy. "Deep Intellect," *Orion Magazine* October 2011: https://orion-magazine.org/article/deep-intellect/.

Moore, Marianne. "Poetry," in *Others for 1919: An Anthology of the New Verse*, ed. Alfred Kreymborg (Nicholas L. Brown, 1920): 131–2.

Morgan, C. Lloyd. *An Introduction to Comparative Psychology* [1894], ed. Daniel N. Robinson (University Publications of America, 1977).

Animal Life and Intelligence (E. Arnold, 1891).

Morin, Alain. "What Are Animals Conscious Of?" in *Experiencing Animal Minds: An Anthology of Animal–Human Encounters*, ed. Julie A. Smith and Robert W. Mitchell (Columbia University Press, 2012): 246–60.

Mortimer-Sandilands, Catriona and Bruce Erickson, eds. *Queer Ecologies: Sex, Nature, Politics, Desire* (Indiana University Press, 2010).

Moses, Michael Valdez. "Disorientalism: Conrad and the Imperial Origins of Modernist Aesthetics," in *Modernism and Colonialism: British and Irish Literature 1899–1939*, ed. Richard Begam and Michael Valdez Moses (Duke University Press, 2007): 43–69.

Møbjerg, N., A. Jørgensen, D. Persson, et al. "Survival in Extreme Environments – On the Current Knowledge of Adaptations in Tardigrades," *Acta Physiologica* 202 (2011): 409–20.

Murfin, Ross C. *The Poetry of D.H. Lawrence: Texts & Contexts* (University of Nebraska Press, 1983).

Murray, Nicholas. *Aldous Huxley: A Biography* (Thomas Dunne, 2002).

Nagel, Thomas. "What Is It Like to Be a Bat?" *The Philosophical Review* 83.4 (1974): 435–50.

Newman, Daniel Aureliano. "'Education of an Amphibian': Anachrony, Neoteny, and Bildung in Huxley's Eyeless in Gaza," *Twentieth Century Literature* 62.4 (2016): 403–28.

Nielsen, Mark and R. H. Day. "William James and the Evolution of Consciousness," *Journal of Theoretical and Philosophical Psychology* 19.1 (1999): 90–113.

Nietzsche, Friedrich. *On the Genealogy of Morality: Revised Student Edition* [1887], ed. Keith Ansell-Pearson, transl. Carol Diethe (Cambridge University Press, 2007).

Oliver, Kelly. *Animal Lessons: How They Teach Us to Be Human* (Columbia University Press, 2009).

Ophir, Ella Zohar. "Toward a Pitiless Fiction: Abstraction, Comedy, and Modernist AntiHumanism," *Modern Fiction Studies* 52.1 (2006): 92–120.

Pandora, Katherine and Karen A. Rader. "Science in the Everyday World: Why Perspectives from the History of Science Matter," *Isis* 99.2 (2008): 350–64.

Parrinder, Patrick. *Shadows of the Future: H.G. Wells, Science Fiction, and Prophecy* (Syracuse University Press, 1995).

Parry, Jovian. "From Beastly Perversions to the Zoological Closet: Animals, Nature, and Homosex," *Journal for Critical Animal Studies* 10.3 (2012): 7–25.

Peppis, Paul. *Sciences of Modernism: Ethnography, Sexology, and Psychology* (Cambridge University Press, 2014).

Pinker, Steven. *The Language Instinct: How the Mind Creates Language* (W. Morrow, 1994).

Premack, David and Guy Woodruff. "Does the Chimpanzee Have a Theory of Mind?" *Behavioral and Brain Sciences* 1.4 (1978): 515–26.

Provine, William B. "Progress in Evolution and Meaning in Life," in *Julian Huxley: Biologist and Statesman of Science*, ed. C. Kenneth Waters and Albert Van Helden (Rice University Press, 1992): 165–80.

Rebecchi, Lorena, Tiziana Altiero, Roberto Guidetti, et al. "Tardigrade Resistance to Space Effects: First Results of Experiments on the LIFE-TARSE Mission on FOTON-M3," *Astrobiology* 9.6 (2007): 581–91.

Richter, Harvena. "Hunting the Moth: Virginia Woolf and the Creative Imagination," in *Virginia Woolf: Revaluation and Continuity*, ed. Ralph Freedman (University of California Press, 1980): 13–28.

Ritvo, Harriet. "Destroyers and Preservers: Big Game in the Victorian Empire," *History Today* 52.1 (2002): 33–9.

Rohman, Carrie. *Stalking the Subject: Modernism and the Animal* (Columbia University Press, 2009).

   "The Voice of the Living: Becoming-Artistic and the Creaturely Refrain in D.H. Lawrence's 'Tortoise Shout,'" in *Experiencing Animal Minds: An Anthology of Animal-Human Encounters*, ed. Julie A. Smith and Robert W. Mitchell (Columbia University Press, 2012): 170–85.

Roughgarden, Joan. *Evolution's Rainbow: Diversity, Gender, and Sexuality in Nature and People* (University of California Press, 2009).

Roy, Eleanor Ainge. "The Great Escape: Inky the Octopus Legs It to Freedom from Aquarium," *The Guardian* April 12, 2016: www.theguardian.com/world/2016/apr/13/the-great-escape-inky-the-octopus-legs-it-to-freedom-from-new-zealand-aquarium.

Royal Commission. *Report of the Royal Commission on the Practice of Subjecting Live Animals to Experiments for Scientific Purposes* (George Edward Eyre and William Spottiswoode, 1876).

Rudacille, Deborah. *The Scalpel and the Butterfly: The Conflict Between Animal Research and Animal Protection* (University of California Press, 2001).

Russell, Bertrand. "Appendix III: Philosophical Books Read in Prison," in *The Collected Papers of Bertrand Russell*, vol. 8, ed. John G. Slater (George Allen & Unwin, 1986): 315–28.

   My Philosophical Development [1959] (Routledge, 1995).

   Mysticism and Logic [1910] (W.W. Norton & Company, 1929).

   Our Knowledge of the External World [1914] (W.W. Norton & Company, 1929).

   Portraits from Memory and Other Essays (Simon & Schuster, 1956).

   The Analysis of Mind [1921] (George Allen & Unwin, 1949).

Ryan, Derek. "From Spaniel Club to Animalous Society: Virginia Woolf's Flush," in *Contradictory Woolf: Selected Papers from the Twenty-First Annual International Conference on Virginia Woolf*, ed. Derek Ryan and Stella Bolaki (Clemson University Digital Press, 2012): 158–65.

Ryan, Judith. *The Vanishing Subject: Early Psychology and Literary Modernism* (University of Chicago Press, 1991).

Rylance, Rick. "Ideas, Histories, Generations and Beliefs: The Early Novels to Sons and Lovers," in *The Cambridge Companion to D.H. Lawrence*, ed. Anne Fernihough (Cambridge University Press, 2001): 15–31.

Sarsfield, Rachel. "From the Chrysalis to the Display Case: The Butterfly's 'Voyage Out' in Virginia Woolf," in *Insect Poetics*, ed. Eric C. Brown (University of Minnesota Press, 2006): 87–111.

Schmithausen, Lambert. "Aldous Huxley's View of Nature," in *Aldous Huxley: Between East and West*, ed. C. C. Barfoot (Rodopi, 2001): 151–74.

Schuster, Joshua. *The Ecology of Modernism: American Environments and Avant-Garde Poetics* (University of Alabama Press, 2015).

Scott, Bonnie Kime. *In the Hollow of the Wave: Virginia Woolf and Modernist Uses of Nature* (University of Virginia Press, 2012).

Selous, Edmund. *Thought-Transference (or What?) in Birds* (Constable, 1931).

Shklovsky, Victor. "Art as Technique" [1917], in *Russian Formalist Criticism: Four Essays*, transl. Lee T. Lemon and Marion J. Reis (University of Nebraska Press, 1965): 3–24.

Simon, Matt. "Absurd Creature of the Week: The Incredible Critter That's Tough Enough to Survive in Space," *Wired* March 21, 2014: www.wired.com/2014/03/absurd-creature-week-water-bear/.

Sleigh, Charlotte. "Empire of the Ants: H.G. Wells and Tropical Entomology," *Science as Culture* 10.1 (2001): 33–71.

Smith, Craig. "Across the Widest Gulf: Nonhuman Subjectivity in Virginia Woolf's Flush," *Twentieth Century Literature* 48.3 (2002): 348–61.

Smith, Jonathan. *Charles Darwin and Victorian Visual Culture* (Cambridge University Press, 2006).

Snaith, Anna. "Of Fanciers, Footnotes, and Fascism: Virginia Woolf's Flush," *Modern Fiction Studies* 48.3 (2002): 614–36.

Snow, C. P. "The Two Cultures" [1959], *Leonardo* 23.2–3 (1990): 169–73.

Stanfield, Paul Scott. "'This Implacable Doctrine': Behaviorism in Wyndham Lewis's Snooty Baronet," *Twentieth Century Literature* 47.2 (2001): 241–67.

Steverding, Dietmar. "The History of African Trypanosomiasis," *Parasites and Vectors* 1.3 (2008): 1–8.

Sultzbach, Kelly. *Ecocriticism in the Modernist Imagination* (Cambridge University Press, 2016).

Sword, Helen. "Lawrence's Poetry," in *The Cambridge Companion to D.H. Lawrence*, ed. Anne Fernihough (Cambridge University Press, 2001): 119–35.

Terry, Jennifer. "'Unnatural Acts' in Nature: The Scientific Fascination with Queer Animals," *GLQ: A Journal of Lesbian and Gay Studies* 6.2 (2000): 151–93.

Thacker, Andrew. "'Mad After Foreign Notions': Ezra Pound, Imagism and the Geography of the Orient," in *Geographies of Modernism: Literatures, Cultures, Spaces*, ed. Peter Brooker and Andrew Thacker (Routledge, 2005): 31–42.

Thoen, Hanne H., Martin J. Howe, Tsyr-Huei Chiou, and Justin Marshall. "A Different Form of Color Vision in Mantis Shrimp," *Science* 343.6169 (2014): 411–13.

Thorndike, Edward Lee. *Animal Intelligence: Experimental Studies* (Macmillan, 1911).

Todes, Daniel P. *Ivan Pavlov: A Russian Life in Science* (Oxford University Press, 2014).

Tsujimoto, Megumu, Satoshi Imura, and Hiroshi Kanda. "Recovery and Reproduction of an Antarctic Tardigrade Retrieved from a Moss Sample Frozen for Over 30 Years," *Cryobiology* 72.1 (2016): 78–81.

Tyson, Neil deGrasse. "Some of the Things that Molecules Do," *Cosmos: A Spacetime Odyssey*, Fox, 16 March 2014.

Uexküll, Jakob von. *A Foray into the Worlds of Animals and Humans, with a Theory of Meaning* [1934], transl. Joseph D. O'Neil (University of Minnesota Press, 2010).

Ulin, Donald. "A Clerisy of Worms in Darwin's Inverted World," *Victorian Studies* 35.3 (1992): 295–308.

Van Dooren, Thom. *Flight Ways: Life and Loss at the Edge of Extinction* (Columbia University Press, 2014).

Vasconellos, Angélica da Silva and César Ades. "Possible Limits and Advances of Environmental Enrichment for Wild Animals," *Revista de Etologia* 11.1 (2012): 37–45.

Wallace, Jeff. *D.H. Lawrence, Science and the Posthuman* (Palgrave Macmillan, 2005).

Walter, Christina. *Optical Impersonality; Science, Images, and Literary Modernism* (Johns Hopkins University Press, 2014).

Washburn, Margaret Floy. *The Animal Mind: A Text-Book of Comparative Psychology*, 1st ed. (Macmillan, 1908).

The Animal Mind: A Text-Book of Comparative Psychology, 3rd ed. (Macmillan, 1926).

Watson, John B. "Psychology as the Behaviorist Views It," *The Psychological Review* 20.2 (1913): 158–77.

Watt, Ian. *Conrad in the Nineteenth Century* (University of California Press, 1981).

Watts, Harold H. *Aldous Huxley* (Hippocrene, 1972).

Weil, Kari. *Thinking Animals: Why Animal Studies Now?* (Columbia University Press, 2012).

Wells, H. G. *The Complete Short Stories of H.G. Wells* (Ernest Benn, 1974).

The Food of the Gods (Charles Scribner's Sons, 1904).

H.G. Wells: Early Writings in Science and Science Fiction, ed. Robert M. Philmus and David Y. Hughes (University of California Press, 1975).

Men Like Gods (Macmillan, 1923).

"The Mind in Animals," *The Saturday Review*, December 22, 1894: 683–4.

The Time Machine [1895] (Penguin, 2005).

The War of the Worlds [1898], ed. David Y. Hughes and Harry M. Geduld (Indiana University Press, 1993).

Wells, H. G., Julian Huxley, and G. P. Wells. *The Science of Life*, vol. 4 (Doran & Company, 1931).

Westling, Louise. "Merleau-Ponty's Human–Animality Intertwining and the Animal Question," *Configurations* 18.1–2 (2010): 161–80.

"Virginia Woolf and the Flesh of the World," *New Literary History* 30 (1999): 855–75.

Whitworth, Michael H. *Einstein's Wake: Relativity, Metaphor, and Modernist Literature* (Oxford University Press, 2001).

Wilson, Edward O. and Robert MacArthur. *The Theory of Island Biogeography* (Princeton University Press, 1967).

Witkowski, J. A. "Julian Huxley in the Laboratory: Embracing Inquisitiveness and Widespread Curiosity," in *Julian Huxley: Biologist and Statesman of Science*, ed. C. Kenneth Waters and Albert Van Helden (Rice University Press, 1992): 79–103.

Wolfe, Cary. *What is Posthumanism?* (University of Minnesota Press, 2009).

Wolsky, Maeia de Issekutz and Alexander A. Wolsky. "Bergson's Vitalism in the Light of Modern Biology," in *The Crisis in Modernism: Bergson and the Vitalist Controversy*, ed. Frederick Burwick and Paul Douglass (Cambridge University Press, 1992): 153–70.

Woolf, Virginia. *A Room of One's Own* [1929] (Harcourt, 1989).

  A Writer's Diary: Being Extracts from the Diary of Virginia Woolf, ed. Leonard Woolf (Harcourt, 2003).

  Between the Acts [1941] (Harcourt Brace Jovanovich, 1969).

  Flush [1933], ed. Elizabeth Steele (Blackwell, 1999).

  The Complete Shorter Fiction of Virginia Woolf, ed. Susan Dick (Harcourt Brace Jovanovich, 1985).

  The Diary of Virginia Woolf, vol. 4, ed. Anne Olivier Bell and Andrew McNeillie (Harcourt Brace Jovanovich, 1982).

  The Essays of Virginia Woolf, vol. 3, ed. Andrew McNeillie (Harcourt Brace Jovanovich, 1988).

Worster, Donald. *Nature's Economy: A History of Ecological Ideas*, 2nd ed. (Cambridge University Press, 1994).

Wylie, Dan. "The Anthropomorphic Ethic: Fiction and the Animal Mind in Virginia Woolf's Flush and Barbara Gowdy's The White Bone," *Interdisciplinary Studies in Literature and Environment* 9.2 (2002): 115–31.

Zuckerman, Solly. "Comments and Recollections," in *Julian Huxley: Biologist and Statesman of Science*, ed. C. Kenneth Waters and Albert Van Helden (Rice University Press, 1992): 161–4.

Index